RACE & POLITICS

RACE & POLITICS

*"Bleeding Kansas" and
the Coming of the Civil War*

by James A. Rawley

UNIVERSITY OF NEBRASKA PRESS
Lincoln and London

First Bison Book printing: 1979

Most recent printing indicated by first digit below:
1   2   3   4   5   6   7   8   9   10

Library of Congress Cataloging in Publication Data

Rawley, James A
  Race & politics.

  Reprint of the ed. published by Lippincott, Philadelphia, in series: Critical periods of history.
  Bibliography: p. 291
  Includes index.
  1. Kansas-Nebraska bill. 2. United States—History—Civil War, 1861–1865—Causes. 3. Kansas—Politics and government—1854–1861. 4. United States—Race relations. I. Title.
[E433.R25 1979]   973.7'113   79–14856
ISBN 0–8032–3854–1
ISBN 0–8032–8901–4 pbk.

Published by arrangement with the author.
Manufactured in the United States of America

CONTENTS

PREFACE

Of making many books on the Civil War there is no end, and it behooves the writer of a new work on the war's background to explain what he is about. I have two purposes in writing this book. One is to demonstrate how the Kansas controversy provided the principal political theme in the United States for a crucial five years. Outwardly it dominated the public scene, and thus formed the drama for a critical period in our history. From 1854 through 1858 Kansas was the keynote of United States politics. Whether the scene was the plains of Kansas Territory, the halls of Congress, the White House, the Supreme Court chamber, or the polling places in the counties and wards of the nation, the Kansas theme—by 1856 "Bleeding Kansas"—prompted the players in the drama. And if the narrative is described as a drama, it must also be depicted as a tragedy. For although the struggle seemed to end in 1858, with Kansas saved from slavery's grasp, its effects persevered in a bitter epilogue until the outbreak of war in April, 1861.

I have said that Kansas outwardly dominated the public scene, but I think only outwardly. My other purpose is to place a fresh emphasis upon the coming of the Civil War. In this book I have not written of state rights, the institution of slavery, conflicting civilizations, and other familiar rubrics for the war's origins. Rather I have exposed the dark streak of racial prejudice in the America of the 1850's. This theme has not been entirely ignored by previous writers, but no book, I believe, has documented anti-Negro sentiment in prewar politics as abundantly as this work essays to do.

Buttressed by contemporary science and almost universally held, though in varying degrees, racial prejudice found political expression in diverse forms. It justified slavery. It justified excluding Negroes from the territories. It justified colonizing Negroes. It justified allowing each state or territory to decide for itself the status of the Negro in the community. It incited men who differed in their justifications to suspect one another of loving or hating Negroes. It prevented that generation from thinking constructively about the racial problem that underlay the crisis of the 1850's.

Racial prejudice—as well as economic, political, and idealistic factors—was a foundation for thinking about slavery in the territories. Proslavery men saw in anti-extension a threat to keeping the institution that preserved existing race relations. Antislavery men saw in extension a threat to wider opportunity for white men. There is scant evidence of public men taking an antiextension or even antislavery position to benefit Negroes. The war's background is complex, and many issues importantly figured, but what I propose to lift from the shadows and to place in the light is the almost universal racial bias of a proud people who boasted to the world of their doctrines of liberty and equality.

Racial thinking in mid-nineteenth-century America was a compound of prejudice, ignorance, anthropology, fear, and jealousy. It usually presupposed the biological inferiority of the Negro. It often sprang from a dread of economic competition and a horror of race mixing. Occasionally blatant and militant, more frequently taken for granted and voiced on occasion, racial inequalitarianism seemed ever implicit—a folk belief which most white Americans held.

Racial prejudice made slavery irremovable for the South. It made impossible Caucasian acceptance of ameliorative measures like enacting civil-rights laws for Negroes. It made impossible a gradual approach to extinction of slavery through education, wardship, or peonage, or freeing the children of slaves upon their reaching the age of twenty-one, as Representative James Tallmadge proposed in 1818—thereby touching off the Missouri controversy. It placed immediate emancipation out of the question. Race relations have rarely been treated rationally by Americans. Discussion of them usually turns to inanities, culminating in the question "Do you want your daughter to marry a Negro?" Race is the one thing in our history that has defied the political genius of the American people. If there had been no color bar, the United States probably could have coped with the issue of slavery.

Belief in Negro inferiority cramped the political choices open to the pre-Sumter generation. It is the unhappy reality of United States history that the institution of slavery was not facing a major attack before the Civil War. Yet slavery itself stood condemned in the Western world. No free state was pioneering in extending civil rights to Negroes; instead there was a reaction against Negro rights that deepened as the decade of the 1850's ran on. No slave state was striving to improve the lot of the blacks; instead there was a reaction against amelioration or emancipation. No major party or major political leader advocated destruction of the peculiar institution. By the 1850's the whole notion of race had taken on a life of its own.

Indeed, from the late 1840's the United States confronted its future as the Negro in the territories might help to shape that future. For a decade the question of the Negro in the territories intermittently threatened the stability of the Union.

Extensionists were moved by a variety of views. Some sought to add land for slavery's economic and political advantage. A few favored diffusing the institution with an eye to ultimate extinction. Others saw in the right to extend a vindication of principle. And there were those who embraced extension in reflex, because antiextension seemed a prelude to dreaded emancipation.

Antiextensionists, too, were prompted by divers views. Many wished to preserve the territories for white men. Many wished to restrict the influence of the South—the slave power—in the nation. And some wished to make a flank attack on an institution which the world had brought to judgment. These last were limited in number, for in general antiextensionists—preponderantly northerners—although they disliked the institution of slavery, believed the system, with all its defects, resolved the problem of race relations and sought neither to overturn it nor expand it.

White America, in such ways, divided over the place of the Negro in the territories. Was he to be there as a slave, as a second-class citizen, or not at all? Almost no one advocated equal opportunity for the Negro in the territories. Almost no one advocated homesteads for Negroes. The quarrel over slavery in the territories was in the main a white man's quarrel over white men's conflicting rights. Antiextension came to be endowed with morality, but it was a morality shaped by ethnic preconceptions.

In summary, this work will examine the Kansas crisis of the 1850's, with more abundant attention to race than previous works have given, but without meaning to exclude the significance of other factors. It underscores race as a premise for the politics of the time and undertakes to show race's crippling effects in coping with the crisis.

For the ordeal of the Union was among other matters a racial ordeal. On the eve of secession a beleaguered generation avoided extending the legacy of the first American Revolution to American Negroes whether free or slave, invoked dogmas of state rights, despised abolitionists, preserved race separateness in the institution of slavery, divided over the question whether the western territories were to be reserved for white men, formed into distinct sections, ruptured its party system, either feared the "Great Conspiracy of the Slave Power" or northern aggressions of the "Black Republicans," and blundered into the irrepressible conflict.

With the larger historiographical dimensions of this interpretation I have dealt in the epilogue. Let it suffice to say here that slavery, to be sure, was toward the center of the American struggle. But what distinguished the institution of slavery in America was the enslavement of Negroes. James Madison, the father of the Constitution, in his old age told Harriet Martineau that if he could work a miracle, he knew what it would be. "He would make all the blacks white and then he could do away with slavery in twenty-four hours." Earlier, in 1821, he had confided to Lafayette, "The repugnance of the whites to their [Negroes'] continuance among them is founded on prejudices themselves founded on physical distinctions, which are not likely soon if ever to be eradicated." Color was the bar to emancipation of American slaves.

As to the Kansas issue, its significance has been diversely defined by past interpreters. That distinguished contemporary, Abraham Lincoln, in his "house divided" speech at Springfield in 1858, saw the Kansas-Nebraska bill as the start of an agitation which he prophesied must pass through a crisis and could end only in the alternatives of extending slavery throughout the nation or extinguishing the institution. "We are now far in to the *fifth* year," he observed, "since a policy was initiated with the *avowed* object and *confident* promise of putting an end to slavery agitation. Under the operation of that policy, that agitation not only has *not ceased,* but has *constantly augmented.* In my opinion, it *will* not cease until a *crisis* shall have been reached, and passed. 'A house divided against itself cannot stand.' . . . I do not expect the house to *fall*—but I *do* expect it will cease to be divided. It will become *all* one thing, or *all* the other."

James Ford Rhodes, the first great scholarly historian of the Civil War, appraised the Kansas-Nebraska Act as "the most momentous measure that passed Congress from the day the senators and representatives first met to the outbreak of the civil war." The Act and the Dred Scott decision, which ruled on the issue of Congressional nonintervention in the territories raised by the Act, together "made the national Democrats a pro-slavery party." The vote taken in Kansas in August, 1858, disposed of the Lecompton constitution, and effectually determined that slavery should not exist in Kansas. "But the question," he maintained, "left an irreconcilable breach in the Democratic party which was big with consequences for the Republicans and for the country."

Ulrich B. Phillips, a pioneer southern scholar, in tracing the interrelationship between Georgia and state rights that culminated in the exercise of the ultimate right of a state—the act of secession—concluded: "From the beginning of the Kansas struggle, secession as a last resort for the protection of Southern rights was never

completely out of the contemplation of Southern statesmen." He found the Lecompton settlement left a "rift in
the Democratic ranks . . . so serious as to render the
Republican triumph almost inevitable in 1860." Lincoln's
victory brought on a crisis necessitating "heroic measures"—military preparations and secession—as Georgians faced the prospect of abolition, enforced racial
equality, and intermarriage.

In 1942 the southern-born historian, Avery Craven,
published *The Coming of the Civil War*. This book, tinged
with sympathy for the southern cause, after making the
usual recognition of the Kansas-Nebraska Act's father-
ing the Republican Party, gave a distinctive interpretation
to Kansas issues. The Act transformed the outlook of
the northern man, who heretofore had generally viewed
abolitionists as "crackpots." Now defining the slavery
issue as nonextension, he accepted the abolitionists'
indictment of slavery. This assumption of morality made
the conflict irrepressible. Actually, the conflict was repressible, Craven suggested. Partisan Republican leaders
used the Kansas dispute not only to build the Republican
Party on the sophistical question of nonextension, but
also nourished the "mushroom-like growth of Republican
strength on emotional issues." The vote taken in Kansas
in August, 1858, vindicated Douglas's popular-sovereignty principle, not Republican nonextensionism. Kansas proved beyond question that popular sovereignty, if
fairly applied, would result in free territories and states.
There was no irrepressible conflict over extension of
slavery into the territories. Lincoln by his "house divided"
doctrine of ultimate extinction gave the Republican Party
a "new slavery formula" which though conservative in its
wording was "deadly in its implications." All the while,
shortsighted politicians, overzealous editors, and pious

reformers emotionalized issues and conjured up distortions in a process by which a repressible conflict was made an irrepressible one.

James G. Randall, a northern historian with southern affiliations, in his *Lincoln the President,* published in 1945, stood on common ground with Craven. The territorial issue was unreal, sectional grievances were magnified through emotionalism, and shadows were given substance, making rational action impossible. "As to the territorial question," he judged, "it is well known that Kansas and Nebraska had been written off for freedom by 1860 . . . it may be truly said that the colossal quarrel concerning slavery in Kansas had practically nothing to do with Kansas itself." Kansas contained only two slaves in 1860, and there was left no territory in the nation to which slavery might be extended. Even so, "intransigents on both sides . . . opposed not only compromise 'terms' but the very idea of any compromise whatever." So far as Republican intransigents were concerned, "artificial difficulties had accumulated to make real obstacles out of shadow objections," and "a problem that seems simple to a later generation was fraught at the time with sectional inhibitions till it was well nigh unsolvable."

A fresh summing up and addition to Civil War scholarship in many volumes began appearing from the pen of Allan Nevins in 1947. A northerner, he excoriated "the gross miscalculations involved in the Kansas-Nebraska Act," and indicted Stephen A. Douglas for renewing the intersectional conflict. He rebuked Presidents Pierce and Buchanan for their failure of "candor, vision, and above all courage in dealing with Kansas affairs." But a deeper failure lay with the American people, who displayed "deplorable partisanship and excitability"; without these traits, "the worst Kansas pages would never have been written." With the territorial vote in August, 1858, "Kansas ceased to haunt the dreams of the nation," but "it left a sinister general heritage in the enhancement of sectional ill-will, and a specific legacy of evil in the Democratic schism." Giving weight to many factors in bringing on war, Nevins stressed a moral strain in Lincoln, brought to leadership by Kansas strife, that portended emancipation of Negroes from slavery and their elevation to equality. The Sumter generation could not face a "curative adjustment." "For Americans in 1861 . . . war was easier than wisdom and courage."

Bleeding Kansas, it is clear, has many interpreters. To Lincoln it was the start of an irrepressible conflict, to Rhodes it was a manifestation of the slavery problem, to Phillips of the state-rights controversy, to Craven and Randall an unreal issue that kindled partisanship and emotions, making rational solutions impossible, and to Nevins a major part of a national ordeal posing real problems of slavery and race adjustment. All agree that Bleeding Kansas served to divide Americans against one another and to bring the divided sections closer to war.

If, then, my purposes differ from those of earlier writers, they alone may be sufficient justification for this book. Beyond this, however, it may be said that since the last masterly synthesis of the 1854–58 period was written by Allan Nevins, much significant new literature has been presented to view. Let me point to the valuable studies by Roy Nichols, James C. Malin, Paul W. Gates, Avery Craven, Larry Gara, W. D. Burnham, T. B. Alexander, Leon Litwack, Eugene Berwanger, William Stanton, W. D. Overdyke, S. A. Johnson, Edmund Wilson, and T. L. Smith, among others published since 1947. Also we have recent biographies of Lincoln, Charles F. Adams, Sumner, Atchison, Walker, Fillmore, Buchanan, Bates, Seward, Greeley, Wade, Peter V. Daniel, Douglas,

S. S. Cox, Wentworth, Hale, Lovejoy, Crittenden, Bell, Garrison, Fessenden, Trumbull, Benton, Joseph Lane, Toombs, Lowell, and others. Articles too numerous to refer to here have been published. Besides these publications I have drawn extensively on the manuscripts and newspapers of the period. My book, accordingly, is my synthesis and interpretation of new and old published materials, and of manuscripts located in the Library of Congress, including the newly opened N. P. Banks papers, the New York Public Library, the New York Historical Society, the New York State Library, the Pennsylvania Historical Society, the University of Chicago Library, the Princeton University Library, and the Kansas State Historical Society.

The scholar, whether sedentary or itinerant, incurs irreparable obligations. Librarians and curators in numerous places have been unfailingly helpful. Special thanks are owed to President Robert D. Cross of Swarthmore College, the skillful editor of the series in which this work appears. Robert W. Johannsen of the University of Illinois gave the manuscript the benefit of his erudition and criticism. But any faults to be found are my responsibility. I am indebted to the University of Nebraska, which has fostered my research and writing, and particularly to its research council, which has twice appointed me to faculty summer research fellowships. And finally, as a husband and father who long engrossed himself in the writing of this book, I recognize as my heaviest creditors my wife and sons, who patiently put faith in me and my labor.

JAMES A. RAWLEY

Lincoln, Nebraska
May, 1969

RACE & POLITICS

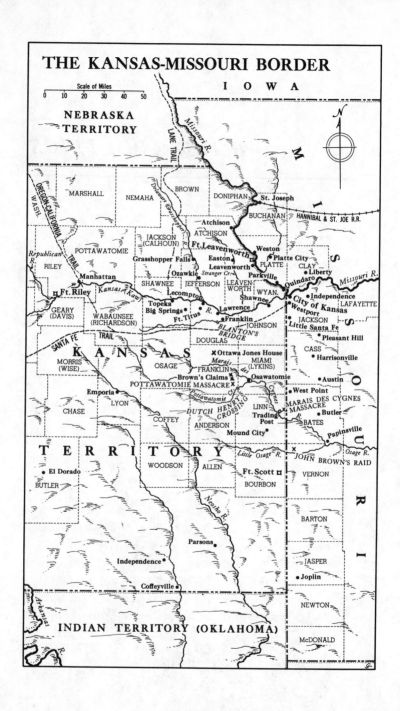

THE KANSAS-MISSOURI BORDER

I O W A

NEBRASKA TERRITORY

Scale of Miles
0 10 20 30 40 50

M I S S O U R I

MARSHALL NEMAHA BROWN DONIPHAN

St. Joseph

BUCHANAN

HANNIBAL & ST. JOE R.R.

Atchison

ATCHISON

JACKSON (CALHOUN)

Ft. Leavenworth

Weston

Platte City

PLATTE

CLAY

Liberty

Grasshopper Falls Easton

Ozawkie Leavenworth Parkville

LEAVEN-WORTH

Quindaro

Missouri R.

POTTAWATOMIE

SHAWNEE JEFFERSON

Lecompton

WYAN.

Shawnee

City of Kansas

Independence

LAFAYETTE

Westport

Ft. Riley

Kansas (Kaw) R.

Topeka Big Springs

Lawrence

Ft. Titus Franklin

JOHNSON

JACKSON

Little Santa Fe

GEARY (DAVIS)

WABAUNSEE (RICHARDSON)

BLANTON'S BRIDGE

DOUGLAS

Pleasant Hill

K A N S A S

MORRIS (WISE)

OSAGE

Ottawa Jones House

CASS

Harrisonville

Marais des Cygnes R.

FRANKLIN

MIAMI (LYKINS)

Brown's Claims

POTTAWATOMIE MASSACRE

Osawatomie

Austin

Emporia

West Point

DUTCH HENRY'S CROSSING

LINN

MARAIS DES CYGNES MASSACRE

CHASE

LYON

COFFEY

Trading Post

Butler

BATES

ANDERSON

Mound City

Papinsville

T E R R I T O R Y

WOODSON ALLEN

Little Osage R.

JOHN BROWN'S RAID

Osage R.

El Dorado

Ft. Scott

VERNON

BUTLER

BOURBON

BARTON

Parsons

Independence

JASPER

Joplin

Coffeyville

NEWTON

INDIAN TERRITORY (OKLAHOMA)

McDONALD

Arkansas R.

Neosho R.

Republican R.

OREGON-CALIFORNIA TRAIL

WASH.

RILEY

Manhattan

LANE TRAIL

Delaware (Grasshopper) R.

Missouri R.

Stranger Cr.

Pottawatomie Cr.

SANTA FE TRAIL

1

Not for the good of the Negroes

A writer in *Blackwood's Magazine* for June, 1854, marveled at "The Recent Growth of the United States of America." He was struck by the contrast between two vast, sprawling nations—Russia and the United States—in the mid-nineteenth century. The United States numbered about 23 million persons, Russia three times that figure or more. The smaller nation was characterized by growth, truly phenomenal growth, and the larger by inertia.

Russia, he observed, had an autocratic government, used her capital in war and pomp, gave little attention to internal improvements, scientific agriculture, foreign commerce, or exploitation of forests, fisheries, fields, and mines.

American history in the first half of the nineteenth century stood in antithesis to this neglect of economic growth. Individual initiative and public enterprise had cooperated in laying the foundation for prosperity. Early in the century a program of public planning and construction of transportation

The chapter title is quoted from *Democracy in America* by Alexis de Tocqueville (1835).

had been initiated. State and local governments in particular had supported an American system for the exchange of goods and the development of mutual interdependence. The State of New York had started digging the Erie Canal in 1817; and the Federal government had subsidized the building of the Illinois Central Railroad in 1850.

If the English journalist perhaps overstated his case, he had nevertheless pointed to a home truth: *growth* was the arresting trait of American life in the midcentury. Within the preceding decade the United States had extended its national frontiers to the Rio Grande, the Golden Gate, and Puget Sound—had become a continental empire, stretching from sea to shining sea.

Its population was exploding at the rate of a one-third increase each decade. Its people were putting new lands to the plow, and the nation was thrusting itself into the world market, pouring grain as well as cotton into Europe's ports. In the years between 1843 and 1860 United States foreign commerce grew by five and a half times, while its domestic commerce multiplied tenfold. Following a western star, pioneers were pushing into Illinois, Wisconsin, Minnesota, and Iowa, and pressing toward the plains region beyond the broad Missouri River. The Americans were migratory beings, and the migration rate grew during the fifties. By 1860 about one in every four lived in a state outside the one in which he had been born.

The whir of machines sounded alongside the advance of the plow. Within this decade industrial production doubled, until it supported about one sixth of the population. In 1852 three main areas of economic production ranked in this order: agriculture $1,752 million, general industry $1,133 million, and household manufactures $30,250,000. By 1860 the United States was perhaps

second only to Great Britain in the value of its manufactures.

Immigration added its masses to the American population. In 1850 one of every nine Americans was foreign
born; ten years later one in every seven. The Irish potato
shortage and the failure of the European revolutions of
1848 had helped impel men of the Old World to venture
to a land of storied plenty and vaunted liberty. By the end
of the decade of the fifties, during which 2,598,214
aliens entered the United States, mostly through the port
of New York, the Irish, numbering 1,611,304, predom-
inated among the foreign-born, and the Germans, numbering 1,276,075, ran second.

Immigrants found employment as laborers, farmers,
mechanics, merchants, and miners in that order. They
contributed not only to the agricultural surge, but even
more numerously to the nation's industry and commerce.
These last-named forms of enterprise forced the
growth of cities; in no decade of the century was the de-
cennial increase in urban population as fast as in the
forties, when it made a spectacular spurt of 99 per cent.
In 1850 one of every eight Americans was a city dweller;
in 1860 one of every six. New York stood first in size
among metropolitan centers, followed by Philadelphia,
Baltimore, and Boston. Only one city in the future Confederacy—New Orleans—took rank (sixth place, count-
ing Brooklyn separately) among the first ten cities of
the country.

Vital and vaulting as the United States was in the fifties, its astounding growth varied in geographic sections.
The Atlantic states were growing less speedily in population than the central, and the central less speedily than
the western. The railroad grid of 1860 reveals similar
variation; of the thirty thousand miles in the nation only
nine thousand lay in the South. The South in 1860 gave

employment in manufacturing to only 111,000 laborers, whereas New England factories hired three and a half times that figure, and a middle zone from the Atlantic to the Midwest retained five times as many. Striking indeed was the contrast between the economic diversification of the North and the persistence of staple agriculture in the South. There was irony in the fact that the South's leading staple, cotton, had provided a strong impetus to the North's economic growth and diversification.

The transatlantic observer of 1854—year of the Kansas-Nebraska act—who wondered at the recent growth of the United States, was pursuing an earlier precedent in comparing the United States and Russia. That astute philosopher, Alexis de Tocqueville, twenty years before had prophesied the eventual polarization of the world between the two great nations: "Each of them seems marked out by the will of Heaven to sway the destinies of half the globe." "The Anglo-American relies upon personal interest to accomplish his ends and gives free scope to the unguided strength and common sense of the people; the Russian centers all the authority of society in a single arm. The principal instrument of the former is freedom; of the latter, servitude."

Nicholas I, Czar of Russia, was an autocrat. In Russia the beliefs that power was limited, that men had rights against government, that power was wrapped in responsibility, were foreign—un-Russian. Nicholas did not govern his empire by law but ruled it by ukase and military repression. The institution of czardom was closely associated with serfdom. Together these two leading institutions of imperial Russia stifled individual initiative, restricted national economic growth, kept the peasantry in ignorance, estranged the intellectuals, and made for a massive immobility. Czarist Russia, only slightly tinged with Western ideas, stood apart from Europe.

The United States in 1854 abided in antithesis to Russian autocracy. It was in fact unlike any other nation. Uniqueness underlay its history. It had carried out the first successful colonial revolt in modern times, ushering in the age of democratic revolutions. It had inaugurated the practice of basing government upon a written compact that prescribed its form, limited its powers, and constituted its organic law. In any political discussion in America, the Federal Constitution figured largely. The great document enhanced the national habit of rationalizing public problems in legal and constitutional terms; and its ambiguity was a source of both strength and strain as the greatest crisis in the Union's life developed in midcentury.

The uniqueness of the United States derived further from the great experiment in imposing a republican form of government over a vast territory. It derived also from the implementation of a federal system, dividing authority between central and state government. It inhered in providing for regular and orderly expressions of the popular will, setting at naught the practice of ages. it sprang, finally, from the attempt to found a government on the rights of man—an effort that invited ridicule and awe and challenged the political capacities of those making the attempt.

If the United States stood unique as an experiment in the form and spirit of government, it presented at the same time to a critical world an anomaly amidst its bright record of progress and liberalism. "Every true American, every real patriot must feel deeply for the honor of his country, and lament the dark plague-spot which has brought upon it the keen reproaches and

scorn of an enlightened universe," Francis Gillette of
Connecticut sadly observed in the Senate in 1855. Negro
slavery reposed securely in the constitutional and social
structure. Upwards of three and a quarter million human beings had been placed beyond the pale—denied
the promises of the Declaration of Independence and the
guarantees of the Constitution. Their numbers were on
the increase; in the fifties three quarters of a million persons were added to the slave system. Under its method
of labor organization, the South seemed to be enjoying a
heady prosperity.

The nation's capital, where Federal policy on servitude
was formulated, was a slaveholding community. Created
from two slaveholding states, the District of Columbia
numbered one of every four inhabitants as blacks. Most
of these, however, were free Negroes, their percentage
having increased thanks to the lax fugitive slave law of
1793. In 1850 the Federal district contained 51,687 persons, of whom 37,941 were white, 10,059 free blacks,
and 3,687 Negro slaves. Slavery actually was on the wane
there, and the auction block disappeared in 1850 when
Congress had outlawed slave trading in the district.

District Negroes did not live in ghettos, but were
scattered from the Navy Yard to Rock Creek. They were
subject to special municipal legislation—a black code
which became more stringent in the 1850's. Though they
were victims of occasional police brutality and various
kinds of discrimination, Washington Negroes were better off than their counterparts in almost any other
American city. A few Negroes prospered as proprietors
of restaurants and shops, but all were beyond the pale
socially. Washington in the fifties, very social and very
southern, was at the same time an unpromising place for
lawmakers of an antislavery persuasion.

By midcentury, efforts had been made both by the

nation and by states to arrest the growth of the slave order. The Constitution had authorized a ban on the importation of slaves that was carried into effect at the earliest opportunity, in 1808, and Congress had declared the international slave trade piracy in 1820. Federal Congresses had prohibited slavery in the Old Northwest and in the Louisiana Territory north of a line drawn at 36°30'. Exercising their state rights, all the states north of the Mason-Dixon line had abolished slavery. The result was the sectionalization of bondage, creating what the South called its "peculiar institution." Within the fifteen slave states there was a variation of distribution, with a high incidence of slaves in the Atlantic and Gulf states. The demography of slavery discloses that five states— Virginia, South Carolina, Georgia, Mississippi, and Alabama—each held over 400,000 slaves by 1860.

Side by side with governmental efforts to contain slavery had gone efforts by private individuals to extirpate it. By midcentury these attempts had become an abysmal failure. The path of colonization, sketched out by the American Colonization Society, had come to a dead end. Rival views in the American Anti-Slavery Society had produced a schism in the organization. When moral suasion and voluntary institutions failed, a small band of politicians addressed themselves to the work. But neither abolition nor containment attracted voters; the peak of political success for the antislavery movement was attained in 1848, when, whipped to a frenzy by the Mexican War and the prospect that its spoils in the Southwest would be turned into further slave areas, 300,000 voters cast their ballots for the Free Soil candidate, ex-President Martin Van Buren. In that election, however, over 1,360,000 voters placed a hero of that war, the slaveholder Zachary Taylor, in the White House.

The American antislavery movement, unlike the British, had failed to find institutions, public or voluntary, that could channel the antislavery impulse. The result was that by midcentury American voices against slavery were scattered, individual, and anti-institutional—moral and abstract in their outlook. Ascendancy in the antislavery movement had come to William Lloyd Garrison, publisher of a small newspaper, strident in word but nonviolent in deed. He and his fellow abolitionists were in low repute among most Americans.

A principal explanation of this low repute of abolitionists was that their goal conflicted with an ideal which nearly all Americans placed above abolition—the ideal of their great experiment, symbolized by the word in common use, the Union. "The Union is part of the religion of this people," wrote Emerson in his Journal. "The Union is a moral and physical, a political and commercial necessity," declared Secretary of the Treasury Robert J. Walker. Twice before 1854 attempts to arrest the advance of slavery had nearly sundered the Union—in 1820 and in 1850. The first crisis had been composed by a Congressional compromise, dividing the Louisiana Territory between freedom and slavery at the line of 36°30′. The second crisis had been composed, in its territorial aspect, by a different tactic—Congressional nonintervention, leaving the question of slavery to local determination, the principle of popular sovereignty.

Thomas Jefferson had feared that the Missouri crisis of 1820 was "the knell of the Union." John C. Calhoun had announced during the crisis of 1850: "I have, Senators, believed from the first that the agitation of the subject of slavery would, if not prevented by some timely and effective measure, end in disunion." New York's conservative Senator Hamilton Fish confided to a friend: "I have *ever* avoided discussing the slavery question." He reprobated both proslavery and antislavery agitators who "will raise the fell spirit of discord, and let loose wild passions, and sectional differences which may rend in sunder the bonds which have hitherto made us one nation." Abraham Lincoln observed that slavery was "the only one thing which ever endangers the Union." "Much as I hate slavery I would consent to the extension of it rather than see the Union dissolved. . . ."

The low repute of abolitionists was also attributable to the conflict in ideals between freedom for Negroes and racial equality in the future social order. Society in America, never wholly equalitarian or uniform but elitist and regionally varied, was, however, less divided by class and section than by the color line. Belief in Negro inferiority was all but universal. This belief was the touchstone for American political action toward slavery and the Negro.

The great equalitarian philosopher Thomas Jefferson in his *Notes on Virginia* commented on the physical differences between the black and white races and judged the former inferior in powers of reasoning and imagination. He noted the deep prejudices entertained by whites, and anticipated "convulsions, which will probably never end but in the extermination of the one or the other race." Racial difference presented a powerful obstacle to emancipation. Intermarriage promptly effected an improvement in the body and the mind of the blacks. These views, held with some diffidence, he never changed.

The first national crisis over slavery occurred when slaveholding Missouri petitioned to be admitted to the Union. Traditionally historians have interpreted this famous episode as a struggle for the balance of political power between free and slave states, then evenly divided. But a recent student of the Missouri controversy has pointed to the overriding significance of race in the achievement of compromise. Reminded by Senator Nathaniel Macon of North Carolina, who said, "There is no place for the free blacks in the United States," northern legislators acquiesced in slavery's existence south of 36°30′—"a profound renunciation of human rights," judged the historian George Dangerfield. Once Congressmen had agreed to this compromise with the principle of equality, they were confronted with race prejudice in Missouri, where the new constitution authorized the legislature to "prevent free Negroes and mulattoes from coming to and settling in this State. . . ." When debate again raged, Charles Pinckney of South Carolina, a Founding Father, terminated discussion by his reminder that Negroes were "created with less intellectual powers than the whites and . . . most probably intended to serve them and be the instruments of their civilization." Led by Clay, Congress accepted the constitution, solemnly declared it could not be construed to mean what it said, and admitted Missouri. Four years later the slave state by statute nullified the Congressional declaration, which had been made a "fundamental condition" of admission. Race prejudice was enthroned in Missouri, neighbor to the Nebraska country.

When antislavery sentiment sought political action through the Free Soil Party, it evaded the issue of Negro rights. Freesoilers in 1848, and again in 1852, declined to insert in the party platform planks for equal rights for Negroes. Few freesoilers believed in racial equality; many believed in the Negro's inferiority. Keeping the territories free for white men was the only antislavery stand northern voters might be expected to support. "The cry of Free Men was raised," Frederick Douglass wrote in his Negro newspaper, *North Star,* "not for the extension of liberty to the black man, but for the protection of the liberty of the white."

Anti-Negro sentiment in the Old Northwest—the region nearest the unorganized territories of the Louisiana Purchase—grew during the years of the Mexican War and the Compromise of 1850. Each of the northwestern states adopted new constitutions between 1845 and 1851. Starting with Iowa, neighbor to the future State of Nebraska, the framers excluded Negroes from the suffrage and militia. Wisconsin, Illinois, Michigan, Indiana, and Ohio also imposed disabilities; and in all these states except Ohio and Iowa, which did not have plebiscites on Negro questions, popular referendums overwhelmingly rejected Negro suffrage.

The potency of race prejudice in the Old Northwest had been remarked upon by Tocqueville. The Frenchman had been deeply impressed by the depth of racialism in America. "It is difficult for us, who have had the good fortune to be born among men like ourselves by nature and equals by law, to conceive the irreconcilable differences that separate the Negro from the European in America." Racial prejudice he found stronger in states that had abolished slavery than those that had maintained it. "And nowhere is it so intolerant as in those states where servitude has never been known."

Why, then, he asked, was there an antislavery movement in the United States? "It is not for the good of the Negroes, but for that of the whites, that measures are taken to abolish slavery in the United States." His answer anticipated Frederick Douglass's charge about the free-soilers.

Racialism as a force in American history has been too little emphasized by American historians. Constitutional, political, and economic factors have been stressed in explaining the coming of the Civil War. But the power of folk prejudice to paralyze statesmanship has not been adequately examined. Perhaps this is because American historians have taken bias for granted; and perhaps they

have been embarrassed by it. Certainly they have ana-
lyzed statesmen's political thought and have reported
speeches omitting the ineradicable racialism of the Civil
War generation.

Foreign observers, especially British travelers and historians, have been more alert than natives to racialism
in America. We have already seen Tocqueville's views.
Travelers in the 1850's recorded the almost universal persuasion that the black man was inferior and the widespread practice of segregation. William Chambers, a
Scot, described the general white repugnance to persons
of color as "an absolute monomania." He thought all efforts at emancipation valueless so long as northern society condemned Negroes to inequality. This fixed opinion
about Negro character, he wrote, "lies at the root of
American slavery. . . ."

"One characteristic of both the Slave States and the
Free—which has been partially noticed by all travellers,"
is the intense sentiment "as regards the aristocracy of
colour," recorded the eminent English journalist Charles
Mackay. Actually, he discovered, white antipathy toward
blacks was stronger in the North than in the South; and
"Northern men, who talk of so much of liberty, and of the
political equality of all men, turn up their scornful noses
at the slightest possibility of contact with an African."
This northern repugnance toward Negroes, thought
Mackay, manager of *The London Illustrated News,*
tended "to deprive the question of the abolition of slavery
of the grace, the force, and the impetus that are derived
from an uncompromising and thoroughly sincere
conviction."

If abolitionists were few as well as unpopular, equali-
tarians were rare. The majority of Americans were little
stirred by the ideal of freedom for the blacks, and less
so by that of equality of the races. Slavery and the Union,

antislavery and disunion—these seemed to be the alternatives facing Americans. In either event the Negro would be kept in his place. Abolitionism threatened the Union and race relations. Racialism, then, ruled out constructive, ameliorative statesmanship.

Confronted with the alternatives, Americans at mid-century put the Union and white supremacy first.

With little love for the Negro, with the great popular churches split by slavery—as we shall see—citizens clung to the republic and what it stood for. Great numbers of Americans equated the Union with three leading ideas: individual rights, free institutions, and prosperity. The tradition of individual rights had been nourished historically by Protestantism, John Locke, and the experience of imposing a civilization upon a frontier. The mid-nineteenth-century American was an "inner-directed" man who associated his rights with free institutions.

A correspondent of J. Sterling Morton, editor of the Nebraska City *News,* summed up this outlook: "It becomes every friend of the Union, and of Free Institutions, to be calm in his deliberations, and decisive in his action, and to see well to it that his position and influence tell favorably upon the prosperity of our country and the permanance of our institutions. Either the right must ultimately prevail, or our prosperity as States, and as a Nation, is at an end. The great law of reciprocity requires that each man leaves his brother as free to enjoy his natural rights as he desires to be left in the exercise of his own. And this doctrine applies equally to the families that compose a State, and to the States that make up a Republic." [1]

The freedom of American institutions inhered in the absence of a feudal past. America was born free, as Tocqueville remarked. Here there was no monarchy, no standing army, no titled nobility, no established church, no land subject to primogeniture, no state monopolies. Taxes were low, suffrage universal, elections frequent, land readily available, tithing a matter of conscience.

American prosperity seemed unbounded. The first years of the decade of the fifties were flush times, as new gold poured from California, rail builders flung their lines west, Yankee clipper ships gave the nation momentary supremacy in Atlantic commerce, and farms, plantations, and factories increased their output. It was the legendary opportunity of the New World that brought the hundreds of thousands of immigrants from Europe where individual rights were often submerged by the state and prescriptive institutions, and where economic opportunity seemed closed by class lines and inherited land. The crisis of the 1850's that we are about to witness occurred during this period of prosperity. It was not the product of hard times, unemployment, low wages, indebtedness, high prices, and economic exploitation. It therefore does not fit the usual pattern of reform, but it resembles the Progressive movement as a happening of good times.

The crisis that was to develop in the fifties was for many Americans not a struggle between freedom and slavery, or between agricultural and industrial economies, or between state rights and nationalism, or between social classes. It was a crisis over the question whether the rights of white men, the freedom of institutions, and the prosperity of a burgeoning economy might endure.

The legislative work of Stephen A. Douglas and the political demeanor of Franklin Pierce would subject the proud, young republic to its severest test. Popular sovereignty and Bleeding Kansas precipitated a critical period of American history.

2

The future is pregnant with strife

The delegates to the Democratic national convention assembled in Baltimore in June, 1852. As they prepared to select a nominee and draft a platform, the recent crisis of the Union could hardly have failed to occupy their minds. Two years earlier the nation had skirted the edge of disaster. The petition of California to be admitted as a free state, combined with the intention of numerous northerners to prohibit slavery in the Mexican Cession, had induced southern Congressmen to form an opposition bloc, inspired a southern-rights movement, and incited cries of disunion.

The fortunate outcome had been the Compromise of 1850. Statesmanship in 1850—personified by Henry Clay and Stephen A. Douglas—granted California's petition and gave the South its sectional equivalent, a draconian Fugitive Slave Law. The heart of the compomise, however, was the disposition of the vexed territorial question. If on the one hand northern extremists were insisting upon Congressional exclusion of

The chapter title is quoted from *The National Era* of November 11, 1852.

17

slavery from the new territories, on the other hand southern extremists were insisting upon Congressional non-interference with slavery in the territories. The first course had precedent in the Northwest Ordinance and the Missouri Compromise. The second course rested on what has been termed the common-property doctrine. This doctrine, championed by John C. Calhoun, asserted that the territories were the common property of the states, that the Federal government was but the agency of the states, and that it was not only powerless to deprive slaveowners of their property but it was also obligated to protect them in their property rights. The Congressmen of 1850 found a middle way between the two extremes, leaving the question of slavery to the territorial legislatures of New Mexico and Utah. This new-found mode of dealing with slavery in the territories was called popular sovereignty. With the decision of 1850 the specter of the expansion of slavery seemed exorcised. An acceptable arrangement with regard to slavery had been made in all the Federal territories.

Behind the compromise lurked danger. Neither extreme was satisfied; the controversy over slavery in the territories had not in point of fact been closed out. And especially offensive to many northerners was the Fugitive Slave Law, which, with almost summary vengeance, denied due process of law to Negroes. Yet its enforcement and northern restraint against encroachment upon slavery were the price of maintaining the Union, warned a special convention in Georgia. Fire-eaters in South Carolina and Mississippi were disappointed that compromise thwarted secession.

By 1852 it seemed clear that only by evading the issue of Negro slavery could a national crisis be deferred. Should a major party menace the stability of the South's biracial society, the republic would be in peril.

The Compromise of 1850, the delegates to the Baltimore convention realized, was the paramount issue of the year 1852. In choosing a Presidential nominee they eventually designated a dark horse, the neutral Franklin Pierce of New Hampshire. Pierce's name was not presented to the convention until Virginia nominated him on the thirty-fifth ballot, and he did not win until the forty-ninth. The key resolution of the platform read: "The Democratic Party . . . will abide by, and adhere to, a faithful execution of the acts known as the Compromise measures settled by the last Congress."

The other major party—the Whigs—also convened in Baltimore, shortly after the Democratic nomination. More grievously rent by sectional rivalries than the Democrats, the Whigs balloted fifty-three times before nominating the Mexican War hero Winfield Scott. The delegates then unanimously approved the platform except for the central plank that pledged "acquiescence" in the Compromise of 1850, "the act known as the Fugitive Slave law included." The plank carried by a vote of 212 to 70, opposition coming largely from Scott's supporters. The old soldier, faced with disarray in the Whig ranks, sought to resolve his dilemma by announcing, "I accept the nomination with the resolutions annexed." To which antislavery Whigs rejoined, "We accept the candidate, but we spit on the platform."

Both major parties had been divided in the previous Presidential contest, when in 1848 "Conscience Whigs" defected and a former Democratic President, Martin Van Buren, accepted the nomination of the Free Soil Party. Now in 1852, the Free Soil Democracy, assembled at Pittsburgh, nominated John P. Hale of New Hampshire for President, and denounced the compromise measures of 1850 as "inconsistent with all the principles and maxims of Democracy."

Historians have traditionally interpreted the election of 1852—a referendum on the compromise—as a resounding victory for Pierce and a mortal blow to the Whig Party. And indeed it was.

The "doughface" Democrat carried all but four of the thirty-one states; "Old Fuss and Feathers" won only the invariably Whig preserves of Massachusetts, Vermont, Tennessee, and Kentucky. Pierce's biographer, Roy F. Nichols, however, has observed that there remained an element of superficiality in his triumph. When the anti-Pierce vote is consolidated, the victor's majority was less than fifty thousand in a vote of more than 3.1 million. Nothwithstanding he carried all but two northern states, Pierce polled a minority of the free-state vote, where voters cast fourteen thousand more ballots against him than for him.

A breakdown of the balloting into county units, however, discloses that Pierce's victory constituted the greatest Democratic Party triumph in the period 1836–92. The Democrats carried four states for the first time in this fifty-six-year span, carried every section of the country for the first time, and carried 127 counties they had not won since 1836. In six of the eight sections of the country, as defined by one analyst, the Whigs did not win one electoral vote; they retained only 434 counties, compared with the 1,110 swept by the Democrats (350 more than they had ever won).

Particularly notable was the fate of the Whig Party in the South. Only one state of the future Confederacy gave its electoral vote to Scott, undeviatingly Whig Tennessee, but only by a margin of 1,880 votes. Traditionally Whig states forsook old loyalties. Louisiana went Democratic by a margin of 1,392 votes, North Carolina by 686. Georgia offered four tickets that cut Scott's vote down to one third that of Taylor in 1848. The returns prefigured the emergence of a one-party South. The Whig Party would never again present an independent slate in a Presidential election.

The Free Soil candidate polled but slightly more than one half the number of ballots given its nominee in 1848. Clearly the country had sustained the Compromise of 1850. Whig questioning and Free Soil denouncing of it had been rebuked. "The Union above all" seemed the sentiment of the electors. Still the election had left the country with only one strong national party. How well suited was it to the maintenance of sectional harmony?

Dr. Gamaliel Bailey's antislavery newspaper, *The National Era,* struck a warning note in an editorial headed "The Presidential Election—Its Result": "The [Democratic] Party is made up of discordant materials. Barnburners, Slavery Propagandists, Disunionists, Compromisers, Hunkers [Conservatives], and Progressives, have united in supporting one man for the Presidency, but will hardly unite upon any great question likely to come up for consideration. . . . The Future is pregnant with strife. General Pierce may calculate on anything but a tranquil Administration."

The new President might at first glance seem admirably adapted to the work of sectional conciliation and national leadership. He had started well in life, the son of a Revolutionary War general and two-term governor of New Hampshire. His father had seen him through Bowdoin College and launched him in politics and law; young Franklin had been elected to the lower house of the state legislature at the same time that his father had been re-elected governor. At the age of twenty-seven he had been elected speaker of the house; and then had gone on to Washington for nine years, first as a Representative and next as United States Senator. He proved a master manipulator of Democratic state politics as well as a skillful pleader before local juries in a successful law practice. During the Mexican War he became a brigadier general, although kept from combat by a combination of illness and accident. Handsome, of middle height but militarily erect, scrupulously polite, convivial, and magnetic, he enjoyed a widespread approbation that he sought to maintain by harmonizing opposing elements. The youngest man ever to that time elected chief executive of the United States, he might appear to possess the capacity for growth and resilience required to cope with the problems posed by rapid national development.

The fourteenth President, however, became known as "poor Pierce" in his own time and was rated "below the average" by historians a century later. The weakness and ineffectuality of a pleasant, pliable man have become a stereotype. His party in 1856 repudiated him, the victim of his disastrous Kansas policy—and he has never recovered the popularity and respect he held in 1852. Today we may recast the stereotype. The handsome, pleasant façade concealed weakness—physical, psychological, and philosophical.

Pierce's conviviality embraced a fondness for alcohol, and this shortcoming contributed to his decision to resign from the United States Senate in 1842. His popularity rested upon a need for approbation, unfitting him for executive firmness. Seemingly strong in body, he was susceptible to respiratory ailments and suffered from malaria during his summers in Washington. His biographer has suggested that he had inner conflicts because of his health, of a sense of alienation from the New England aristocracy to which his wife Jeanie belonged, and of Jeanie's antipathy to the public life he reveled in. Tragedy compounded these tensions. Shortly before his inauguration as President, he and his family were in a railroad accident, and Pierce saw his only remaining son, a boy of eleven, killed before his eyes. In a personal letter to Jefferson Davis, he wrote of "the terrible catastrophe," mourning, "How I shall be able to summon my manhood and gather up my energies for the duties before me it is hard for me to see." Jeanie Pierce believed her husband had deceived her by stealthily seeking the Presidency while denying his ambition to her. Now, numbed by her terrible loss, she would withdraw to her private apartments in the White House. The normally buoyant, engaging Pierce was unnerved.[1]

Beyond these physical and psychical disabilities lay limitations of philosophy. A Jacksonian Democrat, he tempered his nationalism by a devotion to state rights and southern sensibilities. He subscribed to Calhoun's paralyzing view of the Union: "Are we not too prone to forget that the Federal Union is the creature of the States, not they of the Federal Union?" Pierce asked rhetorically in a public message. In his inaugural address he upheld the rights of the South, guaranteed by the Constitution and assured by the Compromise of 1850. He announced it as a part of his creed that Americans had a constitutional right to keep slaves, and he deplored the "fanatical excitement" of foes of involuntary servitude. He differed from many western Democrats in his narrow view of the ability of the central government to assist in internal improvements. "With the Union my best and dearest earthly hopes are entwined," he could say; but it was a Union of sovereign states, of minimum government, premised on a constricting constitutionalism and laissez-faire, respectful of human bondage and hostile to antislavery sentiments.

Nathaniel Hawthorne, his college classmate and friend, in a campaign biography referred to Pierce's hostility to "antislavery agitation," his view of "slavery as one of those evils which divine Providence does not leave to be remedied by human contrivances, but which, in its own good time, by some means impossible to be anticipated, but of the simplest and easiest operation, when all its uses shall have been fulfilled, it causes to vanish like a dream."

Such were the lineaments of Franklin Pierce, one of the two chief executives to preside over the United States during the period of our concern. Would he be tried and found wanting in a time that required him to unite responsibility with his high office, firmness with flexibility, and to search for the national purpose enveloped in separate local interests? Could the United States be governed successfully by a President who believed he was the agent of sovereign states? Who deferred to the special interests of one section of the country? Who accepted the permanence of slavery? Who denounced opponents of slavery?

Pierce's shortcomings were complicated by dissensions in his party. It was of course those dissensions that had brought him to the Presidency—a dark horse. The Democrats' disunity, made up of sectionalism and factionalism, was exemplified in his selection of a cabinet. Pierce sought party harmony, naming the aging leader of one New York faction, William L. Marcy, as his Secretary of State, the champion of southern rights, Jefferson Davis of Mississippi, as his Secretary of War, and the crabbed legal genius, Caleb Cushing of Massachusetts, as his Attorney General. To these he added party wheelhorses. The omissions were conspicuous—James Buchanan, Lewis Cass, Stephen Douglas, John A. Dix, and Howell Cobb. Cobb confided to Alexander H. Stephens on the eve of inauguration: "I have written to my friends—and Gen'l Pierce has been informed—that I would not go into the cabinet with Gen'l Dix or any other free soiler. So you see that in any mongrel programme I am ruled out. . . . the policy of a mongrel cabinet had been strongly urged upon Gen'l Pierce . . ." [2]

Though it would remain intact throughout the Pierce Administration, the Cabinet proved imperceptive—wanting in statesmanship. It endorsed and implemented the Kansas-Nebraska policy—and thereby contributed to embroiling the nation in five years of strife. Largely negative in domestic policy, Pierce and his advisers yielded leadership to Congress. It was a Senator in the Administration party who broke the peace he himself had helped forge in 1850 and make secure in 1852. Let us see how this calamity occurred.

With the Compromise of 1850 a politicial era ended. New men—all born in the nineteenth century, two generations removed from the Founding Fathers—came into power. A new political style emerged. In 1850 nationalism had prevailed over sectionalism, statesmanship over partisanship, compromise over intractability, and the work of Congress had won national acceptance. The new political style would be distinguished by a lack of great leaders, by a tilting of the sectional balance, by Congress's disposition not to compromise, and by the North's disposition not to acquiesce in the work of Congress or (as we will see) of the Supreme Court. Partisanship, acrimony, and occasional fisticuffs characterized the legislators after 1853. The change became startlingly clear as the nation grappled with the politics of settling the Platte country.

Between the wide Missouri and the high Rockies lay a vast territory virtually uninhabited by white men. Long described as "the Great American Desert," it was in actuality a virgin land that rolled and rose from the river valley through the Great Plains to the Mountains. Francisco Vasquez de Coronado had crossed a portion of it in 1541, in his search for the mythical kingdom of gold, Quivira. He found instead the Plains Indians, and in present day Kansas, the area of our special concern, the Kansas, Wichita, and Pawnee tribes. More than two and half centuries later, the country, embraced in the Louisiana Territory, was purchased by the United States. The illusion that the plains were desert wastes was not destroyed by the explorations of Lewis and Clark, Zebulon M. Pike, and Stephen H. Long. The southern part of the Louisiana Territory was more speedily settled than the northern.

Left as unorganized Indian Territory, the area west of the Red River of the North and the Missouri River was occupied by only occasional white men—traders, Indian-fighting soldiers, and missionaries. In the 1840's an increasing flow of settlers moved across the plains along the Santa Fe, Oregon, and California Trails. American acquisition of the Southwest in 1848 and the simultaneous discovery of gold in California quickened the stream of pioneers, intent on the Far West.

Beginning in 1844 western legislators sought to organize the Indian country, at first to afford protection to emigrants and later to open the area to white settlement as an accompaniment to construction of a transcontinental railroad. "In the name of God, how is the railroad to be made if you will never let people live on the lands through which the road passes?" cried a Missouri Congressman. In February, 1853, the chairman of the House Committee on Territories, William A. Richardson of Illinois, reported a measure to organize the country north of 36°30′ as Nebraska Territory. One section provided for extinguishing the Indian land titles. The Nebraska bill said nothing about slavery, but it passed over stiff opposition from the South Atlantic states, where men feared the measure might throw advantages to the northern states. The chairman of the Senate Committee on Territories, Stephen A. Douglas, favorably reported the bill, but it was laid on the table on the final day of the session by a vote of 23–17. No southern Senator except those from Missouri voted aye. It seemed that the organization of Nebraska would continue to be resisted by the South in future sessions.

It was a new Congress that convened in December, 1853, as the last Whig Administration yielded to the fully victorious Democrats. When Pierce had been inaugurated in March, "the pride and power of the Democratic party seemed to be at their flood," observed the Indiana Free Soiler George W. Julian. The party had overwhelming control of both branches of the Thirty-third Congress; the divisions in the House were 159 Democrats, 71 Whigs, and 4 Free Soilers; in the Senate 38 Democrats, 22 Whigs, and 2 Free Soilers. The Whigs had lost 17 members of the House, while the Democrats had gained 19.

Of the two branches, the House of representatives was the less distinguished. In the whirligig of politics only 80 of its 234 members had been returned. It readily re-elected the ponderous Linn Boyd of Kentucky as speaker, and he allocated committee memberships among the nation's sections. The more notable Congressmen included the old Jacksonian Thomas H. Benton of Missouri, Douglas's henchman Richardson of Illinois, the agrarian conservative Alexander H. Stephens of Georgia, and the abolitionist Gerrit Smith of New York. The strongest state delegation hailed from Virginia.

The Senate chamber held distinct groups, of which the most interesting was known as "the Mess." Made up of state righters, it included Virginia's two senators, James M. Mason and Robert M. T. Hunter, the one the author of the Fugitive Slave Law, the second an aspirant for the Presidency. Other members were South Carolina's chivalrous Andrew P. Butler and Missouri's David Rice Atchison, who upon the death of the newly elected Vice-President was chosen presiding officer of the Senate. These four Senators shared a house at 361 F Street, each taking his turn monthly in laying in supplies, directing the household, and keeping accounts. The F Street Mess was one locus of power in Pierce's Washington.

One heartbeat away from the Presidency, the coarse-grained Atchison, a frontier lawyer, had increasingly devoted himself to ultra-Southern principles. His career had been marked by his sharp rivalry with the anti-slavery Benton for supremacy in Missouri state politics and by a passionate belief that Missouri's future hinged on opening the Nebraska region to slavery. During the preceding summer Benton and Atchison had waged a campaign for the Senate in which the Nebraska question had dominated the political dialogue. Benton had advocated construction of a transcontinental railroad through the central route, for which territorial organization was indispensable. Atchison pledged he would support a territorial bill only on the condition it did not restrict slavery. "I will vote for a bill that leaves the slaveholder and non-slaveholder upon terms of equality," he promised. An imposing figure with a florid complexion, Atchison stood six feet two inches tall, straight as an arrow. Popular with his Senatorial colleagues who elected him president pro tem sixteen times, he sometimes belied his Presbyterianism by intemperance in language and liquor.

A second group of Senators led the northwestern Democracy and represented the principle of compromise. Lewis Cass of Michigan, standard-bearer of 1848 and

early exponent of popular sovereignty, now aging, indolent, and fat, was one of these. Jesse Bright, ambitious to control Indiana politics, hostile to Pierce,
placatory to the South, a petty man with a large stomach,
curried favor with Cass.

The most eminent figure in the group, and indeed in
the Democratic party in the decade, was Stephen A.
Douglas. Born in Vermont and educated in the "burned-
over district" (western area fired by religious revivalism)
of New York, he was nevertheless indentified with the
Mississippi Valley. He had emigrated to the West at the
age of nineteen, and in turn taught school, practiced law,
and held public office. He settled in central Illinois,
where northerners and southerners rubbed elbows with
one another. After serving in the House of Representatives, he had been elected U. S. Senator in 1843. He
listed as political tenets his belief in territorial expansion, commercial development, and local autonomy. He
had opposed the partition of Oregon, joining in the cry
for "fifty-four forty or fight." A heavy investor in Chicago
real estate, he looked to encouraging the growth of that
booming lake city by building rail connections with the
South and West. In 1850 he secured a Federal subsidy
for the Illinois Central Railroad in a projected rail link-
age between Chicago and Mobile. In the same year he
had figured importantly in drafting and enacting the
territorial bills for New Mexico and Utah that left the
slavery question to local decision. Ambitious for his
country as well as for himself, optimistic about the future of America, willing to use government as an instrument for furthering individual opportunity, he appealed
powerfully to young Americans. Only five feet four
inches in height, he had a herculean build except for
his small legs. Contemporaries called him "the Little
Giant"; he was a profile in energy, combativeness, and

courage. Few contemporaries could equal him in political debate.

The declining Whig party claimed illustrious leaders. Salmon P. Chase of Ohio, strong-willed, religious if self-righteous, animated by both ambition and a sense of wrong, was a quondam Whig who had joined the Liberty and Free Soil Parties and had been sent to the Senate by a combination of Free Soilers and Democrats. Massive in figure and handsome in feature, he comported himself with gravity, advancing his antislavery convictions with more earnestness than art.

More pro-Negro than most of his contemporaries, he opposed denying suffrage to Negroes as well as proposals to exclude them from entering Ohio and to colonize them. *"True democracy makes no inquiry about the color of the skin,"* he declared. Yet he believed climate would keep Negroes out of Ohio, and said, "Ohio desires a homogeneous population, and does not desire a population of varied character."

His Ohio cohort, Benjamin Franklin Wade, was an impetuous patriot, a gruff reformer, with a bulldog purpose. Sometimes portrayed as a hectoring politician, he was sincere, if overzealous, vehement if not ill-natured in debate, tenderhearted toward his family (as his private correspondence demonstrates) though vituperative to his enemies. Elected Senator because of his opposition to the Fugitive Slave Law, he quickly took his place as a leader of the antislavery group, trying in vain to repeal the objectionable law. Just above the middle height, with strong, nearly savage features, he struck some observers as a cold, unfeeling man. But he was in fact moved by a passionate hatred of slavery, by a deep religious conviction outwardly shown not in church-going but copious quoting of the Bible, and ardent belief in giving land to the landless. His historical reputation deserves rehabilitation. The newly elected Whig Senator, William P. Fessenden of Maine, wrote his wife: "The man of all others that I like best in the Senate is Mr Wade of Ohio. He is rough, but bold and honest—will speak what he thinks, and is pretty apt to be let alone for that reason. I wish we had more such men." [3]

In contrast to Wade's bluff manner and lack of culture (after seeing *Othello* he described it as "gross and barbarous") was Charles Sumner of Massachusetts. A graduate of Harvard College and of Harvard Law School, where he later lectured, he had traveled extensively on the Continent before becoming active in the peace movement and politics. He had opposed the Mexican War, participated in founding the Free Soil Party, and attacked segregated schooling in Boston. A coalition of Free Soilers and Democrats had elected the "Conscience Whig" to the U. S. Senate, where he soon made his famous "Freedom National" speech, indicting slavery and the Fugitive Slave Law. Far short of being an abolitionist, he argued that the Founding Fathers were antislavery in purpose, that the Federal government had no authority to protect slavery in the territories, that each state might determine for itself the extent of its obligation to enforce the Fugitive Slave Law, and that slavery in the United States rested merely upon municipal or state law. Vain, tall, and powerfully knit, a bachelor, "he had nothing but himself to think about," Henry Adams observed. The scholar in politics, handsome in his English Tweeds, "he was the classical ornament of the anti-slavery party," Adams recalled.

Last of all, this portrait gallery of Senators held William H. Seward, the leading Whig of his day. Following a brilliant career as governor of New York and a criminal lawyer, he had gone to Washington in 1849, where his antislavery principles, exerted in advising President

Taylor and in opposing the Compromise of 1850, had helped divide the Whig Party. His reference to "a higher law than the Constitution" in 1850 (merely a rhetorical allusion to commonly accepted divine law) made him appear more extreme than he actually was. He combined in his person the politician and the statesman, a dedicated antislavery man who was alert to party considerations. "A slouching, slender figure; a head like a wise macaw; a beaked nose; shaggy eyebrows; unorderly hair and clothes; hoarse voice; offhand manner; free talk, and perpetual cigar"—so Henry Adams described him.

The foregoing figures numbered among them the nation's best political minds. Just as they did not measure up to the leaders that passed into eclipse in 1850, they were several cuts below the ministry of talents that directed American public affairs in the Revolutionary era. Yet the republic faced an unsuspected peril of a magnitude that had not existed since the 1770's.

Franklin Pierce had been made President upon a pledge to sustain the Compromise of 1850. In his inaugural address he had voiced his hope that the question of slavery "is at rest"; and in his annual message to this new Congress, he recalled the "anxious apprehension" of the year 1850 and pledged that the repose attained by the Compromise would "suffer no shock during my official term, if I have power to avert it. . . ."

If, however, a divisive issue should appear, the prospect of a pragmatic compromise was not strong. Pierce had swiftly forfeited much of his popularity with his own party through his ineffectual handling of the patronage. Politicians, press, and promoters greedy to exploit the Treasury surplus kept the Democratic party in partial disarray.

A little more than a week after the session started, Senator A. C. Dodge of Iowa introduced a bill for the organization of the immense area west of Iowa and Missouri, extending from 36°30′ on the south to 43°30′ on the north to the Rocky Mountains on the west—the Nebraska Territory. Identical with the unsuccessful Richardson bill of the previous session, which made no mention of slavery, it was referred to the Committee on Territories.

When it was reported out of committee on January 4, 1854, by the chairman, Stephen A. Douglas, it had undergone a mystifying change that precipitated the crisis of the Union, gave the lie to Democratic Party pretensions to preserve national harmony, and set the nation on the high road to the Civil War. The substitute bill, now a Douglas measure embracing all the remaining Louisiana Territory, was accompanied by a report which declared that legal opinion was divided on the constitutionality of the Missouri Compromise and which commended to the Senate application of the principles of the Compromise of 1850 to the Nebraska Territory. The report disingenuously asserted that these principles had then been intended to "furnish adequate remedies . . . in all time to come," and to "avoid the perils of a similar agitation, by withdrawing the question of slavery from the halls of Congress. . . ." Not the history of the Compromise of 1850 or of the campaign of 1852 or the nervous, apprehensive approach to ultimate repeal of the Missouri Compromise by this Congress can sustain this assertion. However, the notion "that the Compromise of 1850, being a new compact and treaty between the North and South on the subject of slavery, necessarily abrogated every previous arrangement of a conflicting character," as the Richmond *Enquirer* phrased it, had become a part of a radical southern creed.

The main principle that the Senate was urged to apply to the region once declared forever free was "that all questions pertaining to slavery in the territories . . . are to be left to the decision of the people residing therein. . . ." A few days after the substitute bill was reported, the Washington *Sentinel* published an amended version, giving Douglas's explanation that through a "clerical error" a key section had been omitted. This fresh version transferred the principle of popular sovereignty from the report to the bill itself.

In this opaque process of making law the substitute bill had seemed to suggest that popular sovereignty would become operative only after a court had invalidated the Missouri Compromise; this amended substitute plainly implied that the Missouri Compromise had been set aside. Yet it would not do, in the minds of some lawmakers, to leave the matter of repeal to implication. The Kentucky Whig, Archibald Dixon, on January 16 rose in the Senate to propose outright repeal of the compromise that had helped maintain American nationality since 1820. Douglas, who preferred to work by indirection, was startled. Within a short time, after listening to Dixon's arguments on a carriage drive, he yielded, exclaiming, "By God, sir, you are right, and I will incorporate it in my bill, though I know it will raise a hell of a storm."

It was one thing to get the chairman of the Senate committee to acquiesce in repeal. But it was another to get the chief executive to acquiesce and thereby make repeal a party measure. Douglas apparently had not consulted the head of the government about his bill, so fraught with meaning to the party's future. On Sunday morning, January 22, representatives of the two Congressional committees called on Pierce's confidant, Jefferson Davis, Secretary of War. They described the proposed bill and asked his assistance in securing Pierce's approbation that day. It was necessary to see

The future is pregnant with strife 35

ianism, because they wished to make the committee report the next day. "I went with them to the Executive
mansion," Davis recalled, "and, leaving them in the re-
ception-room, sought the President in his private apartments, and explained to him the occasion of the visit."

The President met with his callers, listened to a reading of the bill and an explanation of it. Pierce was im-
paled on the horns of a dilemma: repeal, to which he
was officially and solemnly opposed, or repudiation of a
powerful group in his party. He was pledged not to reopen the slavery controversy and also to the principles of
1850. He himself subscribed to the doctrine of popular
sovereignty. He may well have reviewed mentally his
own plight as President. His success depended on legislative sanction for his programs, especially an aggressive
foreign policy. He would be a total failure without support from the Senate. Pierce acquiesced and himself
wrote out the repeal amendment. It was agreed to divide
the immense territory into two elements, Kansas and
Nebraska—largely, it would seem, to give persons in the
adjoining states of Missouri and Iowa equal chances to
exploit the territories. The Pierce organ, the Washington
Union, endorsed the Kansas-Nebraska bill as "a test of
democratic orthodoxy"; and it became an Administration
measure.

Though the metamorphosis of the Nebraska bill was
not yet quite complete—there would be further minor
alteration—the vast mischief was done. Douglas, an architect of the peace of 1850, and Pierce, a beneficiary of
the peace, had failed to exorcise the specter of disunion
when it had reappeared. The nation had entered upon a
critical period.

The enormity of what was being done was clearly
grasped by some contemporaries. "REPEAL! is the cry,"

exclaimed the *Commercial Register* of Sandusky, Ohio. "The triumph of the measure is a triumph of Slavery [and] Aristocracy, over Liberty and Republicanism. . . ." it went on, stressing the threat to individualism and the Union. The frontier hero and Texas statesman, Sam Houston, warned the Senate, "My word for it, we shall realize scenes of agitation which are rumbling in the distance now. . . . It will convulse the country from Maine to the Rio Grande."

Henry Wilson of Massachusetts, though he erroneously followed a conspiracy theory of history in interpreting the origins of the bill, wrote in his three volume tome: "No single act of the Slave Power ever spread greater consternation, produced more lasting results upon the popular mind, or did so much to arouse the North and to convince the people of its desperate character." The historian James Ford Rhodes judged: "It is safe to say that in the scope and consequences of the Kansas-Nebraska act, it was the most momentous measure that passed Congress from the day that the senators and representatives first met to the outbreak of the civil war." A more recent historian, G. G. Van Deusen, declared: "More than any other measure passed or threatened during the decade, this bill was responsible for the Civil War."

How are we to explain this headlong rush toward disaster? Historians have spilled much ink in answering this question, focusing much—too much—of their attention on the problem of the motives of Stephen A. Douglas in espousing repeal. They have impeached him of conspiring with the "slave power," and of being its dupe; of Presidential ambition; of pursuing his own pecuniary advantage as a real-estate speculator; of deferring to the wishes of Senator Atchison who was being challenged by Benton for the Senate seat. More friendly interpreters have portrayed him as motivated by a desire to further construction of a Pacific railroad, by the democratic principle of popular sovereignty—a western statesman whose political idea could have made the Civil War a needless conflict.

No one of these explanations is adequate. Taking them with Douglas's own recently found letter about the Nebraska question and with some analysis of Douglas's views, we can, however, come closer to an understanding of the repeal.

In a contemporary letter to citizens of St. Joseph, Missouri, who were interested in immediate organization and settlement of the Nebraska territory, he reviewed his decade of efforts to create a territory on the west bank of the Missouri River. He represented territorial organization as "a national necessity." Three steps were essential: removal of the Indian barrier, peopling the plains and mountains, and construction of railroads and telegraphs across the fifteen hundred miles between the settlements of the Mississippi Valley and the Pacific coast. "How are we to develope [*sic*], cherish, and protect our immense interests and possessions in the Pacific, with a vast wilderness fifteen hundred miles in breadth, filled with hostile savages, and cutting off direct communication." These considerations, and not slavery, he stressed; "so far as the slavery question is concerned," he continued, "all will be willing to sanction and affirm the principle established by the Compromise measures of 1850."

Douglas's letter, dated December 17, 1853—*before* he agreed to repeal—leaves unexplained his willingness to unfasten the bag of winds which he had helped to close in 1850, loosing "a hell of a storm," his insensitivity to antislavery sentiment as a moral force, and his miscalculation of it as a political force. If it is true that Douglas was primarily concerned about western development and building a railroad, it is also true that he made a gigantic misjudgment in exalting these interests above the Union. He impaired national harmony and kindled a sense of outrage among those—North and South—who regarded the settlement of 1820 as a national contract as well as those who opposed the spread of slavery. He misread American values, and it is for this reason he does not stand to the fore in the pantheon of American statesmen.

If Douglas's motives remain puzzling, so also is the question of why the South, which had not asked for repeal and which at first seemed ambivalent to it, at length recklessly and wholeheartedly embraced it, alienating numerous northern Democrats, renewing the sectional conflict that threatened southern security.

Although the measure came from the northerner Douglas, and received the imprimatur of the northern President Pierce, southern leaders including Atchison, Dixon, and Davis contributed to shaping the bill and making it Administration policy. But there were many clear-seeing southern members of Congress who declared there was no immediate necessity to organize the territory, repeal was a firebrand, the South had no interest in the Nebraska region, slavery would never take root there. Sam Houston flatly said of repeal: "I, as a southern man, repudiate it."

Southern history has no record of a demand for repeal; the matter had not been a public issue. A Whig representative from Tennessee asserted in the Committee of the Whole: "No public meeting of the people, no primary assembly, no convention, no legislative body has called for this measure." During the legislative struggle few southern legislatures passed resolutions approving the bill, in contrast to early and numerous protests from northern bodies.

The majority of southern leaders, however, accepted repeal, justifying it on the grounds that it was a northern gift that representatives of slaveholders could not refuse, it was an act of justice, it accorded with the principle of equality among the states. The explanation of southern support of a bill which to many seemed injurious or valueless, the historian Avery Craven believes, seems "to turn on the point that Southern reactions in the long run were not to the Kansas-Nebraska Bill and what it offered but rather to the Northern reaction to that bill."

As storm clouds gathered in the North, southerners sought shelter under a common roof. Repeal, in this view, became a sectional matter. Party considerations figured too; repeal was a Democratic policy invoking party loyalty, and all the while northern Whigs united in opposition to it, estranging southern members of the party.

If Craven is correct in attributing southern adoption of repeal to a sectional reflex, he has suggested an unflattering portrait of the South. The region had justified its slave-based "Athenian democracy" as a school for statesmen. Now was the time for statesmanship—statesmanship that entailed rejection of repeal, even as southern Whigs and Calhoun and many Democrats had rejected the annexation of all Mexico in 1848. Craven sees the South in 1854 drawing together, thin-skinned, defensive, abandoning common sense. Douglas, Dixon, and Pierce were culpable, but so too were southern leaders.

What warped counsel the Richmond *Enquirer* gave when, once the issue had been joined, it wrote: "While the restriction of 1820 remains to attest the jurisdiction of Congress over slavery, there is no security for the rights of the South. The South then should be content with nothing less than a surrender of the usurped power and a repeal of the odious statute. This concession is essential as well as to the dignity of its character as to the security of its rights." And finally, in assessing the South's response one may ponder Alexander H. Stephens's words uttered in 1860: "never was an act of Congress so generally and so unanimously hailed with delight at the South. . . ."

What of Douglas's attitude toward slavery? It has often been said that he disapproved of it; and biographers have quoted his private conversation of this year 1854 in which he called slavery "a curse beyond computation" and "a dangerous tumor" afflicting the country. Critics have pointed out that his first wife inherited slaves from her father and they were bequeathed to Douglas's two sons; under provisions of the will Douglas received one fifth of the net profit from the slaves and the Mississippi plantations. He managed this property from 1848 until his death, never seizing the opportunities afforded to sell the slaves, though as early as 1850 he told a friend he intended to transfer all the property to Illinois "as soon as possible." It is difficult, to square Douglas's practice with his pronouncement; and it is to be borne in mind that Douglas never publicly condemned slavery. Its morality did not disturb him; its profitability impressed him. Speaking in Memphis in 1858 he said: "Whenever a territory has a climate, soil, and productions making it the interest of the inhabitants to encourage slave property, they will pass a slave code and give it encouragement. Whenever the climate, soil and productions preclude the possibility of slavery being profitable, they will not permit it. You come right back to the principle of dollars and cents."

As to Negroes he shared the prevalent notion of white superiority over blacks. Defending the Fugitive Slave Law before a hostile audience in Chicago, where the city council had denounced the act and branded its makers traitors and Iscariots, Douglas declaimed: "The civilized world have always held that when any race of men have shown themselves so degraded by ignorance, superstition, cruelty, and barbarism as to be utterly incapable of governing themselves, they must, in the nature of things, be governed by others, by such laws as are deemed applicable to their condition."

What of Douglas's role in repeal? He had earlier in public life been an ardent defender of the Missouri Compromise. It had "become canonized in the hearts of the American people as a sacred thing, which no ruthless hand would ever be reckless enough to disturb," he had told a Springfield audience in 1849. His subscription to the Missouri Compromise of course entailed endorsement of the principle that Congress may rightly exclude slavery from the territories, instead of the new notion of Congressional nonintervention. The story of his espousal of repeal of this "sacred thing" during the first three weeks of January, 1854, does not reveal qualities of deliberation, judiciousness, or foresight. Rather, it reveals rashness and callousness to national harmony. He was overly willing to adapt means to ends, earning Jefferson Davis's description of him as a "plastic and constructive genius." In some respects the fateful repeal remains one of the riddles of American historiography.[4]

If repeal had been unintended by Douglas, it was not wholly unanticipated by others. Senator Atchison, as we have seen, had made repeal an issue in Missouri politics.

Although the South as a section had not asked for repeal, there had been restless southern spirits favoring it. Weeks before the Dixon amendment, a member of the House of Representatives in a little-noticed letter wrote to Alexander H. Stephens's brother of "the repeal of 'the Missouri restriction' which will be offered to the bill organizing the Territory of Nebraska. . . ." [5]

If repeal was unintended by Douglas, it was also unnecessary for the organization of Nebraska. Time was on the side of eventual organization as well as on the side of freedom. John Bell of Tennessee said in a sagacious speech in the Senate that he saw no need to create a territorial government. There was "no white population to demand the protection and security of a territorial government," he pointed out. The preceding October there had been only three white persons in the territory, apart from officials, soldiers, missionaries, and traders. "Wait a season," he wisely counseled, "be not so impatient to build up a great northwestern empire. In due time all your plans of development will be accomplished. . . ."

Bell could see no "practical advantage or benefit to the country, generally, or the South in particular," in repeal. Moreover, would not repeal provoke a "deep-rooted hostility to slavery and the whole South?" Should one of the proposed territories establish slavery, he presciently asked, would not this sound the "tocsin for a general rally of all the worst elements of the Abolition faction . . . stimulated and supported by northern citizens who have heretofore given no countenance to their excesses?"

So far as the railroad explanation of repeal is concerned, it may be observed that there was no urgency in 1854 greater than that of insuring domestic tranquility. A transcontinental line was not completed, in point of fact, until 1869—fifteen years after the Act;

and it appears not only that the nation did not suffer unduly for the delay but also that the construction of the Union Pacific may have been a case of premature enterprise. Passage of the Kansas-Nebraska bill was a disaster, a national tragedy, one of the greatest political follies ever wrought by an American Congress, for which a transcontinental railroad was a cheap seduction.

Douglas's notion of popular sovereignty was itself an *ignis fatuus*. National action on slavery in the territories had been taken repeatedly. Recurring crises over slavery had demonstrated that slavery was not a local issue, but national. Problems of slavery extension, of petition gags, of fugitive slaves, all pointed to the impossibility of leaving slavery to local resolution. The territories themselves were the creatures of Congress, their officials appointees of the President. Frederick Douglass, a slave who after escaping to freedom became the leading Negro in the United States, speaking of the Kansas-Nebraska bill in 1854 charged: "The only shadow of popular sovereignty is the power given to the people of the territories by this bill to have, hold, buy and sell human beings."

"In all else," Douglass continued, pointing to Federal sovereignty over territories, "popular sovereignty means only what the boy meant when he said he was going to live with his uncle Robert. He said he was going there, and that he meant while there, to do just as he pleased, if his uncle Robert would let him." Although it has been argued that the slavery provisions of the Kansas-Nebraska bill were a compromise, this is true only in a peculiar sense. Slave interests compromised on new demands that went beyond and repudiated an earlier compromise. They accepted the lesser extreme of two new pro-Southern views that had come forward only in the 1840's. They took half a new loaf in place of a full one.

They took popular sovereignty in place of national protection of slaveowners in the territories, which the common-property doctrine entailed. In doing so they gained
an opportunity earlier yielded in exchange for national
immunity for slavery south of 36°30′! At the same time
the free states lost the exclusion of slavery from the
upper part of the Louisiana Territory, and gained nothing. Strange compromise!

It was precisely because the measure was not a compromise that the North erupted against it. Douglas reported his bill to the Senate on January 23—the day
after Pierce had placed his imprimatur upon it. Chase
asked to have consideration postponed for a week. Meanwhile he prepared his attack. The next morning the
press carried his "Appeal of the Independent Democrats
in Congress to the People of the United States." The
opening gun of the verbal war that continued until the
guns of the Charleston batteries opened fire on Fort
Sumter, it takes rank among the most famous pieces of
propaganda in United States history.

Eminent historians have divided over interpreting the
Appeal. James Ford Rhodes praised it as a "brave, truth-
ful, earnest exposition," whereas Allan Nevins condemned it as "grossly exaggerated," hasty, and
unnecessary. Signed by one other Senator, Charles Sumner, and by four Representatives—antislavery men or
abolitionists all—it rang the changes on many emotional
themes. It also pleaded a historical interpretation of the
bill that was widely accepted by northerners.

The signers of the Appeal warned of imminent danger to free institutions and the Union. They arraigned
the bill as a "gross violation of a sacred pledge"; and,
going beyond this, charged it was part of "an atrocious
plot" to convert the unoccupied territories "into a dreary
region of despotism." They reviewed the history of Con-

gressional exclusion from the territories and denied claims that the Compromise of 1850 had superseded the Missouri Compromise. Looking to both railroad promoters and white farmers, they predicted that introduction of slavery would present "almost insuperable obstacles to building the road" and make a homestead law, if enacted, "worthless." They appealed to the people to resist the conspiracy of the "slave power"; they implored Christian ministers in particular to interpose. They called for protest, "by correspondence, through the press, by memorials, by resolutions" against "this enormous crime." They pledged their own resistance by speech and vote. "We will not despair; for the cause of human freedom is the cause of God," they concluded their impassioned address. Moralistic, accusatory, outraged, hyperbolical, the Appeal contained enough sincerity and truth to be taken up by countless newspapers in the Northern states.

Incensed by the personal calumny in the Appeal and by the conviction that he had been duped into granting a delay on his bill to enable Chase and his fellow signers a chance to spread their poison, Douglas took the floor of the Senate on January 30 to open debate and reply to his critics. To a thronged chamber he explained that his committee had taken the principles of the Compromise of 1850 as its guide—the great principle of self-government: "That the people should be allowed to decide the questions of their domestic institutions for themselves." He rejected the assumption of the manifesto that the Founding Fathers had intended to ban slavery from all the territories, declaring that their purpose had been to draw a line recognizing climate and production as the dividing boundary between free and slave states. This policy had been persisted in until 1848, when northern Congressmen defeated attempts to extend the line to the

Pacific Ocean. That defeat "reopened the slavery agitation," he charged, and "created the necessity for making
a new compromise in 1850."

"The leading feature of the compromise of 1850 was
congressional nonintervention as to slavery in the Territories. . . ." This feature, he claimed, had superseded
the Missouri Compromise; and it had won endorsement
from both major parties in 1852. This same feature of
self-government had characterized the progress of emancipation in the states, where state action, not "the dic-
tates of the Federal Government," had freed the slaves.
He challenged the Congress to show him a man who had
favored the Compromise of 1850 that did not now favor
popular sovereignty for Kansas and Nebraska. "This
tornado has been raised by Abolitionists and Abolitionists alone," he cried. As for the prospect of slavery in
the Nebraska territory, "in that climate, with its production, it is worse than folly to think of its being a
slave-holding country."

It was an impressive performance on the part of the
Little Giant, alternating between indignation and cogent
argument, flawed by his assertion that the Compromise
of 1850 had superseded that of 1820. The speech was
weakened further by his assumption that slavery was a
local matter and repeal the concern of abolitionists
alone.

The great debate had begun. Leadership of the forces
of resistance fell largely upon Chase, who now rose,
looking like a Roman senator, to defend the Appeal.
That document had not meant to be soft, he said; there
had been "a criminal betrayal of precious rights." "What
rights are precious, if those secured to free labor and
free laborers in that vast Territory are not?" A few days
later he made a major speech; "Let Us Maintain Our
Plighted Faith" was his theme. He recalled how, when

this Congress had convened, "no agitation seemed to disturb the political elements. . . . It is slavery that renews the strife," he charged. He excoriated Douglas's claim that the Missouri Compromise had been superseded; this "statement is untrue in fact and without foundation in history." Prophesying that the nation was on the verge of an "Era of Reaction," he urged the Senate to "reject the whole proposition which looks toward a violation of the plighted faith and solemn compact which our fathers made. . . ." Chase had good cause to write a friend he was gratified by "the profound attention . . . and the immense audience . . . by which I was listened to."

Wade, Chase's Ohio colleague, on February 6 joined in attacking the notion of supersession: "I hardly know what a man means when he tells me that an act of legislation is superseded by a principle." Recurring to the intention of "our forefathers" with respect to the territory, he evinced his belief that "it should be fenced up from the intrusion of this accursed scourge of mankind, human slavery." What would be the fearful outcome, if, "You of the South, all of you, propose to go for repudiating this obligation?" Conflict and disunion, he answered. "I am an advocate for the continuance of this Union; but . . . I do not believe this Union can survive ten years the act of perfidy that will repudiate the great compromise of 1820."

Dixon of Kentucky interrupted to raise the question of racial equality. "Does the Senator consider the free negroes in his State as equal to the free white people?"

"Yes," answered Wade. "I say in the language of the Declaration of Independence, that they were 'created equal.'. . ." Under this doctrine slavery was wrong, and in this sense he was an abolitionist, who preferred a gradual system of emancipation. Wade had refrained from saying he believed in the biological equality of the two races.

Senator George E. Badger of North Carolina made his "old mammy" speech a short time later. "Why, therefore, if some southern gentleman wishes to take the nurse that takes charge of his little baby, or the old woman that nursed him in childhood, and whom he called 'mammy' until he returned from college, and . . . whom he wishes to take with him in her old age when he is moving into one of these new Territories for the betterment of the fortunes of his whole family, why, in the name of God, should anybody prevent it?"

To this, "Bluff Ben" Wade blisteringly replied: "We have not the least objection to the Senator's migrating to Kansas and taking his old mammy along with him. We only insist that he shall not be empowered to sell her after taking her there." Wade doubtless did a disservice to Badger, termed "the ablest Whig then in public life," because the North Carolinian was arguing for the diffusion of slavery, and he did not anticipate that slaves would be taken into Kansas except as domestic servants.

Seward, canny and oracular, disposed of Badger's diffusionist argument with his question, "whether slavery has gained or lost strength by the diffusion of it over a larger surface than it formerly covered?" Pleas that only a few slaves would enter the territory did not convince him. "One slaveholder in a new territory, with access to the executive ear at Washington, exercises more political influence than five hundred freemen." There was no necessity for the bill. "Who, indeed, demands territorial organization in Nebraska at all?" He joined opponents of the measure in denying that the Missouri Compromise had been abrogated in 1850. Then he sounded a defiant, lofty note: "Senators from the slaveholding states . . . you may legislate, and abrogate, and abnegate as you will; but there is a Superior Power that overrules all your actions." With clearer vision than Douglas, he affirmed, "The slavery agitation you deprecate so much is an eternal struggle between conservatism and progress, between truth and error, and between right and wrong."

In his studious, eloquent address "The Landmark of Freedom," Sumner rejected Badger's "delusive suggestion" about "a beneficent diffusion of slavery," contrasting the free state of Illinois where the Northwest Ordinance had banned slavery and the adjacent slaveholding State of Missouri where Congress had accepted slavery. The way to establish tranquillity throughout the country was not by passing the bill but by defeating it.

Sumner's fears about the spread of slavery were shared by numerous colleagues. A recent student of the proposition that "all well-informed contemporaries" knew that slavery had already reached its natural limits of expansion found that fifty-six members of the Congress addressed themselves to this question. Of these exactly half apprehended expansion, thinking slavery could extend into Kansas. To these contemporaries conflict over slavery in the territories was not repressible through the operation of nature. Legislation was a realistic—not emotional, least of all fanatical—measure to arrest the advance of slavery.*

The South made its defense of slavery not alone upon

* Some historians, arguing that slavery had reached its natural limits of expansion, point to the census findings of only two slaves in Kansas in 1860 as proof positive of slavery's inability to secure a foothold. To state the circumstance of 1860 as proof that it was impossible for slavery to expand into Kansas is both a logical and an historical fallacy. It may also be noted that slavery, far from being on the wane in neighboring Missouri, grew in the 1850's by more than 30 per cent, from 87,422 slaves to 114,931.

the traditional textbook abstraction of state rights, but also upon the less familiar cry of white supremacy. Southern Senators frequently recurred to racial themes: the inferiority of Negroes, the impossibility of racial equality, the pervasiveness of race prejudice among northern whites, and the belief in American freedoms for whites only. "You pursue it [abolition], you say," Virginia's Hunter retorted to the North, "because slavery is an evil—a great evil. Suppose that it is. To turn the slaves loose upon the community would be a still greater evil, both to blacks and whites, as all experience proves. What, then, is to be done?" he asked, and went on to answer that by popular sovereignty, "we have removed from this great Confederacy a sore cause of strife, disturbance, and collision. . . ."

South Carolina's Butler asked whether abolitionists would themselves consent to a "domestic relation" with a Negro? If the South's 3 million slaves were freed and sent North, would the northern people welcome them? "No, sir; they would resist them with the bayonet." The great Georgia leader, Robert Toombs, affirmed as an article of Caucasian faith, "The liberties of America were won by white men for white men, by our race for our race."

Historians have stressed the constitutional issues aired in the debate; they have ignored the anthropological assumptions by the lawmakers. Senator John Pettit of Indiana presented the traditional view of plenary Congressional power over the territories. It flowed, he said, from the power to acquire territory; and he cited the precedents of the Northwest Ordinance, the Missouri Compromise, and the authority of Justice Story and Chancellor Kent. But he would not exercise the power in the new territory, and he favored passage of the bill.

But also he rejected "ultra extreme Abolitionism"

with its appeal to the Declaration's claim all men are created equal. "Tell me, sir, that the slave in the South, who is born a slave, and with but little over one half the volume of brain that attaches to the European race, is his [the European's] equal, and you tell me what is physically a falsehood. . . . The idea that negroes, if they are to go there [the Nebraska territory] are to be free and freemen, is to my mind preposterous."

The common-property doctrine had a spokesman in Butler. "The territory of the United States is the common property of all the States. . . . I have always taken the ground that we are, *as States, tenants in common* in the territory which is the property of the United States." With thrusts at Sumner and Wade he went on to raise the specter of race mixing and affirm God's intention to make Negroes inferior beings. "That He has made the blacks unequal to the whites, human history, as far as it can take cognizance of the matter, has pronounced its human judgment."

The Senate debate, taken in entirety, was attended by as much heat as light. The opponents' major speeches, together with Badger's, were widely disseminated in a booklet entitled "The Nebraska Question." The debate awakened the nation to the crisis; it contributed to sectionalizing the country; and it ventilated the issues.

What of Cass and repeal? He was the author of the doctrine of popular sovereignty, the Democratic Party nominee for the Presidency in 1848—the Nestor of his party. He believed slavery to be a great social and political evil, and he hoped it may end "peacefully and justly," but he went on lamely, "I see no way in which this can be effected but by leaving it to those most interested in it, and to the process they may find it best to adopt. Any external interference would only aggravate the evils and the dangers. . . ." With his passivity to-

ward the national government's power to limit an acknowledged misfortune, Cass threw away a claim to
statesmanship.

The South was solidifying behind the bill. "The Whigs
of the South—Where Are They?" asked the Richmond
Enquirer. "We would rejoice to see the South present an
unbroken front in defence of its rights. . . . Can it be
possible that any man will go over to the enemy?"

Behind the scenes a series of bipartisan caucuses was
held, revealing almost complete southern support for the
measure. Toombs from his desk in the Senate, while
Chase was speaking, wrote to a Baltimore editor: "We
had a caucus this morning of the friends of the bill,
Every Southern Whig Senator for the bill and every
Southern Democrat whose opinions are known also for
it. The meeting was composed of a large majority of the
Senate—who unanimously determined to carry the bill
as it stands on the slavery issue." Northern assault had
helped produce this southern unity.

Senatorial approval was a foregone conclusion. Debate
was closed on March 3 in an all-night sitting—"that
noche triste of our history"—as Longfellow described it.
Bell, Fessenden, Wade, Seward, Houston all spoke. Violent feelings and vulgarity marked the long night. Liquor
flowed in an anteroom; Mason of Virginia threatened
Fessenden, and Wade gave the Virginian a verbal wal-
loping. Shortly before midnight Douglas took the floor to
deliver a speech that lasted nearly four hours. Having the
last word, he answered his critics vigorously. By this
time he had subordinated his claim that the Compromise
of 1850 had superseded that of 1820, and he amended
the bill to say that the latter agreement was "inconsistent" with the principle recognized in 1850. Douglas
predicted that given time, despite abolitionist agitation
and northern misunderstanding, his principles of pop-

ular sovereignty and nonintervention would be as popular in the North as in the South.

It was nearly daybreak when the Senate voted. The outcome was ominous for national and party unity. Only two southerners—honored in history for their courage and vision—opposed the bill, the Democrat Houston of Texas and the Whig Bell of Tennessee. Four northern Democrats, on the other hand, refused to make the bill a "test of democratic orthodoxy." The division was 37 to 14—an overwhelming victory for the Administration, with the help of nine southern Whigs. But the South had united, and the northern Democrats had divided. With a peculiar myopia the administration organ pronounced that now, "the Union will stand as safe from peril, and last as long as

> 'The hills,
> Rock-ribbed and ancient as the sun!' "

The House of Representatives lacked illustrious names; its work, done not in wordy debate but in committee and in complicated parliamentary process, is less easy to record. The bill's labyrinthine progress, however, was attended by greater public excitement than was the oratory and celerity of action in the Senate. By early March, the northern public had become aroused, and there were signs of Democratic disruption and fears for the Union. Anxious about House action on the bill, the Ohio editor Samuel S. Cox tried to reassure Douglas: "The sentiment of this state is misrepresented. We can today, whip the Whigs & Abolitionists cleanout—niggers too." [6]

A worried correspondent of Kentucky Congressman John C. Breckinridge, future Vice-President of the United States, declared he was unable to see the necessity for raising one question of repeal. It "will lead to a fatal di-

vision in the democratic ranks, and engulph [sic] it in ir-
retrievable defeat . . . this Nebraska business is with
me a matter of conscience, as well as one of policy so far
as the party is concerned. I can respect neither the motive which has prompted the step, nor the man who first
put it in motion." [7]

Although the Democrats had a two-to-one majority in
the House, ninety-two of the 158 Democrats were northerners. The northern Democrats were restive under
party discipline, partly because of the ferment among
their constituents and partly because of sectional and
factional considerations. Southerners dominated the
House Committee on the Territories, 4 to 2, and its
chairman, William A. Richardson of Illinois, was Douglas's ally. The second northern member, William English
of Indiana, and most northern Democrats wanted the
House version of the bill reworded to incorporate a positive statement of popular sovereignty that would define
the issue for the forthcoming campaign as self-government in the territories and not repeal of the Missouri
Compromise. The committee would not agree to English's
wording. Moreover resentment against Pierce lurked
among New York Democrats, who disliked his giving patronage to men who had bolted the party in 1848 to follow
Martin Van Buren.

An early outcome of these considerations was the
House's refusal to refer the Senate bill to Richardson's
committee; instead, on March 21 it buried it at the foot
of the calendar of the Committee of the Whole. Pierce
now exerted himself. He wrote editors, held interviews
with politicians, used the patronage.

On May 8 Richardson, confident he had recovered
enough dissident Democrats to force the issue, moved
that the House resolve itself into the Committee of the
Whole on the State of the Union. He candidly declared he

intended to have the committee lay aside all the bills
that were ahead of the Kansas-Nebraska bill. He won this
first victory, 109–88; and then one by one he had the
question put eighteen times until he had reached the
House version of the bill. Now he proposed the Senate
version as a substitute. This was debated for two days
until party discipline broke when he moved that debate
close the following day at noon. Opponents of the bill
had been playing for time, believing they could block
the Nebraska measure. Tempers erupted, names were
hurled, and filibustering began; the sergeant-at-arms was
ordered to arrest one member who seemed about to use
a weapon against another. Douglas appeared on the
floor of the House and worked indefatigably. After a
week of stormy scenes and one hundred speeches, the
astute little parliamentarian, Stephens of Georgia, in an
intoxication of excitement, executed an intricate pro-
cedural maneuver that brought the Kansas-Nebraska bill
to a vote. Shortly before midnight, Monday May 22, the
House approved the momentous law by the narrow vote
of 113 to 100. "I feel as if the *Mission* of my life was
performed," Stephens exulted.

The House vote, as analysis shows, had not been an
Administration victory. More than a third of the Democratic Party had refused the cup described as a test of
orthodoxy. Of the 158 Democrats only 100 had given
their yeas. Sectional allegiance, not party loyalty, animated the legislators. Only nine slave-state Representatives had voted nay, seven Whigs, of whom but one was
from the Deep South, and two Democrats—John Millson
of Virginia and Benton of Missouri. The bill had won by
enlisting 13 southern Whigs among its supporters; two-
thirds of the southern Whigs had sustained the Democrats. But every northern Whig had voted nay. Only three
New Englanders—one each from Maine, New Hamp-

shire, and Connecticut—had voted for the bill. Together, the votes in Congress disclosed a house dividing against itself.

The Kansas-Nebraska Act, approved by the President May 30, shattered party allegiances. It metamorphosed the Democratic Party from an apostle of national harmony into an agent of sectional discord. It transmuted the character of the party, as northern Democrats withdrew and southern Whigs joined. It gave rise to a northern antislavery party and to a solid South. It renewed the peril of disunion.

The clearest immediate meaning of the Congressional vote lay in the realignment of political parties. Governor Horatio Seymour of New York, looking at freesoil losses in the Democratic Party, lamented, "The only party left therefore to sustain it [the bill] at the North is that of the Old Line Democracy.' [8] Three days after the House passed the law, Wade, a lifelong Whig, renounced his party, proclaiming to the Senate, "We certainly cannot have any further political connection with the Whigs of the South. . . . I am an abolitionist. . . ."

Douglas proved to be plainly wrong in judgment when he told Howell Cobb of Georgia, "The storm will soon spend its fury and the people of the North will sustain the measure when they come to understand it." Equally dim-visioned was the Washington *Union*: "We . . . congratulate the country upon the removal from the halls of Congress, for all time to come, of those embarrassing and irritating controversies which have grown out of the agitation of the slave question."

Beyond further sectionalizing the Union and disrupting political parties, the Kansas-Nebraska Act had made Stephen A. Douglas a controversial figure and had lessened the reputation of Franklin Pierce. "Never before has a public man been so hunted and hounded," commented the Washington *Union* on the Senator. "Pierce is a runt miserable dog, and seems bent on destroying his country, as well as himself," Fessenden wrote home.[9] The specter of an aggressive slavocracy antagonized northerners, curbing the prospects of annexing Cuba, inspiring the formation of the Republican Party, and thrusting the sectional struggle upon Kansas Territory. Most evil of all its effects, the measure had envenomed an ancient conflict and invited national strife.

3

A hell of a storm

The Kansas issue erupted during an age of romanticism. Americans of the fifties saw their past and their future in romantic terms. They gave fealty to the Declaration of Independence and the Constitution, albeit they read these eighteenth-century scrolls diversely, according to their needs.

They looked upon old Europe as decadent and upon young America as the wave of the future. They believed the United States should not interfere in European affairs but should be a beacon of freedom for benighted European governments and peoples. They regarded as their manifest destiny the duty to extend the blessings of liberty over less fortunate people in the Western Hemisphere.

American letters of the fifties expressed American values. At the beginning of the decade Nathaniel Hawthorne established his fame by his novel *The Scarlet Letter*. With a wonderful moral intensity, Hawthorne brooded upon sin and guilt in Puritan New England. The following year Herman

---

The chapter title is a remark by Stephen A. Douglas in 1854, quoted in *The True History of the Missouri Compromise and Its Repeal* by Mrs. Archibald Dixon.

Melville, who had sailed before the mast and had lived with the natives in the South Seas, produced *Moby Dick,* a magnificent allegorical tale of the struggle between one-legged Captain Ahab, obsessed with revenge, and a huge and ferocious whale—an ambiguous conflict between good and evil. Against this monster, man's only choice was to fight heroically. In 1855 Walt Whitman sent forth his "letter to the world," *Leaves of Grass.* A great poet and prophet of democracy, Whitman eschewed formal creeds and institutions, finding man's future in an intuitive individualism. His activism fostered rebellion against social wrong.

Out of such romanticism, with its sense of sin, its belief in the necessity to fight evil, its faith in man's capacity to shape a better future, came that remarkable novel *Uncle Tom's Cabin.* Penned by the daughter of an eminent Calvinist clergyman, it originally appeared as a serial in the abolition newspaper, *The National Era.* By the spring of 1854 her indictment of slavery had been read by millions. Untold numbers became familiar with the dramatized version, first presented in August, 1852.

Harriet Beecher Stowe's concern was condemnation of slavery, not of the South; she was national rather than sectional in her outlook. She believed slavery endangered the ideal of the unexampled American republic—the Union established under Christian principles. The institution of slavery, for which the North was responsible as well as the South, violated the republican ideal and Christian teaching. If Mrs. Stowe did not make "this big war," as President Lincoln is supposed to have said when she called on him at the White House, she was, nevertheless, perhaps the most influential figure in the antislavery reformation of the fifties.

Even before the Senate had approved the Kansas-Nebraska bill, Mrs. Stowe joined in outraged protest. She helped organize the New England preachers who—3,050 strong—signed a two-hundred-foot petition against the bill. She prophesied "such an uprising of the country as never has been heard of since the days of the Revolution." She wrote for the leading organ among the religious press, *The Independent,* a stirring "Appeal to the Women of the Free States of America," inciting them to protest the iniquity proposed by Congress. "Shall the whole power of these United States go into the hands of slavery?" she demanded.

Though Douglas, insensitive to the immorality of slavery, scorned the clergy's protest, the spiritual warfare against slavery, waged in the thirties, silent in the forties, had been renewed. Previously the struggle for men's souls had been fought in the rural areas; now the battleground, as T. L. Smith has emphasized, was the great cities, where revivalists were at work. Great national denominations, Presbyterian, Methodist, and Baptist, had been sectionalized by slavery, and by 1854 evangelical Christianity was more free in the North to attack slavery. A new religious press, of which *The Independent,* founded in New York City by Congregational ministers, was foremost, molded antislavery sentiment at the hearthsides of countless northern readers. After the Nebraska bill had passed Congress, *The Independent* foresaw only divine retribution upon the hapless republic: "The Fugitive-Slave Law and the Nebraska bill have assumed the conservation of slavery by the national arm. And a Christian nation that in this age has voluntarily given itself to the crime of oppression must suffer the judgments of heaven. . . ." Revivalists in the cities "carried the brunt of the religious attack upon the Negro's bondage."

The northern secular press also joined the antislavery rising. The power of the press had markedly increased by midcentury. Published cheaply and plenteously by Hoe's rotary press, daily newspapers had almost doubled in number between 1840 and 1850 and continued to climb in the fifties. They became big business in metropolitan centers, competing with one another for circulation and employing special correspondents for wide coverage. Intensely partisan, the press was presided over by a galaxy of distinguished editors the like of whom the nation never saw again. The three greatest newspapers, Horace Greeley's *New-York* Tribune, William Cullen Bryant's New York *Evening Post,* and Samuel Bowles's Springfield, Massachusetts, *Republican* formed the cutting edge of press assault on the Kansas-Nebraska measure and its aftermath. The *Tribune,* in particular, through its semiweekly and weekly editions, had a readership far into the interior of the republic.

The abolitionists, that antislavery vanguard, of course fell upon the bill. On May 22, 1854, "against the strongest popular remonstrances—against an unprecedented demonstration of religious sentiment—against the laws of God and the rights of universal man—in subversion of plighted faith, in utter disregard of the scorn of the world, and for purposes as diabolical as can be conceived of or consummated here on earth," Garrison raged in *The Liberator,* the House of Representatives passed the Nebraska measure. At the same time Henry Ward Beecher, Harriet's ministerial brother, was crying in *The Independent,* "For the last time God has called upon the north. . . . Let the *conscience* of the North settle this question, not her *fears.* God calls us to a religious duty!"

Douglas had miscalculated the depth and durableness of antislavery feeling in America when he repealed the Missouri Compromise. He anticipated abolitionist objection, but he did not foresee that so fundamentally conservative a group as the northern merchants would oppose repeal. Yet conservatism demanded maintenance of the *status quo*, and the mercantile interest demanded that the West be kept freesoil and that the South not be allowed to grow in power. In New York City, the greatest mercantile community in the nation, merchants held protest meetings, adopted anti-Nebraska resolutions, and organized to correspond with other cities and to aid in sending free emigrants to Kansas. To some extent also, though historians have heretofore exaggerated the extent, German-Americans, who had earlier identified their political fortunes with the Democratic Party, now began to reconsider their allegiance.

If Mrs. Stowe had summoned the spirit of the American Revolution, and if the New York merchants had formed a committee of correspondence reminiscent of that earlier time, still another ominous sign appeared as Americans willfully obstructed law. Even as Bostonians had flouted the Tea Act in 1773, so now they flouted the Fugitive Slave Act. Two days after the House approved the Kansas-Nebraska bill, Anthony Burns, who had escaped from slavery in Virginia, was seized in the heart of Boston. His master had come to demand his return.

"Yesterday a fugitive slave was arrested in Boston!" Longfellow exclaimed. "To-day there is an eclipse of the sun. 'Hung be the heavens in black.'" The repeal of the Missouri Compromise had incensed Boston. Intending to prevent rendition, leading abolitionists came to Burns's aid. At a great gathering in Faneuil Hall, scene of Revolutionary meetings—"the cradle of liberty"—the passionate agitator Wendell Phillips cried, "Nebraska, I call knocking a man down, and this is spitting in his face after he is down." The meeting broke up when it was learned that an attempt was just then being made to rescue the fugitive, and Faneuil Hall men rushed to join in. The Federal marshal managed to thwart the mob, but only after it had battered down the door to the courthouse and killed one of his posse.

Commissioner Loring, after a hearing, ordered the rendition to bondage of Anthony Burns. Would Boston submit? With unwonted firmness President Pierce telegraphed the district attorney: "Incur any expense deemed necessary . . . to insure execution of the law." He provided a revenue cutter to carry the slave back to Virginia. On the day Burns was to be escorted to the wharf, twenty-two companies of Massachusetts soldiers and a large number of city police guarded the streets. Fifty thousand people witnessed the procession past houses draped in mourning.

"And, as I thought of Liberty/Marched handcuffed down that sworded street/The solid earth beneath my feet/Reeled fluid as the sea," wrote Whittier. There was no incident, but plainly Boston was in an ugly mood; and so was much of the North. Pierce soon found in his correspondence a letter addressed, "To the chief slave catcher of the United States."

Garrison despaired of a government that surrendered a human being to the slave power. Slavery, he thought, would be insatiable in its demands for expansion. "Our Union, all confess, must sever finally on this question." At an open-air celebration of the Fourth of July held by abolitionists at Framingham, Massachusetts, he made a melodramatic performance as a "testimony of his own soul." One by one he burned copies of the Fugitive Slave Law, the decision of Commissioner Loring in the Burns case, and the charge of the Federal judge to the grand jury in respect to the assault upon the courthouse—the audience shouting "Amen" after each immolation. Then he held aloft the U. S. Constitution, branding it "a covenant with death and an agreement with hell," and burned it to ashes—the audience sending up a tremendous shout of "Amen!" Disunionism was not a southern monopoly; but it must be recognized that disunionism was not widespread in the North, not espoused by political leaders, and was aimed at disassociating the republic from slavery.

If all Massachusetts did not like Garrison's pyrotechnics, the state did enact in the wake of the Burns case a stringent measure ostensibly intended to safeguard free Negroes against being sent into slavery, but actually to impede the execution of the Fugitive Act. The Kansas-Nebraska Act, in fact, inspired a general northern assault upon the Fugitive Slave Law. Only one state, Vermont, had enacted a personal-liberty law in response to the 1850 measure; and its action had been offset by Pennsylvania, which moderated its famous statute. Now six states within two years passed personal-liberty laws: Connecticut, Vermont, and Rhode Island in 1854, and Michigan, Maine, and Massachusetts in 1855. The Dred Scott decision would bring yet another wave of statutory resistance to the rendition of fugitives.[1]

The laws came perilously close to nullifying the Act that formed an integral part of the Compromise of 1850. Nullification was not a southern monopoly, and the laws which combined justice with its obstruction exacerbated the exchange of accusations about sectional bad faith.

If Anthony Burns was marched down a public street to slavery, other slaves were furtively being spirited to freedom by the "Underground Railroad." The famous "Liberty Line" has come down to us in history as a highly organized network of routes, conductors, and hiding places, supported by all abolitionists, dominated by Quakers and New Englanders, successful in engineering the escape of immense numbers of slaves. As for the slaves themselves, tradition relates that they escaped by following the North Star to Canada and that they all yearned for freedom. So runs the myth.

The historical fact, according to Larry Gara, author of *The Liberty Line*, is that the "railroad" was never well organized but was a loose, shifting local network, often managed by free Negroes, often opposed by abolitionists who regarded this tactic of assisting escape as a prolongation of slavery instead of a root-and-branch reform. Moreover, the number of fugitives was never large, the census of 1850 reported a total of 1,011 slaves missing for the preceding year, and the number actually declined during the decade of controversy to 803 in 1860. In the ten years the number of free Negroes in the North increased by less than 13 per cent, while the number of slaves in the South grew by 23.5 per cent. The number of free Negroes in the State of New York diminished by 2,583, and in New England stabilized after 1840. The entire Negro population of Canada West was only slightly more than 11,000 in 1860. The slaves often seem not to have been inspired by an abstract love for freedom, but by a desire to run away from work. Not the abolitionists but the slaves, who risked capture and punishment and who received minimal assistance, were the true heroes of the underground.

But this is mere sober fact, and the important historical point is that the fancy was believed in the South, aggravating mistrust. Less than a month before Lincoln's election *The Charleston Mercury* fulminated: "When a party is enthroned at Washington . . . whose credit is, to repeal the Fugitive Slave Laws, the *under*ground railroad, will become an *over*ground railroad."

The measure of race prejudice in the North before the Civil War has only recently been taken. Proscription was the rule. Free Negroes were forbidden to migrate from state to state; they were denied the ballot in most states, denied the right to serve as jurors or witnesses or even to sue in courts. They were segregated in chuches, public carriers, and in public schools. The famous "separate but equal" doctrine, accepted by the U. S. Supreme Court in 1896, originated in a Massachusetts court ruling in 1849, when Charles Sumner as attorney vainly challenged segregation in Boston. Job competition between white and black menial labor was keen. On the eve of the Civil War, historian Leon Litwack has concluded, "the northern Negro remained largely disfranchised, segregated, and economically depressed."

The most influential and esteemed moulders of northern thought believed Negroes were different from whites. Harriet Beecher Stowe, in a little-noticed passage in *Uncle Tom's Cabin*, wrote: "The negro, it must be remembered, is an exotic of the most gorgeous and superb countries of the world, and he has, deep in his heart, a passion for all that is splendid, rich, and fanciful; a passion which, rudely indulged in by an untrained taste, draws on them [*sic*] the ridicule of the colder and more correct white race." Nevertheless, she believed the exotic and less correct Negro entitled to his freedom.

Emerson, in an arresting passage from his chapter on race in *English Traits*, observed: "Race is a controlling influence in the Jew, who, for two milleniums, under every climate, has preserved the same character and employments. Race in the negro is of appalling importance." However, he believed there were powerful countering forces; and in the long view, "The fixity or inconvertibleness of races as we see them, is a weak argument for the eternity of these frail boundaries. . . ."

The great Unitarian clergyman, Theodore Parker, declared, "Of all races the Caucasian has hitherto shown the most . . . instinct of progress." In a sermon to his Boston congregation he fixed fault for racial oppression upon the nation. "If the nation play the tyrant over her weakest child, if she plunder and rob the feeble Indian, the feebler Mexican, the Negro, feebler yet, why the blame is yours."

The science of anthropology sustained the all but universal belief in the Negro's inherent inferiority. An "American school" of anthropologists rejected the notion of the unity of the human race, with its equalitarian implication, and held the notion of polygenism—the separate creation of the various human races as distinct species. There had been a black Adam and Eve. The American group reached a pinnacle of prestige when the great Swiss-American scientist Louis Agassiz adhered to it.

Southerners, paradoxical as it may seem, generally rejected this anthropological bulwark of white supremacy, because it conflicted with Scripture. In 1854 two leading members of the "American school" of anthropology, Dr. Josiah Nott, a Mobile physician, and George Gliddon, an Egyptologist, published a ponderous tome of more than eight hundred pages, *Types of Mankind*, meant to be a compendium of anthropological evidence proving polygenism. Later that year a principal defender of slavery, George Fitzhugh, repudiated the widely discussed book.

"We abhor the doctrine of the *Types of Mankind;* first, because it is at war with scripture, which teaches us that the whole human race is descended from a common parentage; and, secondly, because it encourages and incites brutal masters to treat negroes, not as weak, ignorant and dependent brethren, but as wicked beasts, without the pale of humanity. The Southerner," he continued, "is the negro's friend, his only friend. Let no inter-meddling abolitionist, no refined philosophy, dissolve this friendship."

Fitzhugh's book, *Sociology for the South; or, the Failure of a Free Society* (published in Richmond in 1854), was an important statement of the proslavery argument. Fitzhugh justified slavery on three major grounds. First, he compared the South to ancient Athens, a democracy governed by its free citizens. "Now, it is clear the Athenian democracy would not suit a negro nation, nor will the government of mere law suffice for the individual negro. He is but a grown up child. . . ." Secondly, because the Negro is improvident, society has a right to prevent his becoming "an insufferable burden . . . and can only do so by subjecting him to domestic slavery." The third justification for slavery was that in character "the negro race is inferior to the white race. . . ." American slavery relieves the Negro "from a far more cruel slavery in Africa, or from idolatry and cannibalism, and every brutal vice and crime that can disgrace humanity; and . . . it christianizes, protects, supports, and civilizes him . . . it governs him far better than free laborers at the North are governed. . . ." "Negro slavery would be changed immediately to some form of peonage, serfdom or villeinage, if the negroes were sufficiently intelligent and provident to manage a farm."

Fitzhugh disowned the philosophy of Thomas Jefferson, arraigning John Locke and indicting the Declaration of Independence. The latter-day Virginian denied the contract theory, life, liberty, and equality as inalienable rights, laissez-faire, and the idea of progress. Two philosophies were locked in combat; slavery, he believed, would be everywhere reinstituted; they could not coexist. Abraham Lincoln conceived of his "house divided" prophesy after reading an editorial by Fitzhugh.

The apologist had adverted to a common theme—the

wage-slavery argument—in extolling the virtues of slavery. This contrast between the miseries of the industrial wage slave and the carefree security of the southern bondslave inspired the long poem, cast in heroic couplets, by the South Carolina classicist and public man, William Grayson. "The Hireling and the Slave" published in 1854, summed up its message in the pithy line, "The Slave escapes the perils of the poor."

Racial antipathy ran deep. It was an old folk prejudice, understandable in unsophisticated terms to the non-slaveholding poor whites of the South. The northern traveler, Frederick Law Olmsted, recorded his conversation with a poor farmer who had emigrated from Alabama to Texas. Slavery was a bad institution, the farmer acknowledged, but he feared emancipation of the slaves.

"It wouldn't do no good to free 'em," he declared, "and let em' hang round, because they is so monstrous lazy; if they hadn't nobody to take keer of 'em, you see, they wouldn't do nothin' but juss natrally laze round, and steal, and pilfer, and no man couldn't live, you see, whar they was—if they was free no man couldn't live." Then came the clinching argument: "Now just suppose you had a family of children, how would you like to hev a nigger feeling just as good as a white man? how'd you like to hev a niggar steppin' up to your darter?"

With upwards of three millions of slaves imbedded in the structure of its society and economy, with northern hostility to slavery erupting in a manner unexampled in the history of the republic, with a liberticidal philosophy to draw upon, with an insurmountable color bar, the South was prepared to embrace repeal of the Missouri Compromise.

Outstanding historians have crossed swords over the South's first response to repeal. Avery Craven had described a state of apathy, whereas Allan Nevins has judged, "actually it would be misleading to call the South indifferent." The truth of course is that there was no united southern opinion at the beginning of the legislative struggle. The currents of southern thought about repeal and popular sovereignty may be said to have flowed through a funnel, not narrowing to the small neck until Kansas began to bleed. Wise spokesmen of the region saw no advantage and much danger in repeal; rash heads cried that opponents of the bill should "be hanged in chains as an example and warning to traitors."

In 1854 the South was not solid in its espousal of repeal. Yet it did not actively oppose it. Apathy, doubt, and enthusiasm were exhibited by its publicists. In the end, however, as in the case of their lawmakers, the preponderance of the southern people supported the ill-fated law.

The Nebraska issue produced the greatest political party convulsion in United States history. The disruptive bill appeared at a time when, as we have seen, the Democratic Party was a precarious coalition; the bill almost sundered the party. The bill appeared at a time when the Whigs were disintegrating; the bill sundered the party—all northern Whigs voting nay, twenty-one of twenty-nine southern Whigs voting yea. A correspondent of John C. Breckinridge correctly predicted on March 12, 1854: "The course of the Northern Whigs . . . will surely kill the party in the South. If it does not, it seems to me a sensible man will be bound to conclude that the whig party of the South have abolition sympathies." [2]

The Georgia Whig, Alexander H. Stephens, opposed the suggestion to start a ticket of southern men for President and Vice-President. But his alternative was inauspicious for national unity: "hold no affiliation with any party North or South which does not make these prin-

ciples [of 1850 and 1854] the test of their organization.
. . ." Like the Democratic national Administration, he
had added repeal to the 1852 platform.

A political reformation was under way. At the time it
would have been impossible to predict the emergence of
a new major party that would displace the Whigs and
endure as a permanent element in the American two-
party system. The actual birth of the Republican Party
was unimpressive, all the more so since its progenitors
argued over where the infant was born. A small knot of
citizens, incensed by "the Nebraska swindle," met at the
Congregational Church in the village of Ripon, Wisconsin, on February 28, 1854 to adopt resolutions opposing
repeal and predicting the creation of "a great Northern
Party," should the Nebraska bill pass. A result of the
Ripon gathering was a state convention in Madison on
July 13—anniversary of the adoption of the Northwest
Ordinance—which used the name Republican. One week
earlier a convention at Jackson, Michigan, organized the
first state Republican Party. As independent political
meetings proliferated, the influential *New-York Tribune*
recommended use of the name Republican—once used
by the party of Thomas Jefferson.

The third-party movement had begun in the Old Northwest, a section dedicated to freedom by the national
decision of 1787. What was "the Nebraska issue"? It was
not at the beginning an effort to extirpate slavery from
the territories. The Ripon resolutions merely called for
keeping the Missouri Compromise: "we deem that compact irrepealable as the Constitution itself." The Jackson
convention's platform was more militant, demanding repeal of both the Kansas-Nebraska Act and the Fugitive
Slave Law, and abolition of slavery in the District of
Columbia.

Indignation over the breaking of a national contract,

accompanied by charges of treachery and villainy, burst forth in the ebullition of passion in 1854. "I have little faith in the principle of the North," Greeley wrote a friend, "but some in its pride. To be overreached in a bargain is not pleasant to Yankees. . . ." [3]

Northern anger found a target in Douglas, who was compared with Judas Iscariot and presented with thirty pieces of silver. "I could travel from Boston to Chicago by the light of my own effigy," he said. He addressed a belligerent crowd in Chicago in September, standing his ground against boos and catcalls for two hours before giving up. (It is an oft-repeated myth of United States history that he ended his speech, shouting: "It is now Sunday morning; I'll go to church, and you may go to hell." He ended his speech at half past ten on a Friday night).

The Republican movement of 1854 had no great leaders like Madison and Jefferson who had brought into being the first Republican Party, or like Theodore Roosevelt who created singlehanded the Bull Moose Party. It was a grass-roots movement, starting in the Northwest and sprouting elsewhere in the North. Recent investigators of American political behavior have stressed socio-cultural factors as determinants of voting, but it is difficult to explain the vast national upheaval of 1854 merely in terms of ethnic allegiances, the temperance issue, and similar local variances. One common theme animated the Republican organization—opposition to the Kansas-Nebraska measure.

To be sure, other themes commingled in the party chaos. "The Maine law" of 1851 had initiated the prohibition movement in America; and this social reform was being debated in numerous northern states. If some Americans were apprehensive about the effects of Demon Rum upon American society, greater numbers feared the influence of the foreigner upon the republic. The flow of immigrants reached flood tide in 1854, when 405,000 Europeans arrived in the United States. Nativism—hostility to immigrants—had been spreading in preceding years; and now in June, 1854, a national convention, with thirteen states represented, met in New York City to devise an organization whose members were sworn to vote only for native-born Americans. The American, or Know Nothing, Party which became virtually national in compass, had two fundamental themes: opposition to foreigners and opposition to Roman Catholics. It made a strong appeal in states with large foreign-born and Catholic populations that fostered native, Protestant distrust. Nativist ranks swelled to abnormal proportions because of the splintering in Democratic and Whig ranks, fears that the positive slavery stands of other parties might break up the Union, and the long-standing fear of the foreigner that reached back to the Alien and Sedition Laws.

Besides Republicans, temperance men, and Know Nothings there were anti-Nebraska men and members of People's parties, Free Soilers, and factions of Democrats. To the dismay of regular Democrats, antislavery men successfully sought to unite these disparate forces. "The fusionists are playing the D - - - l in the North East," wailed Breckinridge to Douglas.[4]

In the election campaigns of 1854 excitement over the Kansas-Nebraska issue, liquor legislation, foreigners, and Catholics was compounded, especially in the Northwest, by two additional issues of great future importance. The House of Representatives in March, 1854, had passed a homestead bill—a measure long sought by agrarian reformers. Following its introduction, the bill was amended in a significant aspect, ignored by historians: homestead grants were to be restricted to white persons. Gerrit Smith, who had spoken in favor of the original version, now exclaimed, "The curse of God is upon the bill," and voted against it.

The House vote revealed a sectional cleavage: 74–3 for it in the free states, 41–33 against it in the slave states. The Senate did not approve this bill, but passed a substitute providing that free white persons, after five years' occupation of the land, should be entitled to buy a quarter section at twenty-five cents an acre. The House did not act on the Senate substitute, and a homestead law, embodying the dream of land for the landless, was not realized until 1862. There was an East-West as well as a North-South cleavage, but plainly the slave states, though not solid, looked with disfavor on a measure that would have encouraged free white migration into Kansas, Nebraska, and the other territories.

A second aggravant to the Northwest was Pierce's terse veto in early August of a river-and-harbor-improvement bill. Approved by both houses of the Congress, it was regarded as important to the economic growth of the nation. At the end of the year the President made a long exposition of his reasons. He reaffirmed his cramped belief that "the Federal Government is the creature of the individual States and of the people of the States severally; that the sovereign power was in them alone. . . ." In a protracted historical and constitutional disquisition he asserted he could find no authority in the Constitution to justify Federal appropriations for river-and-harbor improvements. He suggested, in concluding, that the Congress leave such works "to individual enterprise or to the separate States." In the future the Republican Party would capitalize upon the eastern Democracy's indifference to these issues, incorporating an internal-improvements plank in its 1856 platform and a homestead plank in its 1860 platform.

The state elections took the measure of northern sentiment. As early as March President Pierce's native New Hampshire placed anti-Nebraska legislators in control of the state's lower chamber. "We have effected one object—rebuked treason, condemned the Nebraska Bill, and discarded the President," rejoiced former Congressman Amos Tuck.[5] The following month the Administration lost both Connecticut and Rhode Island. The August election in Iowa held special interest, for the state was contiguous to the new Nebraska Territory, and in its brief history this western state had been steadfastly Democratic. Now the Whigs elected an opponent of the Kansas-Nebraska Act, James W. Grimes, who had been endorsed by the Free Soilers, won control of the legislature, and filled one of the two seats in Congress.

The fall elections were the true test of popular reaction. Vermont and Maine conducted their voting in September; and fusion organizations of anti-Nebraska men carried their slates. Disaster struck the Democratic Party on October 10. "On that one day half the party majority in the House was lost," Roy Nichols has observed. Fusion tickets in the three states of Indiana, Ohio, and Pennsylvania had overwhelmed the Democracy.

The Illinois canvass, in perspective, was highlighted by the return to public life of Abraham Lincoln. After his one term in Congress, he had retired from politics; news that the Kansas-Nebraska bill had been passed roused him, he said, "as he had never been before." As a candidate for the state legislature, he debated in October with the architect of the bill, Douglas. Lincoln's Peoria address is a notable expression of his views on the Kansas-Nebraska Act, the South, slavery, race, popular sovereignty, and his political faith.

He began with an historical review of the slavery question before repeal of the Missouri Compromise. Repeal was wrong, he asserted, and he hated its indifference to the spread of slavery. "I hate it because of the monstrous injustice of slavery itself. I hate it because it deprives our republican example of its just influence in the world. . . ." He emphasized that he had no prejudice against the southern people. "They are just what we would be in their situation." They were not more responsible for introducing slavery than northerners; and so far as its future was concerned, "If all earthly power were given me, I should not know what to do, as to the existing institution." The race bias held by the great mass of white people prevented making Negroes equals. Though he thought gradual emancipation might be adopted, he would not judge the southerners for their tardiness in this; and he respected their constitutional right to reclaim fugitive slaves under a fair law.

Lincoln did not, however, believe slavery should be permitted to go into free territory; he could see no difference in moral principle between a law prohibiting the African slave trade and one prohibiting slavery in the territories. The argument of popular sovereignty, used to support repeal, he said did not apply because the Negro is a *man*, and the American republic was founded on the principles of the Declaration of Independence, including "all men are created equal." Beyond this, the localism of popular sovereignty ignored the fact that the whole nation was interested in the territories. "We want them for the homes of free white people."

Lastly, he opposed the Nebraska bill because it simultaneously threatened the security of the Union and stained the republican ideal. "Already the liberal party throughout the world, express the apprehension 'that the one retrograde institution in America, is undermining the principles of progress, and fatally violating the noblest political system the world ever saw.' "

What was to be done? "The Missouri Compromise ought to be restored. For the sake of the Union, it ought to be restored." It was a statesman's speech, cutting to the heart of public issues, moderate, sympathetic with the South, yet affirmative as to the future. The electoral outcome in Illinois was a decided Democratic setback. Anti-Nebraska voters captured the lower house of the legislature and five of the state's nine seats in Congress.

In New York the caldron of politics contained many elements, but as ex-Congressman Preston King predicted, "This State will boil over at the Election. They [the opposition] may be split and curve and mystify as much as they can [,] the State is thoroughly Anti Nebraska." [6] Fusionists placed in the governor's chair a Whig with nativist and temperance sympathies, and filled twenty-nine of the state's thirty-one Congressional seats.

In Massachusetts the Know Nothings, allied with the Free Soilers, swept the state, electing the governor and all the state's eleven Congressmen.

The Kansas-Nebraska Act had proved the solvent of old political loyalties. The Whig Party was disintegrating in the North and, as subsequent elections were to show, was almost defunct in the South. Republican Parties existed in a handful of northern states, and fusionist organizations in several others. The historic alliance between the South and the West was impaired as the West defected from the Democracy. The Democratic Party had been weakened in the North and strengthened in the South.

Issues other than slavery, to be sure, had figured in the balloting. When Wade, speaking to his fellow Senators, referred to "the rebuke which they have received at the hands of the people," Douglas shot back: "What is that rebuke?" The essential element in the fusion parties, he insisted, was Know Nothingism. Time, however, would show that Douglas was substantially wrong. The overarching issue was Nebraska.

The election of 1854 was a turning point in the anti-slavery struggle. The Democrats had lost control of the next House of Representatives, dropping to a minority of seventy-five. Only seven of the forty-two northern Democrats who had voted for the dissentious law had been re-elected. The American people, for the first time, had enlisted the popular arm of their government on the side of containment. If the anti-Nebraska forces could hold together, they could elect the speaker and organize the House committees, block admission of a slave-holding Kansas, and order investigation of frauds in Kansas territorial elections.

The sectional schism had been widened; in 1852 the Democrats had carried all but two northern states; in 1854 they had lost all but two. The Kansas-Nebraska Act had touched off a political revolution that would not run its course until 1860.

The Washington *Union,* fearful for the prospects of the Democratic party, declared: *"We must bury all our dissensions if we would triumph at all in the future. A common impulse must lead to a common union;* and those who think other wise will either be carried forward by the current or will go down with it."

In early December the Illinois Whig leader, O. H. Browning, wrote to Supreme Court Justice John McLean: "Every free State in the Union has now declared against the violation of the Missouri Compromise, but notwithstanding all this [,] Kansas will yet be a slave state." [7] To see what was happening we must now turn to the operation of popular sovereignty in Kansas Territory.

4

Negroes are dangerous to the state

In northeastern Kansas the Smoky Hill and Republican Rivers join to form the Kaw—or more formally, the Kansas River. It flows generally eastward about 170 miles, down undulating grasslands into the last fringe of forested prairie, past cottonwood and walnut trees, until it empties into the mighty Missouri opposite the river port of Kansas City, Missouri. Once the land of the Kansas Indians, or Kaws, the region in 1854 was peopled by numerous tribes, placed there a generation earlier by the Federal govern-government. Trappers had already taken the best of the fur-bearing animals, and the buffalo—Coronado's "crook-backed oxen"—had fled to western Kansas. Quail, wild turkeys, and prairie chickens still winged above sunflowers, gooseberry, and grape.

The Indian barrier and the myth of a Great American Desert had combined to repel the white man until 1854. The eastern third of the new territory was a garden spot, well-watered, abundantly timbered, and richly fertile—capable of growing grain in a

The chapter title is a remark made by a Kansas immigrant in 1855.

plenitude to gratify Croesus. Beyond lay "the fruited plain"—ideal for grazing—and westward rose the upland, reaching toward the distant mountains.

To the north was Nebraska Territory, watered by the Platte, less lush, more rigorous in climate, less attractive to settlers. To the south was Indian territory, present-day Oklahoma, occupied by the Five Civilized Tribes. Eastward extended a band of slaveholding states —Missouri, Kentucky, Virginia, Maryland, and Delaware. In the same zone of latitude lay large portions of Illinois, Indiana, and Ohio.

The key to the immediate future of Kansas Territory was the State of Missouri, whose breadth wholly dominated all the approaches. And the key question about the future of Kansas was, Would it become slave or free? During the Congressional debate over territorial organization, many southerners had said slavery could not find a foothold in Kansas. The Richmond *Enquirer,* ardent champion of repeal, had editorialized that climate would prevent rooting slavery in Kansas soil, saying the South favored repeal, "solely for the reason that it would vindicate the equality and sovereignty of the states."

But Sumner and others had pointed to slavery in Missouri as proof that the institution could flourish in adjacent Kansas. The census takers of 1850 counted 87,422 slaves in Missouri—an increase of 50 per cent over 1840. Of this number 17,357 lived in six western counties, along the Missouri River, bordering Kansas, where they worked on hemp and tobacco farms. Estimated to have a value of at least $10 million, these border slaves formed nearly a quarter of their counties' population, compared with a slave–white proportion of one in seven for the state.

Proslavery sentiment was particularly strong in this part of Missouri, Senator Atchison's home. And the potential loss to slaveholders, if their bondservants should flee to a free Kansas, was great. "The State of Missouri is now bounded on two sides by free States," Atchison pointed out; "organize this Territory as free territory, then we are bounded on three sides by free States or Territories." Moreover, the spectacular growth of Missouri's population encouraged restive spirits to sell out at a profit and go west. Population nearly doubled every decade: 384,702 in 1840, 682,044 in 1850, and 1,067,081 in 1860.

Economically, Kansas promised to be a colony of Missouri. The Missouri River, which separated the territory from the state, met the Kaw at Kansas City and flowed sinuously southeast to the metropolis of St. Louis. Transport, trade, and services would be a Missouri monopoly. If the peculiar institution should be fixed in Kansas, the security of slavery in the border state Missouri—an investment of millions—would be enhanced. And beyond beckoned an empire: "We are playing for a mightly [*sic*] stake," Atchison told Hunter, "if we win we carry slavery to the Pacific Ocean, if we fail we lose Missouri Arkansas and Texas and all the territories, the game must be played boldly." "I know that the Union as it exists is in the other scale," he recklessly acknowledged.

Notwithstanding these advantages, Missourians did not hold all the trump cards. The Boston *Evening Traveler* reminded Missouri that she had only two persons per square mile, while Massachusetts had 126; "Missouri cannot, therefore, send many emigrants to Kansas without making her own territory a wilderness.' And the Natchez *Courier* dolefully admitted: "Property is very timid; it moves not with rapidity, it seldom runs risks, especially where no extraordinary motive induces; and, therefore, long before the first five hundred slaveholders reach those regions, fifty thousand Northern men and foreign emigrants—all opposed to slavery in the abstract, and utterly unwilling to associate with the system in practice—will have flocked there, formed territorial laws for exclusion, and set on foot the machinery of State government, which make that exclusion perpetual." The populous North, then, possessed the greater opportunity to dispatch settlers into Kansas; and the South owned the handicap of the cost and hazard of removing slaves to a territory where competition with free farmers might be keen.

Nor may it be assumed that all Missourians were proslave in their philosophy. The venerable Benton, the powerful Blair clan, and the moderate Edward Bates, together with others including many Germans in St. Louis, opposed slavery's spread.

A final dampener of slavery's prospects in Kansas was the environmental peculiarity of the problem of settlement. Kansas was not the Great American Desert, but west of the prairie, which comprised the eastern third of the territory, began the Great Plains—subhumid, treeless, semiarid—a challenge to farm makers accustomed to water and wood. More immediately meaningful, agriculture was undergoing a transformation as rail transport, mechanical harvesters, and frenzied land speculation, placed midwestern Americans in a capitalistic world setting.

If Congress had blundered in repealing the Missouri Compromise, it added to its sorry record in opening Kansas Territory to settlers before disposing of the more than ten thousand Indians in the region or devising a land policy. On May 30, 1854, when the territory was thrown open, Congress had not ratified any of the treaties providing for cessions of land by the Indians. Equally egregious in this story of pre-Civil War failure of statecraft was the neglect to provide for the survey of lands or to establish the land rights of settlers or Indians. "When, therefore, the first land-seekers crossed into Kansas in June, 1854, not an acre of land was legally open to them and they were subject to heavy penalties for invasion of the reserves," Paul W. Gates, the historian of these fifty million acres, has pointed out. The surveying went forward snail-like, attended by incompetence and bungling administration; a year and a half after the territory had been opened, not a single township had been finished.

Intensifying the land troubles was the speculative fever that raged in America in the fifties. Abetted by the gold discoveries in California and the opulence produced by war in the Crimea, the inpouring of immigrants, and high commodity prices, speculators did not tarry to establish claims. Investors back East in both free and slave states acquired extensive claims: great Washington bankers, Virginia gentlemen, New England capitalists. The officers and enlisted men at Fort Leavenworth filed claims the Delaware Indian trust lands. Nearby Missourians eagerly laid their claims, astutely seizing the timbered tracts, coal lands, and prospective town sites. With these strategic resources they hoped to control Kansas Territory. In addition to owning favored lands, they looked to holding public office, keeping hotels for emigrants, becoming merchants and millers, and elsewhere to share in the boom times acoming. Kansas became a frontier cockpit of laissez-faire capitalism.

To establish squatter's rights under the Pre-emption Law that gave actual settlers priority to purchase, claimants often contented themselves with thrusting a marked stick in the earth or laying a foundation of four logs. Claim rivalry promptly broke out. "Throughout eastern Kansas, but especially south of the Kansas

River," commented Paul Gates, "claim warfare spread until it threatened to engulf the people in chaos. The slavery issue was deeply involved in claim jumping, with the slavery people repelling the 'antis' and the antislavery people trying to drive off the 'pros.' "

The contest for Kansas, beginning during the national paroxysm over repeal, elicited the interest of a Massachusetts educator and entrepreneur, Eli Thayer. A critic of abolitionists, a believer in popular sovereignty, he spied his opportunity for profit in promoting emigration to Kansas. He secured a charter on April 26, 1854—more than a month before the Kansas-Nebraska law was enacted—for the Massachusetts Emigrant Aid Society. Thayer's first purpose was to make money, and only incidentally to make Kansas free. His society encouraged emigration to the plains by assisting with travel arrangements, block purchasing of tickets, and like services. Contrary to legend, it did not pay the passage of emigrants or furnish them with rifles. The society expected to make profits in land and by operating hotels and mills.

The promoter Thayer sold stock to prominent Bostonians and New York merchant princes. He won the powerful aid of Greeley's *New-York Tribune* as well as Bryant's *Evening Post*. The organization was reincorporated in 1855 as the New England Emigrant Aid Company. The philanthropist Amos Lawrence served as treasurer, differing with Thayer over the prospect of profits, and selling stock as a patriotic and charitable opportunity for the buyers. Lawrence, descended from an old Boston family, was a large-souled man interested in the care of the ill and insane, education, colonization of free Negroes in Africa, and restricting the growth of slavery. The town of Lawrence, Kansas, and the little college located there that later became a state university were both named for him, as was Lawrence University in Appleton, Wisconsin.

The Kansas aid movement made exciting news for the eastern press, created apprehensions in Missouri and the slaveholding South, encouraged a freestate movement, but made little contribution to the population of Kansas. In the year 1854 it assisted about 450 persons; and by the end of 1855 it had aided a total of 1,240 settlers. In October, 1855, "the enterprise seemed dangerously close to ruin." Nevertheless it played a large role in enhancing the national hysteria over the fate of Kansas. It issued a pamphlet stating that the immense sum of $5 million would be raised and that twenty thousand settlers would be sent to Kansas. It inspired Whittier to pen' his "Song of the Kansas Emigrant."

> We cross the prairie as of old
> The pilgrims crossed the sea,
> To make the West, as they the East,
> The homestead of the free!

The historian of the company, Samuel A. Johnson, has estimated that in all it aided "probably under 2,000 [persons], of whom a considerable number, probably a third, returned."

Border Missourians, with exaggerated fears, began to organize vigilance committees and secret lodges, in order to stem the anticipated tide of Yankee abolitionists. The truculent Senator Atchison called a meeting that formed the Platte County Self-Defensive Association, which interpreted self-defense to embrace removal from Kansas of settlers aided by emigrant-aid societies. Soon Atchison was writing Secretary of War Jefferson Davis: "We will have difficulty with the Negro heroes in Kansas; they are resolved to go in and take their 'niggers' with them. Now the men who are hired by the Boston Abolitionists, to settle and abolitionize Kansas will not hesitate to steal our slaves, taking this for granted, I on the 21st of this month advised in a public speech the squatters in Kansas and the people in Missouri, to give a horse thief, robber, or homicide a fair trial, but to hang a negro thief or Abolitionist, without judge or jury; this sentiment met with almost universal applause. . . ."

Territorial government was established late in 1854. As the first governor Pierce selected Andrew H. Reeder, a Pennsylvania lawyer and popular-sovereignty Democrat. Reeder had never held public office; his main claim to preferment seemed the expectation he might strengthen the Democratic Party in northeastern Pennsylvania. Generous and sincere in manner, corpulent and erect in appearance, undistinguished and inexperienced, he had little about him to suggest he could cope with turbulent frontier politics. In implementing the Kansas-Nebraska law, "His appointment of Reeder to that pivotal position was Pierce's initial mistake," Roy Nichols has judged.

Reeder arrived in the territory October 7—more than three months after he had been commissioned—to take a census, designate a temporary capital, and make arrangements to elect a territorial legislature. Though not unsympathetic with slavery (he reportedly had said he had no more scruples about buying a slave than a horse) he early disappointed the proslavery folk, who were keen to act before freesoil settlers arrived, by deferring election of a legislature (which required a census and apportionment) and providing merely for choosing a territorial delegate to Congress.

Among its shortcomings the poorly drafted Kansas-Nebraska Act had neglected to prescribe a term of residence for voting. Three weeks before the election Atchison harangued an audience in Weston, Missouri: "When you reside within one day's journey of the territory, and when your peace, your quiet and your property depend upon your action, you can, without an exertion, send 500 of your young men who will vote in favor of your institutions." The Senator moved up and down the border speaking in this irresponsible vein; he also presided over a "blue lodge" meeting that nominated his proslavery friend, John W. Whitfield, as candidate for territorial delegate. The night before the election he conducted a band of Missourians into Kansas, where they camped overnight and next day voted in the territorial election.

The "border ruffians," to use the pejorative term promptly applied to the illegal voters, cast a majority of the total vote. A Congressional committee subsequently reported 1,114 legal ballots and 1,729 fraudulent ones, and branded the "systematic invasion" a "crime of great magnitude." "Its immediate effect," the report continued, "was to further excite the people of the Northern States—induce acts of retaliation, and exasperate the actual settlers against their neighbors in Missouri."

The election of a territorial legislature on March 30, 1855, further exposed the intransigence of proslavery Missourians, the weakness of Governor Reeder, and the incompetence of President Pierce; and it raised grave questions about Douglas's doctrines of Congressional nonintervention and popular sovereignty. Preparatory to the election, Reeder ordered an enumeration of inhabitants and qualified voters. The return showed a total of 8,501 persons, of whom 2,905 were voters, nearly half of these, in turn (47.6 per cent), from Missouri. It also showed the presence of 242 slaves and 151 free Negroes. Reeder in a proclamation prescribed the manner of voting in terms which, if they had been carried out, would have insured a fair election.

Rumor, however, was rife that the New England Emigrant Aid Company and other northerners were inducing settlers to go to Kansas to vote. Slavery partisans believed Reeder had delayed the election to permit this eastern influx to arrive. On election day armed Missourians again invaded the Kansas polls, threatening officials and balloting plentifully. The returns listed 5,427 proslavery votes and 791 antislavery. Atchison had excused himself from the Senate early, and once more participated in making a mockery of popular sovereignty, leading eighty men and twenty-four wagons into the territory. "There are eleven hundred coming over from Platte County to vote," he shouted to his band, "and if that ain't enough we can send five thousand—enough to kill every God-damned abolitionist in the Territory." Send five thousand they did, as the Congressional investigation disclosed there had been 4,968 illegal votes, against 1,210 lawful ones.

"Can such outrageous conduct from Missourians be longer tolerated?" stormed Dr. Charles Robinson, an agent for the Emigrant Aid Society. "Our people are forming military companies," he wrote from Lawrence, "& are determined to protect their rights even should it set the Union in a blaze.

"We want 200 of Sharp's rifles & two cannon for Lawrence people," Robinson continued, "& I have written in regard to it to Mr. Thayer. Cannot your secret organizations *loan* them to us till this question is settled, or till they can be paid for by the people here?" Later, when Kansas began to bleed, it was charged the company had supplied weapons to freestate settlers. The company denied the charge, but the truth is that the officers and directors individually contributed substantially to furnishing rifles to emigrants.[1]

"My person and my life were continuously threatened from the month of November, 1854," Reeder later testified. Because of the threats, much distressed, he arranged to have protection when he announced his decision about the validity of the election returns. "Upon the one side of the room were arrayed the members elect, nearly if not quite all armed, and on the other side about fourteen of my friends, who, with myself, were also well armed," he described the scene of frontier government. In this tense atmosphere Reeder accepted most of the election certificates, ordering fresh elections in only one third of the districts. He did not then know, he later said, of frauds in other districts, because no complaints had yet been filed. At the new elections the freestate voters were in the majority, but a proslavery legislature, made up almost entirely of natives of slave states, which the antislavery press styled the "bogus legislature," would meet in July.

The Kansas frauds stirred the country, inciting indignation in the free states while inspiring justification in the slave ones. Clearly the struggle for Kansas was no mere local affair. The Massachusetts moderate Edward Everett orated on the Fourth of July: "it has lately been maintained, by the sharp logic of the revolver and the bowie-knife, that the people of Missouri are the people of Kansas."

"Missourians have nobly defended *our* rights," proclaimed the Jacksonville, Alabama, *Republican*. The cause of that State is the common cause of all the Southern states." Events in Kansas were contributing to Southern unity.

If the first fraudulent election in November had not

underscored the imperative need for Federal intervention in the territory, surely the second fraud in March had. Under threats against his life Reeder hastened East, delivering a disenchanted address in Pennsylvania before going on to Washington. The question whether President Pierce would support a policy of impartiality in Kansas had become compounded by charges, presented to the chief executive, that the governor was speculating in land. Moreover, Atchison in a rage had determined to have Reeder's head.

Opinion in the country was divided and sharp about Pierce's anticipated attitude toward Reeder. "Can it be true that President Pierce will not sustain the executive of his own appointment in his [Reeder's] efforts to maintain the supremacy of the laws in the new territory?" asked *The New York Times*. It predicted civil war unless a new election was held. The proslavery *New York Herald* charged Pierce had appointed Reeder in order to make Kansas a free state. Would Pierce have the hardihood to send Reeder back to Kansas? "Upon that question may depend the controlling movement of the approaching Presidential election, and the ultimate issue of the Union or a dissolution."

The President, more anguished by the Kansas troubles than anything since the loss of his son, spent two weeks in earnest conversations with the governor, trying to thrash out Administration policy. Reeder sought to impress upon Pierce the need for executive action to protect the actual settlers from the Missourians. Pierce asked what action could he take; and in response Reeder outlined a three-point program. The President should let all his appointees understand they were to set their faces against out-of-state interference; he should issue a proclamation reciting and disapproving the lawless acts, and pledging the Administration against outside interference as violations of the organic act; and, if necessary, he should use troops. Reeder said such an Administration position would have salutary moral effects upon Congress and the nation.

Pierce countered this policy with his condemnation of the "illegalities" of the emigrant-aid society, not the Missourians, with objections to issuing such a proclamation, and with doubts about his authority to support a proclamation if he did issue it. His manner, Reeder asserted, "made me very distrustful of any sincere intention . . . to give adequate protection to our [Kansas] people. . . ."

The President's weaknesses lay exposed: his partiality shown by unwarranted charges of illegality against the emigrant-aid society and his complacency about the illegality of Missourians' interference, and above all his unwillingness to exert executive authority to discharge the Kansas-Nebraska Act.

Pierce sought to secure Reeder's resignation, promising him another public office, but Reeder declined, and in the end the President let the governor return to Kansas with the understanding that, if he were removed, it would be for his land speculations.

Reeder had directed the legislature to meet far in the interior at Pawnee, his own townsite. The legislature defied him, moving back east to Shawnee Mission. Having unseated the freestate members, it set about adopting Missouri statutes over Reeder's vetoes. It assumed slavery to exist and imposed prison sentences on anyone who claimed the institution had no legal standing and death for advising or inducing slaves to rebel. Officeholding was restricted to proslavery men. The Shawnee slave code passed by the "bogus legislature" aggravated northerners' sense of outrage. "There is no doubt that some of the statutes passed by the Legislature of Kansas are a disgrace to the age and the country," Cass stormed in the Senate. At the end of the month Pierce removed Reeder, stressing the speculative improprieties.

Pierce was fully justified in dismissing Reeder for his land deals, but the dismissal was commingled with pro-slavery opposition to the governor. By this time Pierce's reputation had sunk very low. Former Vice-President George M. Dallas told Richard Rush at the beginning of the year: "We have literally no administration:—the men fill the office, but do not constitute a government." He had spent five days in Washington, and "The only official call I made was at the White House, and as I turned to look back after having left my card, I thought I perceived on the pale front the fatal Mene, Mene, &c." [2]

Another Democrat took an equally doleful view of Pierce. "It is melancholy," he informed James Buchanan, "to hear the contemptuous manner he is personally alluded to by some of the most distinguished Senators and members of our party." [3]

The son of an old Jacksonian Democrat, Frank P. Blair, Jr., fumed to his brother Montgomery of "my contempt for Pierce, his meanness, his cowardice & his ingratitude, his weakness in truckling to the nullifiers, his folly in taking all the corrupt men of the party to his councils & his stupidity in permitting the Democratic party to be ruled & ruined by renegades & nullifiers. . . ." [4]

Pierce sought a replacement for Reeder in Wilson Shannon, who had served as governor of Ohio, minister to Mexico, and as a member of Congress where he had voted for the Kansas-Nebraska bill. Actually a small-bore politician, noted for his tactlessness, he was another poor appointment. He promptly sided with the slavery partisans in Kansas and entertained suspicions of the freestaters.

The progress of slavery, attended by fraud and Federal laxity, appalled those who wished to see Kansas become free. Freestate leadership devolved largely upon two remarkable men—James H. Lane and Dr. Charles Robinson. They found a supporter in ex-governor Reeder.

Jim Lane—picturesque, ambitious, provocative—was the very portrait of a frontier politician. Lean and sinewy, careless about his dress and hair, he spoke in a raspy voice, gesturing crudely, while hurling invective and sarcasm. Essentially an agitator, he was a magnetic stump orator who combined opportunism and principle. He had been born in Indiana, the son of a Congressman, and he had served in the Mexican War and in Congress where he had voted for the Kansas-Nebraska law. With an eye to the main chance he had emigrated to Kansas in April, 1855, where he had failed to organize the Democratic Party. He then joined the freestate movement, and was called the "Liberator of Kansas." In 1861 he would be elected as a Republican to the United States Senate, where he advocated colonization of Negroes (as a solution of the race problem). "Our prejudices against them are unconquerable," he declared. In 1863 he raised one of the first regiments of Negro troops. He died by his own hand in 1866.

Charles Robinson had been bred in an abolition atmosphere in Massachusetts and had practiced medicine. In 1849 he had emigrated to California, where he had figured in a frontier scrape that nearly cost him his life and briefly placed him under indictment for murder. He had served both as president of a squatters' association and as a member of the California legislature. In 1851 he returned to Massachusetts, marrying the cultivated Sara Lawrence, whose book, *Kansas; Its Interior and Exterior Life,* published in 1856, is a fascinating firsthand narrative of the Kansas struggle, marked by a freestate bias. He had been sent to Kansas in 1854 as an agent for the New England Emigrant Aid Company. Of purer metal than Lane, he would become the first governor of the State of Kansas.

What could be done to oppose slavery in the face of Border Ruffians and Presidential weakness? How best to organize antislavery opinion? Violence and fraud had been the vehicles of slavery's partisans. Slavery's foes were divided between forming a freestate party or striking directly for statehood; either course avoided illegality and would be in the American grain. The necessity to unite was plain; and on September 5, 1855, freesoil elements met at Big Springs, a camping ground not far from Lawrence. The day of organized opposition to slavery in Kansas Territory had dawned.

The work of the Big Springs convention was fourfold. It created a Free-state Party, thereby institutionalizing antagonism to slavery. It nominated its own delegate to Congress, Reeder, and fixed a day for his election. And thirdly, it adopted resolutions, written by Reeder, and a platform, reported by Lane. The resolutions condemned the legislature as representing "demagogues of Missouri," and repudiated its work. The platform countered accusations that the Free-state Party was abolitionist, and sought to consolidate all men, Whig and Democratic, who looked to the eventual exclusion of all Negroes, slave and free, from Kansas. Finally, the convention called a new convention to meet at Topeka on September 19, "to consider the propriety of forming a state constitution."

These transactions incurred the censure of the Administration organ, the Washington *Union*. "It strikes us as remarkable," it editorialized, "that whilst the illegal and forcible interference of non-residents of Kansas is denounced and resisted, the remedy by which the evil is sought to be met is no less violent and revolting than

the proceedings of which they complain. We confess that
the acceptance of the nomination for delegate by Gov.
Reeder has surprised us."

Equipped with leaders, a party, and a platform, the
freesoil movement strode forward rapidly. The Topeka
convention made the decision to seek statehood, calling
a constitutional convention at Topeka for October 23, and
naming an executive committee, with Lane as chairman,
that was to act as a provisional government and manage
the movement for statehood. In inaugurating a rump
government and seeking, without authorization, to form
a state, the Topeka movement was moving beyond the
confines of legality.

Of the thirty-seven delegates who were to sign the
Topeka constitution, thirteen were natives of southern
states, and twenty-one had previously been Democrats.
Jim Lane, the opportunist who had earlier presented himself as a friend of "Frank" Pierce, was elected president
of the convention; he, "with characteristic modesty, had
demanded the place for himself." Factions quickly appeared among the delegates, Dr. Robinson leading the
opposition to Lane, who, it was reported, wished to rush
Kansas to statehood and become U. S. Senator.

For the most part the proposed constitution was like
those of other western states. The issues were drawn,
however, on a proposed endorsement of popular sovereignty on slavery and discriminatory provisions against
Negroes. Robinson obtained indefinite postponement of
the resolution favoring popular sovereignty but was
obliged to refer the question of the status of free Negroes
to voters along with the constitution. The document prohibited slavery after July 4, 1857. It was submitted to
popular vote December 15. The constitution was adopted
1,731 to 46, and the proposal to exclude free Negroes
and mulattoes was approved 1,287 to 453.

Settlers from New England voted against exclusion, while those from the Midwest staunchly favored it. Midwesterners, a *New York Times* reporter explained, "are terribly frightened at the idea of being overrun by negroes. They hold to the idea that negroes are dangerous to the State and a nuisance, and measures have to be taken to prevent them from migrating to the territory." Free soil for white men dominated political antislavery in Kansas. The frontier has often been interpreted as a liberal force in American history, but it does not appear to have eradicated race prejudice.

Two days after the Topeka convention adjourned, proslavery men held a "law and order" convention at Leavenworth. They appointed Governor Shannon himself as president. Taking the chair, Shannon declared that the Shawnee legislature was a legal body, and persons who disobeyed its laws would be guilty of treason against the state. He branded Reeder's election as delegate to Congress a revolutionary movement; and charged that the freestate men, by calling a convention, had taken a step which, if approved by Congress, must lead to civil war. He assured those present that the Administration would sustain them. The governor's remarks were incorporated in resolutions adopted by the convention. A Law and Order Party was organized.

One week later the murder of a young freestate settler led to the famous "Wakarusa War" and inaugurated a time of violence in Kansas. Emotions were already at a high pitch before the murder, the proslavery men believing their rival forces to have a secret military organization. Though this was not the case, the freestate men did indeed by this time have a quantity of Sharps rifles. The incident became a crisis when freestate men rescued one of their leaders who had been arrested by the sheriff of Douglas County.

The sheriff now appealed to Governor Shannon for three thousand men to enforce the laws. Shannon ordered out the Kansas militia, which as it was only partially organized reported in small numbers; but twelve hundred armed Missourians, spoiling for a fight, assembled south of Lawrence on the Wakarusa River, a branch of the Kaw. They intended to destroy the hated town of Lawrence, and the sheriff, on becoming convinced by freestate emissaries of this hostile purpose, requested Federal troops from Fort Leavenworth. The commander refused to comply without orders from Washington. The Missourians, Shannon acknowledged, *"are beyond my power, or at* least soon will be."

In this exigency Shannon himself went to Lawrence. A collision loomed. Had warfare flared on the Wakarusa, the nation would have been aroused. A proslavery assault upon Lawrence would have inflamed the free states, produced a defensive reflex in the slave states, and played into the hands of antislavery politicians. The alarmed Atchison supported Shannon in seeking a peaceful settlement. The extraordinary outcome of executive intervention was a treaty signed by Shannon and Robinson and Lane in which the governor denied he had summoned the Missourians and the two freestate leaders denied they had knowledge of any organization to resist the laws. Shannon then succeeded in getting both sides to disband their forces.

Such was the Wakarusa War, storied in Kansas history. A sack of Lawrence had been averted—postponed only, as events demonstrated. From Osawatomie the zealous settler John Brown wrote a long letter to his wife and children, describing the episode, and exulting: "Free State men have only hereafter to retain the footing they have gained; *And Kansas is Free."* [5] Throughout the winter discontent persisted on the prairie, sporadically crackling in small disturbances. In the month of May guerrilla bands would again encircle the little town of Lawrence.

By the end of the year 1855 the situation in Kansas was complex and threatening. Much of the difficulty could be attributed to normal frontier violence. A willingness to wink at the law was widespread. The popular notion of the struggle for Kansas as a simplistic contest between slavery and freedom—a notion nourished by certain contemporaries and long naïvely maintained by historians—will not wash. To the Kansan of the mid-fifties anti- and proslavery ideals figured less in his life than his appetite for land, material advantages, patronage, and party advancement. Abolition of slavery in America—even more, equal rights for Negroes—was alien to most frontiersmen.

By early 1856 the preponderance of settlers were westerners, who wished to see Kansas become a free state yet did not desire freedom for Negro slaves or welcome the coming of Negroes. The Osawatomie settler John Everett wrote his father. a former Welsh Congregational minister who had translated *Uncle Tom's Cabin* into Welsh, an illuminating letter: "The community here are very nearly united on the free-state question. But the majority would dislike and resent being called abolitionists. . . . Our community here are mostly Western people, some from Slave States. There is a prevailing sentiment against admitting negroes into the territory at all, slave or free. The Western people are far the most numerous in the territory."

But normal frontier turbulence does not account for Bleeding Kansas as a cause of the Civil War. The question of slavery did not arise in the frontier territory to the north; there is no history of a "Bleeding Nebraska." Studies of economic conflicts in Kansas are valueless in explaining the origins of the irrepressible conflict unless they recognize that it was the slavery issue, as seen by contemporaries, that made the Kansas struggle a cause of national controversy.

Whether Kansas would be slave or free drew the dividing line between clashing conceptions of the state's future. The question arrayed Americans against one another in political parties; it embittered personal relations, exacerbating the settlers' quarrels over land claims and like matters. It reared the emotion-laden issue that was to make Kansas a bloody battleground.

5

The government has been nothing but an obstruction

The year 1855 was political chaos. It witnessed the advance of the Republican Party, the partial recovery of the Democracy, the disruption of the Know Nothings, the increasing solidification of the South, significant Senatorial elections, and the convening of Congress for a renewal of the struggle over Kansas. Shadowed by the dark cloud cast by Kansas, it was not an auspicious year for the American republic. Walt Whitman, penning the preface in this year to his *Leaves of Grass*, conceded: "Other states indicate themselves in their deputies . . . but the genius of the United States is not best or more in its executives or legislatures . . . but always most in the common people."

In January the Massachusetts legislature, predominantly Know Nothing, elected Henry Wilson, son of a day laborer, United States Senator. Born in 1812 and bound out at the age of ten by indenture to a neighboring farmer for ten years, he had "inwardly digested" nearly a thousand books of

The chapter title is a remark made by Ralph Waldo Emerson (1856).

biography and history by the end of his service. He followed the shoemaker's trade (later as Vice-President of the United States he was called "the Natick cobbler"), continued his self-education, and discovered he was an able public speaker. Entering politics in 1840 as a Whig, he served in the Massachusetts legislature for several years, joined the Free Soil Party in 1848 and the Know Nothing Party in 1852. He had abhorred slavery since 1836, when on a visit to Washington, "I saw slavery beneath the shadow of the flag over the Capitol," as he later said. "I saw the slave-pen, and men, women, and children herded for the markets of the far South. . . ." His first Senate speech placed him with those who favored the abolition of slavery "wherever we are morally or legally responsible for its existence" (*i.e.*, the District of Columbia and the territories), and the repeal of the Fugitive Slave Law. He believed that if the Federal government should dissociate itself from sustaining slavery, "the men of the South who are opposed to the existence of that institution, would get rid of it in their own States at no distant day." In this same speech he excoriated colleagues from Indiana and Tennessee, who had just proclaimed their pride in white supremacy, and announced, "If the African race is inferior, this proud race of ours should educate and elevate it. . . ." Replacing the moderate Everett, he took his place with the ardent Sumner, and figured conspicuously in the Kansas struggle. During the Civil War he would serve as chairman of the Senate Military Affairs Committee, and in 1872 he would be chosen Vice-President of the United States.

Early in February the New York legislature re-elected Seward, still a Whig, U. S. Senator. Two days later the Illinois legislature dealt a blow to Stephen A. Douglas by refusing to return to the U. S. Senate his colleague and supporter, James A. Shields. Anti-Nebraska legislators, after dividing their votes between the Whig Abraham Lincoln and Lyman Trumbull, an anti-Nebraska Democrat, united upon Trumbull who had denounced Douglas as a demagogue. J. W. Sheahan, editor of the Chicago *Times* and a loyal friend of Douglas, lugubriously wrote the Little Giant, "The deed is done. The severest blow we have recieved [sic] has been given us." [1]

Above the middle height, well-knit, with bright sandy hair, piercing blue eyes, and gold-rimmed spectacles, Senator Trumbull would be a clarion voice for freedom in Kansas. During the 1860's he would take advanced ground in behalf of emancipation and civil rights for Negroes. For his part, Lincoln, deeply disappointed, had withdrawn his candidacy before the final ballot, unwilling, as he said, to "let the whole political result go to ruin, on a point merely personal to myself."

Meanwhile, nullification had reared its head in the northern State of Wisconsin. An abolitionist editor, Sherman Booth, had been arrested for aiding a Negro's escape from a United States deputy marshal who had arrested him as a fugitive. The Wisconsin supreme court ordered Booth's release on the ground that the Fugitive Slave Law of 1850 was unconstitutional. The clash between state and national authority was appealed to the United States Supreme Court. In 1859 that court not only sustained the paramountcy of the Supreme Court over the state courts, but also the constitutionality of the Fugitive Slave Law.

Reviewing these exciting weeks Senator Chase in Washington wrote a friend: "The elections of the last few weeks have produced a marked effect here. Harlan [Iowa], Wilson, Durkee [Wisconsin], Seward, are all regarded as hot shot from abolition cannon. Then the action of the Supreme Court of Wisconsin has startled the politicians—& the Judges too—not a little. And now even while I am writing comes the election of Trumbull in Illinois—Anti Douglas & Anti Nebraska at all costs & an election which is thus far at least a triumph. Everything indicates that the Anti Slavery Sentiment will sweep on soon to its final triumph now." [2]

The selection of antislavery Senators reflected the popular vote of 1854. A better index of sentiment in 1855 than the Senatorial choices is the series of state elections held that year. There was no uniform date for congressional elections, and as a result, besides state offices, there were many seats in Congress yet to be filled. The elections would measure Know Nothing power, Democratic disarray, and Republican growth. Of special interest was the election in the President's home state, New Hampshire, where a coalition of Know Nothings, Whigs, and Independent Democrats strove to keep foremost the "invidious" repeal of the Missouri Compromise. On March 13 the coalition captured every office, electing a Know Nothing governor, the Congressional slate, and the legislature that was soon to choose a United States Senator. Three months later the legislature made its choice, portly, resonant-voiced John P. Hale, who had been the Free Soil Party candidate for the Presidency in 1852. New Hampshire's rebuke to Pierce was severe.

Thirty-two thousand Know Nothings had turned out at the polls in New Hampshire, and within less than a month Know Nothings prevailed in Rhode Island and Connecticut. How far would the Know Nothing Party advance? What would be its appeal in the South, where it had replaced the Whig Party? Though there were few foreigners and Roman Catholics in the South and it was localized in the valleys of the Potomac, Ohio, and lower Mississippi Rivers, the Know Nothing, or American,

Party attracted many southerners because of its patriotism, conservatism, and hostility toward foreigners who swelled northern strength.

The spring canvass in Virginia seemed to foreshadow the future of southern politics as well as that of the American party. It was the first and greatest test of Know Nothingism in the Old South. "I am fearful of the result of our election," wrote a correspondent of Democratic Senator R. M. T. Hunter. "Think of loosing [sic] the old dominion." [3] To forestall losing the Old Dominion the Democrats nominated Henry A. Wise, a scholarly gentleman and orator, who carried the battle against Thomas Flournoy, the American candidate. "All eyes were turned toward the Old Dominion as the natural gateway, or 'entering wedge,' to the Southern States," Wise's grandson has observed. The outcome of the exciting campaign on May 24 was a clear majority for Wise. "I have met the Black Knight with his visor down, and his shield and lance are broken," he rejoiced. And Franklin Pierce, vastly relieved, wrote Stephen A. Douglas: "The result of the election in Virginia has put a new face upon the prospects of the Democratic party—the only party which carries no dark lantern & gives its time honored banner to the breeze." [4] The Know Nothings did succeed, however, in electing one Congressman and sixty members of the state legislature.

Within a fortnight the probable fate of the Know Nothing Party, which the previous autumn had elected nine governors and 104 of the 234 members of the House of Representatives, seemed clearer. The national council of the Know Nothings, with nearly every state represented, met in Philadelphia to adopt a national platform. The resolutions committee experienced no difficulty in drafting anti-Catholic and anti-immigrant planks, but it split on the issue of slavery. The largely southern majority recommended resolutions denying the power of Congress to prohibit slavery in the territories, while the minority proposed resolutions favoring immediate restoration of the Missouri Compromise, protection of actual settlers, and admission of Kansas and Nebraska as free states. The rival resolutions were debated by the entire council, with Henry Wilson, whose earlier history had made him appear a political chameleon, leading the northern forces. In a flaming speech he implored: "Reject this majority platform, adopt the proposition to restore freedom to Kansas and Nebraska, and to protect the actual settlers from violence and outrage . . . make an open organization, banish all bigotry and intolerance from your ranks. . . ." Wilson did not prevail, and upon adoption of the majority platform, he and the delegations from twelve northern states withdrew from the convention. The slavery issue had taken precedence over all other questions; it had divided the Know Nothing Party. The party, astonishing as its rise and strength in 1854 had appeared, would prove to be a halfway house for voters in transit between old and new allegiances.

Party disorder at this time is reflected in letters written by Robert Toombs of Georgia and Abraham Lincoln of Illinois. An old-line Whig, Toombs now was declaring: "The true policy of the South is to unite; to lay aside all party divisions. Whigs, Democrats and Know Nothings should come together and combine for the common safety. If we are wise enough to do this, to present one unbroken column of fifteen states united for the preservation of their own rights, the Constitution and the Union, and to uphold and support that noble band of patriots at the North who have stood for the Constitution and the right against the tempest of fanaticism, folly and treason which has assailed them, we shall succeed."

Late in the summer, Lincoln, replying to a Kentucky

friend, wrote a letter in which he seemed to be musing aloud: "You enquire where I now stand. That is a disputed point. I think I am a whig; but others say there are no whigs, and that I am an abolitionist. . . . I now do no more than oppose the *extension* of slavery.

"I am not a Know-Nothing. That is certain. How could I be? How can any one who abhors the oppression of negroes, be in favor of degrading classes of white people?"

As the summer wore on the Pierce Administration could find solace in scattered victories in the South. Also the recovery of control over Pennsylvania, with a platform stressing party orthodoxy on Kansas and Nebraska, pointed to making it the "keystone" state in the arch of Democratic triumph in the Presidential contest of 1856.

The month of September was notable for the fusion of Whigs into the Republican Party in the State of New York, where Greeley had shifted parties and was beating the drums for the new organization. Although the united party lost to the Know Nothings by a thin margin, and the election "exhibited a total derangement of old organizations," [5] fusion was propitious for the future. Three weeks after the union the North's foremost Whig, Seward, who in May had avowed he would die a Whig, announced his apostasy from the old party and his embrace of the new one. On the day of his announcement the Washington *Union* affirmed: "Nothing is more certain than that Wm. H. Seward is the great presiding genius of black republicanism, nor is it less certain that Henry Wilson is its chief champion and missionary." The enlarged party named as its state chairman the taciturn New York merchant prince Edwin D. Morgan, destined soon to become the first national chairman of the Republican Party.

That Kansas, with its ruffians and outrages, was shak-

ing the political parties as in a kaleidoscope, was best demonstrated in Ohio. There an anti-Nebraska convention,
made up preponderantly of Know Nothings, nominated
for governor Salmon P. Chase, the independent Democrat
and embodiment of opposition to repeal of the Missouri
Compromise. Again antislavery sentiment had tran-
scended hostility to Catholics and immigrants. The delegates adopted an anti-Nebraska platform, the name
Republican, and appointed a committee to help organize
a national party. The stalwart Chase said in his acceptance speech: "Slavery in the territories must be prohibited by law. . . . Kansas must be saved from slavery
by the voters of the free States." Chase in a three-
cornered race ran for the governor's chair against Whig
and Democratic rivals. His success and the choice of a
Republican legislature represented the principal triumph
of the Republican Party in 1855.

What was the political situation in the slave states at
the year's end? A staggering development was the commitment to a proslavery creed of the Whig successor
party, now called American. Congressman Humphrey
Marshall of Kentucky, ponderous leader of the pro-Ne-
braska Americans, remarked in December that there was
almost no issue of nativism—it was "all nigger." In Kentucky, traditionally a Whig State, there was a particularly bitter canvass, with election-day riots between Irish
and Americans in Louisville. The outcome of the voting
was American victories in state offices and six of the ten
Congressional districts. The Americans won four of the
six Congressional seats in Maryland, where a substantial
Catholic population lived. Tennessee, which had retained
its loyalty to the Whig faith in 1852, filled five of its ten
seats with Americans, but re-elected a Democrat, An-

drew Johnson, future President of the United States, as governor, and gave the Pierce Administration two additional Congressmen.

Virginia's leadership in repulsing the American Party was influential in the lower South. "Thank God Old Virginia like a rock in a tempest tossed Ocean broke the wave as it rolled South," a Mississippi friend rejoiced to Douglas.[6] The old Whig states of North Carolina and Georgia had now definitely arrayed themselves with the Democracy. The Old North State sent six Democrats (two more than in the previous session) to Congress. In Georgia Stephens wrote his powerful "Letter on Know-Nothingism," which scored "the insane cry against foreigners and Catholics"; and Toombs, following him, decried the party of prejudice. Both men this fall formally forsook their old allegiance and entered the Democratic Party. After Stephens appeared in Washington in December, he reported, "The Northern Democrats seem to think more of me than of their old party-line men." The Georgia electorate sent seven Democrats and one American to Congress, returned Herschel V. Johnson, a Democrat, to the governor's chair, and gave him a Democratic legislature. Louisiana, in spite of its Catholic element, filled its state offices with Democrats and sent three Democrats and one American to Congress. Elsewhere in the South the Democrats won victories, but the Americans retained strength in the section's representation in Congress.

The Whig party was defunct, and Senator John Bell of Tennessee urged in a speech at Knoxville that the American Party be looked on as permanent. But many signs indicated that other southerners would pursue the course of Stephens and Toombs in taking their places in the Democratic Party.

The strife in Kansas and northern nullification had

widened the cleavage between North and South. When
the legislature of South Carolina met on November 26,
Governor Adams reprobated the state of Massachusetts
for obstructing the Fugitive Slave Law, and ominously
concluded that South Carolina would risk the dangers
of civil war rather than submit to the degradation and
ruin threatened by agitation over slavery.

By the close of the year various antislavery politicians
were deliberating organization of a national antislavery
party. Kansas had been the major chord in American
politics in 1855, and repeal had been the refrain in the
northern states. The rebuke to Douglas in Illinois and to
Pierce in New Hampshire, the rift in the Know Nothing
organization, the election of Chase as a Republican governor, and the accession of Seward to the new party—all
these had been auspicious signs. Chase, ever a brides-
maid for a Presidential nomination, was striving to create
a national party that he might lead to victory in 1856.
Seward, in the sensational and widely read speech that
declared his Republicanism and became the keynote of
the new party, had asked, Shall we form a new party?
Slavery, he said, was the special foundation of a privileged class, which might work the subversion of the
Constitution. His cardinal theme was abridgment of majority rights by the slaveholding minority. The Republicans had no purpose to abolish slavery; they proposed to
"avert the extension of slavery in the territories of the
Union, and that is enough." A united Republican Party
could check the growth of the privileged class's power
and restore the virtue of a demoralized nation. Seward
was not an abolitionist. Plainly he was concerned with
the rights of white Americans, endangered by an oligarchy, more than with the wrongs of slaves. "What, then,
is wanted? Organization. . . . The Republican organi-

zation has . . . laid a new, sound, and liberal platform broad enough" for true Democrats and true Whigs to stand upon.

The convening of Congress in Washington in December made that city headquarters of the movement to launch a national antislavery party. A Republican Association of Washington had been organized in June. The venerable Francis P. Blair, former editor of the *Globe*, Jacksonian Democrat and later Free Soil Democrat, declined the presidency of the association, but in a letter published on December 1 gave it his blessing, and wrote: "The extension of slavery over the new Territories would prove fatal to their prosperity; but the greatest calamity to be apprehended from it is the destruction of the Confederacy, on which the welfare of the whole country reposes." Toward the end of the month he was entertaining political friends at his Silver Spring residence to plan "a national organization of the friends of freedom." [7] By that time events in Congress, to which we must now turn, had given impetus to the movement.

"The tendency to form geographical parties on the Slavery questions," [8] which Minister James Buchanan watched with alarm from London, became all the more evident when the Thirty-fourth Congress of the United States assembled on December 3, 1855. The Democrats comfortably controlled the Senate by a two-to-one majority; however fifteen members belonged to the new Republican Party. Senator Trumbull recalled: "It was a time of high party excitement. The majority were domineering and often offensive to members of the minority. They controlled the business of the Senate and could take their own time to assail minority Senators . . . . it was not uncommon for the members of the dominant party to go out of their way to seek controversies with and assail certain Senators in the minority." Atchison had not been returned, and the Missouri legislature had dead-locked over his successor. Jesse D. Bright of Indiana served as president pro tempore.

The parliamentary situation in the House of Repre-sentatives pointed up the decomposition of the party sys-tem. The editor of the *Congressional Globe* (official record of debates) abandoned his custom of classifying members by parties. Heroically the *Tribune Almanac* ad-dressed itself to the analysis, finding 79 Pierce Demo-crats, of whom 20 were northerners, 117 anti-Nebraska men, all of whom were northerners, 37 Whigs or Amer-icans of proslavery tendencies all but 3 of whom were from slave states. Of the 117 anti-Nebraska Congress-men, 75 had been elected as Know-Nothings.

The body that assembled on the first Monday of De-cember in 1855 was the first Congress elected since the passage of the Kansas-Nebraska Act. The contrast be-tween an Administration majority of 158 in the previous House and an anti-Nebraska plurality of perhaps 117 in the present House exposed the popular revulsion.

The House held a broad spectrum of political factions: Administration democrats, anti-Administration Demo-crats, northern Whigs, Free Soilers, antislavery Know Nothings (or Americans), proslavery Americans, and Republicans. This array was vastly confusing to a po-litical process that was customarily operated by two par-ties. The first task of the House was to organize itself by electing a speaker, who then would appoint the standing committees. At immediate issue was control of the Con-gress. Under the rules a majority was needed to elect. Could the various shades of anti-Nebraska sentiment unite in the choice of a speaker? Until the House orga-nized, the business of the national legislature could not be conducted.

The Administration's candidate for speaker was the

House manager of the Nebraska bill, Douglas's hench-man, William A. Richardson of Illinois. Jovial and obese, he appeared in Washington months before the session opened, surrounded himself with friends, and, chewing tobacco and telling frontier jokes, plotted his candidacy. A leading candidate of the anti-Nebraska men was Na-thaniel P. Banks of Massachusetts, who had served in the previous House as a Democrat, had been elected to this House as an American, and had subsequently be-come a Republican. Well-groomed, erect, and dignified, he was sagacious in counsel and impressive in speech, his aristocratic appearance belying his humble origin as a bobbin boy in a cotton factory. A third important can-didate was the American Party's Henry M. Fuller of Pennsylvania.

On the first ballot Richardson, the caucus candidate of the Democrats, received 74 votes; and no anti-Ne-braska nominee, of whom there were 17, came within 20 votes of that figure. A majority was required for elec-tion. A prolonged deadlock set in. The American govern-ment was paralyzed, and Pierce was long prevented from sending his annual message to Congress. More than five weeks later the House resolved to ascertain the candi-dates' views on slavery issues.

On the day of catechism, January 12, 1856, questions were addressed to the aspirants, including the topics of slavery in the territories and race. Richardson defended popular sovereignty and gave his opinion that the Negro is inferior to the white man. Fuller expounded the com-mon-property doctrine that denied to both Congress and the territorial legislature power over slavery, and stated his belief in white supremacy.

Before this time Banks had come within less than half a dozen votes of victory. Caucus upon caucus, vote upon vote had revealed the assiduity of his supporters and the strength of his stand. Sponsors of the nascent Republican organization regarded his success as fundamental to their plans. The New Yorker Preston King wrote the elder Blair: "the election of Banks will contribute to consolidate the union of our friends. It is possible that his Election is indispensable for union." [9]

Banks in response to questions now stoutly affirmed his conviction that Congress could constitutionally prohibit slavery in the territories. With regard to Kansas and Nebraska, "I am for the substantial restoration of the prohibition as it has existed since 1820." When a Mississippian asked his views on racial equality, he replied, "Whether the black race . . . is equal to the white race, can only be determined by the absorption or disappearance of one or the other, and I propose to wait until the respective races can be properly subjected to this philosophical test before I give a decisive answer." This statement, perhaps meant as a jest, elicited howls of laughter; but when it brought the charge that he was an "amalgamationist," he publicly revised it.

The whole nation had its eye on the House during the long stalemate. New York's political boss Thurlow Weed came down from Albany to pull wires, and Greeley came from New York to wield his influence. The Banks men's unity was enhanced by hostility to the slave power, "our opponents who only know nigger in the morning, nigger at noon, nigger at night, & until broad daylight." Southerners talked freely of disunion, but the House kept goodnatured during the long prorogation, northern members deriding dissolution threats with laughter and singing out, "Good-by, John." The only violence occurred outside the chamber, when Albert Rust, member from Arkansas, assaulted Greeley on the street.

Following the catechism, parliamentarians began to scheme to replace the requirement of a majority to elect with that of a plurality. Not until February 2 was there agreement that a minority might name the speaker, but speedily after agreement Banks was elected under the plurality rule on the 133d ballot with 103 votes.

"Got 'em, boys," exulted a Banks backer. "Licked, by thunder!" wailed a southern member. It was fitting that Father Giddings, dean of the House—old Joshua Giddings, whom Douglas branded "the high priest of abolitionism"—administered the oath of office to the exuberant Banks.

It was a famous victory. More than the election of a speaker and the organization of the House was at stake. The antislavery men in the nation's lower chamber had successfully fused. A new alignment of political parties loomed in prospect, and already the election could be hailed as a Republican triumph. Greeley termed it the first northern victory within the memory of men now living.

Thurlow Weed wrote Banks the day after the decision: "This triumph is worth all it cost in time, toil, and solicitude. For *once* the North has been faithful. *One* conflict with slavery has been settled without a *compromise;* though we trembled all of yesterday, lest the *one* or *two* should be on the wrong side.

"The Republican Party is now Inaugurated. We can now work 'with a will.'" The editor of the Boston *Atlas* exultantly wrote Banks, "Thank God, there is at last a great United North!" Another constituent, an aged farmer who described himself as an "illiterate stranger," congratulated Banks: "Never, since the day John Q Adams dared to stand up in his place, and plead for the Right of purtician [petition], has this country felt such intense anxiety. With what joy, and lightning spede, was Telligraphed, through the free States, that *Justice*

& *Principal,* had once tryumphed, in the Halls of Congress." [10]

Alexander H. Stephens, defeated in his plan to unite southern Know-Nothings with the Democrats, sadly observed that Banks' election was the first of its kind in the history of the country that was purely sectional. His fellow Georgian Toombs declared, "The election of Banks has given great hopes to our enemies, and their policy is dangerous in the extreme to us." The Washington *Union* regretfully acquiesced in the outcome, "inasmuch as it enables the machinery of government to move on."

The nine weeks' struggle had intensified sectionalism in the North and South. It had weakened the American Party in both sections. It had promoted the rise of the Republican Party and served to solidify the Democratic Party in the slave states. It had fostered sectional ill will, aggravating southerners and buoying up northerners. In summary, it had highlighted the rending effects of the Kansas-Nebraska issue upon the American polity.

While the national legislature seemed dissolved in debate over the choice of a speaker, President Franklin Pierce had waited impatiently for the customary advice from the Congress that it was ready to receive his annual message. On the last day of December, as debate persisted, he sent the message, breaking precedent and provoking a "terrible uproar in the House." His purpose was threefold: to demonstrate his leadership, to put himself at the head of the Democratic Party, and to get ready for the campaign of 1856.

The message dwelt upon two themes—foreign relations and domestic politics. With regard to the first theme Pierce examined two minor crises in Anglo-American affairs, one concerning Central America and the other British recruiting in the United States for the Crimean War. The President insisted upon an American interpretation of the Clayton-Bulwer Treaty, providing for British-American relinquishment of domination in Central America, and upon British respect for American neutrality in the Russian war.

Turning to Kansas Territory, where, it will be remembered, one faction had come into power by virtue of Border Ruffians and another had extralegally framed a constitution, Pierce conceded "there have been acts prejudicial to good order, but," he continued, "as yet none have occurred under circumstances to justify the interposition of the Federal Executive." His intervention could be justified only by obstruction to Federal law or by organized resistance to territorial law, assuming the form of insurrection.

Thus Pierce extenuated executive failure to enforce the Kansas-Nebraska Act. He heedlessly threw aside his opportunity for constructive statesmanship. Now was his time to insist upon a new, fair election in Kansas, with safeguards for the rights of actual settlers. Firm executive leadership was needed for the troubled territory and for the troubled country. Nor did he expect Congress to act. "The Congress of the United States is in effect that congress of sovereignties which good men in the Old World have sought for, but could never attain. . . ." Beyond all this, the fathers of the Constitution, "being engaged in no extravagant scheme of social change," made the matter of the colored population a "question of local rights." The President defended incorporation of the principle of nonintervention in the Kansas-Nebraska Act, and deplored the sectional agitation that he said would lead to disunion or civil war.

"Disunion for what?" he asked. "If the passionate rage of fanaticism and partisan spirit did not force the fact upon our attention, it would be difficult to believe that any considerable portion of the people of this enlightened country could have so surrendered themselves to a fanatical devotion to the supposed interests of the relatively few Africans in the United States as totally to abandon and disregard the interests of the 25,000,000 Americans. . . ." Continuing his indictment of abolitionists, he said, "I know that the Union is stronger a thousand times than all the wild and chimerical schemes of social change which are generated one after another in the unstable minds of visionary sophists and interested agitators."

The Union of the Fathers above social change was his creed—an obdurate conservatism blind to the movement of historical forces. The Free Soiler John P. Hale replied to the President in a Senate speech so "savage and uncharacteristic" that Pierce turned his back on Hale at a White House reception. Hale objected bitterly to Pierce's terming opponents of slavery in Kansas as enemies of the Constitution and the Union. "I tell him, when he undertakes to designate these men as enemies of the Constitution, he abuses and defames men whose shoe-latchets he is not worthy to untie." The sharp difference between Pierce and antislavery men in Congress would persist throughout the long, turbulent session of Congress that lasted into the dog days of summer.

A fortnight following the Annual Message, the free-soil men in Kansas took another step toward making the territory a free state. In an election held January 15 Charles Robinson was named governor and a "state" legislature was chosen. Kansas now had two sets of officials—Shawnee and Topeka—and rival territorial delegates—Whitfield and Reeder.

Meanwhile, strife, started in the Wakarusa War, continued in Kansas, and Pierce became obliged to send Congress a special message. He reviewed the process of organizing the territory, upheld the right of the inhabitants to determine their own domestic institutions, and reproved former Governor Reeder for dilatoriness in establishing a government and for not "exercising constant vigilance" in putting down illegal acts. But he pinned most of the blame for the lawlessness, which now threatened the peace of the Union, upon "propagandist colonization" of the territory. This unnatural emigration endangered the peace of Missouri, though it did not justify the "reprehensible counter-movements which ensued."

The Topeka movement he condemned as "revolutionary"; but he went on to say, without turning a hair, "it is not the duty of the President of the United States to volunteer interposition by force to preserve the purity of elections either in a State or Territory." To interpose against revolutionary acts, he blandly asserted, "would be subversive of public freedom."

What, then, was to be done? He asked Congress to enact a law authorizing the people of Kansas, when numerous enough to constitute a state, to elect a convention that would frame a constitution, and thus prepare for lawful admission into the Union.

Pierce had evaded his responsibility. Kansas had only one third the population requisite for statehood, and for several years could anticipate having territorial government. Although he had repudiated Reeder, he refused to look into irregularities in the Kansas elections. Recognizing revolution, he refused to intervene. Faced with fraud, he gave his sanction to a territorial government that did not represent the consent of the governed. A strong President would have asked for a Congressional investigation of the frauds, would have maintained law' and order with Federal garrisons, and would have called for an early, honest election to ascertain the will of the majority.

Within three weeks, however, events forced Pierce to act without waiting for Congress. The freestate elections of January 15 were attended by disorder that continued. The impending session of the first "state" legislature, thus elected, and the threat of further Border Ruffianism combined to cause Lane and Robinson to appeal to the President to order the invading Missourians to disperse.

Pierce now issued a proclamation. He commanded the irregular combinations in the territory to disperse and placed the Federal troops at Forts Riley and Leavenworth at the disposal of Governor Shannon. The proclamation seemed to many persons to mean Pierce would use force to support a proslavery program. John C. Frémont wrote Governor Robinson: "It is to be feared from the proclamation of the President that he intends to recognize the usurpation in Kansas as the legitimate government." Andrew H. Reeder, who had asked friends having the ear of the President to impress upon him the danger of bloodshed, described the proclamation as "just the low contemptable [sic] trickstering affair which [you] might expect from Pierce . . ." [11]

If the President would offer no constructive program for Kansas, it was left to Congress to act. On January 26 George G. Dunn of Indiana had moved in the House to settle the agitation by restoring the Missouri Compromise. Dunn's conservative measure carried by one vote, 101–100, but failed in the Senate. Pierce's proclamation ignited controversy in the House, where "cut and thrust debates" became common. "The country anxiously waits for the action of Congress on the Kansas subject," a friend wrote the speaker.[12]

The immediate issue confronting the House was whether to seat the Shawnee delegate Whitfield or the Topeka delegate Reeder. When the Committee on Elections asked for authority to send for papers and persons in the dispute, southerners objected. Orr of South Carolina proposed what amounted to an ex parte investigation by two southern lawyers. On March 19 the House, against the unanimous objection by members from the slave states, by a 101–93 vote took a constructive step —the first one taken by the national legislature in implementing the Kansas-Nebraska Act. Acting upon a resolution introduced by Dunn, it authorized the speaker to appoint a committee of three "to inquire into and collect evidence in regard to the troubles in Kansas." It gave the committee ample powers to conduct its research and requested the President to furnish military protection, if necessary. Three members of the House, William A. Howard of Michigan, John Sherman of Ohio, both Republicans, and Mordecai Oliver, Democrat of Missouri, formed this important fact-finding committee.

Senate proceedings took another turn when on March 12 Douglas submitted a report for his Committee on Territories. The report, intended to implement Pierce's special message on Kansas, began with an exposition of Douglas's political philosophy. Keenly aware that his party would draft a platform and nominate a Presidential candidate within less than three months, he expounded his doctrine of Congressional nonintervention in the territories. Slavery, he insisted, was a local concern, and until they were admitted as states, the territories had a right to prohibit or establish slavery. In the American federal system Congress was powerless to interfere in purely internal affairs. The report sustained the legality of the Shawnee government, without inquiring into its bastard birth, and condemned the illegitimate Topeka government. Douglas poured the vials of his satirical wrath upon the emigrant-aid societies and threatened employment of Federal force to uphold the existing regime. The Senator promised to bring in a bill to prepare

Kansas to become a state in accordance with Pierce's request.

The Republican member of the committee, Collamer of Vermont, brought in his own report. Aiming at the Achilles heel of the majority report, he related how the invasion of Kansas had resulted in a usurpation of the powers of government by the Shawnee legislature. Both the executive and the Congress had refused redress; and thus far, he argued questionably, the Topeka effort was "peaceable, constitutional, and right." The true remedy, he declared, lay in the repeal of the Kansas-Nebraska Act. "Let Kansas be organized anew as a Free Territory, and all will be put right." But if Congress would not do that, it should declare all this spurious, foreign legislation void and "direct a reorganization, providing proper safeguards for legal voting and against foreign force." One other way to end the trouble in the territory and the nation was by admitting Kansas as a state, with her free constitution.

Collamer's speech had suggested alternatives to Administration policy. The clash between Democratic and Republican solutions of the Kansas struggle was sharpened on March 20 when Douglas spoke in behalf of the Administration bill and Seward announced he would introduce a substitute providing for immediate admission of Kansas under the Topeka constitution. Partisan rivalry was prompting reckless actions.

Douglas, the master of the Democratic majority, was in the prime of his life. We have a vivid portrait of him at this time from the pen of the author of *Uncle Tom's Cabin*. "This Douglas is the very ideal of vitality. Short, broad, and thickset, every inch of him has its own alertness and motion. He has a good head and face, thick black hair, heavy black brows and a keen eye. . . . He has two requisites of a debator—a melodious voice and a clear, sharply defined enunciation. . . . His sp eches, instead of being like an arrow sent at a mark, resemble rather a bomb which hits nothing in particular, but bursts and sends red-hot nails in every direction. . . . Douglas moves about the house as the recognized leader of Southern men."

The Little Giant now vigorously argued in behalf of his bill. He urged settlement of Kansas affairs by beginning with a census taken under the supervision of the governor. When the territory reached the population necessary for statehood, the legislature was to provide for the election, by bona fide white male settlers, of a constitutional convention. The trouble in Kansas, he iterated, had been caused by emigrant-aid societies, not by popular sovereignty as antislavery men charged. His great doctrine of local option could yet be made to work.

The Douglas proposal lacked statesmanship. A glaring fault was that it propped up the present regime. The "bogus legislature" with its "bogus laws" and a proslavery governor would exercise their "tyranny" for a long period of time, and when the population of Kansas had grown threefold, they would control the arrangements for statehood, including processes previously abused like taking a census and supervising the elections.

The Republican proposal, sponsored by Seward, was equally blundering. It provided for the immediate admission of Kansas, with its small population, under the Topeka constitution, drafted by a fraction of the settlers in an extralegal fashion. It accepted the exclusion of Negroes, both free and slave, from the state. If Douglas's advocacy of his measure had been a skillful barrister's plea, Seward's speech of April 9 in behalf of his measure was a piece of Republican eloquence. Seward indicted the Pierce Administration; he examined the evidence of Missourian interference mercilessly; he upheld the right of northerners to colonize Kansas, and argued that the Topeka constitution rested upon the popular will. The prophet shone through the politician when he declared, "He who found a river in his path, and sat down to wait for the flood to pass away, was not more unwise than he who expects the agitation of slavery to cease while the love of freedom animates the bosoms of mankind."

The speeches of both men as well as those of many other members of Congress were disseminated throughout the country in this election year. The debate—the second of three Congressional debates on Kansas, 1854, 1856, and 1858—doggedly persisted. It was not as searching as the first debate. The impending Presidential campaign overhung the proceedings. The times cried out for statesmanship and firmness, but there was no Henry Clay, no Andrew Jackson on the political scene.

"The government has been an obstruction, and nothing but an obstruction," Emerson grumbled. "The people by themselves would have settled Iowa, and Utah, and Kansas, in a sufficient way. The government has made all the mischief."

In the spring of 1856 the Kansas chicken had come home to roost. A weak President had first cooperated in the foolish destruction of the statecraft of 1820 and had then compounded his folly by inertly allowing a crisis to develop in the execution of his new policy. Two governments—one having the form of law but the spirit of lawlessness, the other having the spirit of law but the form of lawlessness—glared at one another in Kansas Territory.

The national legislature was bidden to formulate a policy. In 1854 Congress had withdrawn the ban on slavery agreed upon three decades earlier. In 1856 there was a new Congress, whose lower chamber contained a plurality elected in opposition to the withdrawal. The electorate of one section of the nation had given strong indications of favoring restoration of the Missouri Compromise. Dunn and Collamer, men of the second rank, had advocated a strategic retreat to the *status quo ante* 1854. But the Senate and executive continued to be under Democratic control, making restoration impossible. The American political system, unlike a parliamentary one, was rigid, not responsive to the popular will; terms of office were fixed by the Constitution. And although the House had been reformed, the Senate and President remained in power, immune to a vote of no confidence.

In the circumstances, the wise alternative was to insist that the policy of popular sovereignty truly reflect the sovereignty of the people of Kansas. This could only be accomplished by holding a fair election, at an early date, under impartial, Federal supervision. Unfortunately, however, on the eve of national nominating conventions, partisanship was the spirit of the hour. One party was disposed to wink at fraud and maintain a proslavery faction in control of the territory. The other party was disposed to ignore the proslavery faction and the sparseness of population and insist upon immediate admission as a free state.

Stalemate and personal abuse typified the Senate this spring. On March 4 the Topeka legislature had adopted a memorial requesting statehood and had elected Andrew Reeder and James H. Lane United States Senators. The freestate men commissioned Lane to carry its memorial to the Congress. When it was presented to the State, Douglas discovered that the signatures were all in one handwriting and that revisions of the document had been made following passage. Douglas branded the document a fraud and, pinning the blame on Lane, heaped sarcasm upon him. Lane explained that the memorial had been recopied, and improved in phrasing, with the approval of the governor. The Senate rejected the memorial by a partisan vote, whereupon Lane, who had been accused of fraud and forgery, called upon Douglas for an explanation of his language. Douglas coolly turned aside the demand, leaving Lane to his humiliation. The Kansan with his crude methods had exposed the Topeka movement to ridicule, and had turned his cause into a personal controversy.

The climax of personal vilification came in late May with Senator Charles Sumner's philippic "The Crime Against Kansas." When he took the floor of the Senate on May 21, he delivered an ornate oration that must be viewed against the background of persisting disorder in Kansas, Democratic demands for acceptance of the Shawnee government, the rise of Republicanism, and Sumner's sense of vanity and moral outrage. His oration contrasted with the conservatism found in earlier addresses, where, in order to effect emancipation he had expressed a willingness to compensate slaveowners at national expense and to examine plans for colonizing freedmen in the tropics. And although he had championed *legal* equality for Negroes, he did not strive for or anticipate *social* equality between the races. He expected, he had said, that most Negroes when freed would remain in the southern states as "a dependent and amiable peasantry."

Sumner spoke to the Senate on two days, spending May 21 castigating the Kansas "swindle," and May 22 examining the various remedies, of which the only one acceptable to him was immediate admission as a free state. Measures are one thing, but men another, and unhappily on both days he dealt in personalities, especially assailing Senator Andrew P. Butler of South Carolina. The absent Butler he described as the Don Quixote of slavery, who "has chosen a mistress to whom he has made his vows, and who, though ugly to others, is always lovely to him; though polluted in the sight of the world, is chaste in his sight . . . the harlot Slavery."

This coarse tirade created a sensation. The venerable Cass immediately rose to denounce it. But the sad sequel was a savage physical onslaught on Sumner. Butler had a younger cousin, Congressman Preston S. Brooks of South Carolina, devoted to his family and to the southern code. "I felt it to be my duty to relieve Butler and avenge the insult to my State," he explained to his brother. He waited for Sumner outside the Capitol for two days, before finally going to the Senate chamber after its adjournment on May 22. Brooks vividly recounted his deed to his brother, "I then went to S's seat and said, 'Mr. Sumner, I have read your Speech with care and as much impartiality as was possible and I feel it my duty to tell you that you have libeled my State and slandered a relative who is aged and absent and I am come to punish you for it."

Sumner was sitting at his desk, and as he was about to rise, "I struck him with my cane and gave him about 30 first rate stripes. . . . Every lick went where I intended. For about the first five or six licks he offered to make fight but I plied him so rapidly that he did not touch me. Towards the last he bellowed like a calf."

After less than a minute a Congressman appeared and prevented Brooks from inflicting further injury. Sumner remained senseless for several minutes. The exact extent of his injuries is hard to determine, and subject to the same kind of controversy, contemporary and historiographical, that surrounds Kansas affairs. He absented himself from his Senate chair until December, 1859, for three and a half years, undergoing treatment and at the same time seeming in vigorous physical shape.

Accused of shamming at the time by political foes and later by critical historians, he appears to have suffered wounds more gravely psychic than physical.

Sumner's empty Senate chair remained as a symbol of northern feeling about the attacks. In the press, in private letters and diaries, in public meetings the North vented its opinion. "Never was the country in such a crazy state as just now," the New York lawyer George Templeton Strong wrote in his diary. "Civil war impending over Kansas . . . North and South farther alienated than ever before. I believe civilization at the South is retrograde and that the Carolinas are decaying into barbarism." With disgust he noted that, "Southern editors and Congressmen talk about the 'chivalry,' 'gallantry,' and manliness" of Brooks' deed.

"Another Southern outrage, which is causing more talk and action than anything which has ever transpired in either House of Congress before," a correspondent wrote to Banks. "I am glad to see that Northern people are waking up. . . ." [13] From distant Dresden, Germany, James Russell Lowell wrote his brother-in-law: "Kansas seems in a bad way, and the last thing I read was about the assault upon Sumner, which shocked me more than I can tell. There never was anything so brutal. How long are such things to be borne?"

Greeley's *New-York Tribune* exploited the episode to partisan advantage. Seward called a caucus of Republican Senators, who agreed to have Sumner's Massachusetts colleague, Wilson, address the Senate and call for action. John P. Hale saw a stiffening of northerners' resolve to maintain their position in the Senate at all hazards as the result of the outrage.

There were indignation meetings in nearly every northern city. An estimated five thousand persons thronged Faneuil Hall in Boston; and after the gentle

Emerson spoke in Concord, dispraising the assault, the Quaker poet Whittier wrote: "A thousand thanks for the speech at the Concord meeting." The most notable meeting took place in the Tabernacle in New York City on May 30, where men of moderate political views and much property cheered every mention of Sumner and hissed every mention of Brooks. Republican chairman Edwin D. Morgan glowed: "The changes *now taking place* in our city are very great. The Sumner meeting on Friday night was glorious." [14]

"Bully Brooks" he was in the North, but in the South he was a hero. "Every Southern man is delighted," Brooks told his brother. "The fragments of the stick are begged for as *sacred* relicts [*sic*]." The southern press widely supported the assault. The Richmond *Enquirer* declared it was a choice of "shameful submission to insult" or "the finding of some adequate redress"; because a gentleman could not reply to abolitionists in the language of "the brothel," there was little else to do than inflict personal chastisement. Toombs, who had come upon the scene while Brooks was still struggling with the Congressman who was restraining him, later said of the affray, "I approved it."

Wilson's call for Senate action ended only in a purely Democratic committee report. Nothing could be done, as Brooks was a member of the other house. A motion to expel Brooks from the House passed 121 to 95, every southern Congressman save one opposing, but the vote failed to secure the necessary two-thirds majority. Brooks resigned and was re-elected by his admiring constituents. He was fined $300 by a Baltimore court for his assault, and died the following January, aged thirty-seven, heartsick at his role.

The Sumner-Brooks episode, giving the North a dubious martyr and the South a dubious hero, revealed a dualism in American values. It inflamed feeling, at a crucial time, on the eve of party conventions. It widened the rift between North and South, and at the same time intensified sectional self-consciousness.

The day before the assault on Sumner the freestate town of Lawrence had been attacked, inaugurating frontier warfare, giving the nation the agony of Bleeding Kansas throughout the long hot summer of 1856. Behind "the Sack of Lawrence," as the Republican press promptly labeled it, was the building up of tension in the territory throughout the spring. The winter of 1855–56 had been more severe than any winter Indians and traders who had lived for years in the territory could remember. Deep, drifting snows and subzero temperatures probably served to abate violence. By the end of March, however, the grass was growing and tiny flower bells, adder's tongue, were swaying in the breeze.

The annual spring emigration to the West began. Every year's passing augmented the freestate population of Kansas and diminished the possibility that Kansas might become a slave state. Partisans on both sides sought to turn the migration into a militant campaign. "Let your young men come forth to Missouri and Kansas!" Atchison had exhorted the editor of the Atlanta *Examiner.* "Let them come well armed!" Throughout the South a program to assist emigration to Kansas was advocated, without much success. The most notable band was raised by Colonel Jefferson Buford of Alabama. A planter who sold his slaves and enlisted some four hundred defenders of slavery to colonize Kansas, he crossed the Kansas line on May 2. The proslavery company attracted wide attention, the northern press branding the men Border Ruffians, but as Paul W. Gates has suggested,

"Buford seemed as much interested in his land activities as in the slavery question."

In the North *The New-York Tribune* shrilly asserted that "the duty of the people of the free States is to send more true men, more Sharpe's [sic] rifles, and more field pieces and howitzers to Kansas." The New England Emigrant Aid Company was busy with its futile but inflammatory activities. Northern churches witnessed warlike preparations for the Kansas Crusade. Henry Ward Beecher's Plymouth Church in Brooklyn began to furnish Sharps rifles, Beecher declaring that in Kansas the Sharps rifle was a greater moral agency than the Bible. From then on this weapon of northern emigrants was called "Beecher's Bible." Despite southern reproaches, it appears that probably not more than 316 Sharps rifles ever reached fighting freestate men. By late spring settlers were streaming onto the prairies, intent on improving their lot in life, most of them unconcerned about slavery.

In April, while the Congressional committee was conducting its hearings, an incident in the town of Lawrence precipitated a crisis. Sheriff Jones of Wakarusa War renown was shot in the back, while in town to arrest some freestate leaders. Though only slightly wounded, he was reported dead, igniting a rough element's demand that the "abolition" town be destroyed. The notoriously partisan chief justice of the territory, Judge Lecompte, sprang to the aid of the proslavery men, charging the grand jury in language that encouraged finding bills for treason. Without gathering evidence the grand jury indicted Reeder, Robinson, Lane, and others for treason. The jury also recommended that the freestate hotel in Lawrence, constructed of stone for military purposes, be demolished, and that the freestate papers, published at

Lawrence, the *Herald of Freedom* and *The Kansas Free State*, be abated as nuisances. Robinson started east, but was arrested in Missouri and taken to Lecompton in Kansas Territory, where for four months he was detained.

The United States marshal for Kansas issued a proclamation declaring he had warrants to serve in Lawrence and calling upon all law-abiding citizens to come to Lawrence to aid in executing the law. It was an invitation to violence. Lawrence, founded by the Emigrant Aid Company, with its fortress hotel and antislavery press, was the detestable symbol of the Yankee interlopers. Gleefully, men came from the countryside: the Douglas County * (Kansas) Militia, the Kickapoo Rangers, Buford's troop, the Doniphan Tigers, the Missouri Platte County Rifles with two artillery pieces commanded by ex-Senator Atchison, and others.

A deputy marshal's posse encountered no difficulty in arresting the men they had come for. The posse dissolved and Atchison and the marshal accepted the invitation of the Free State Hotel proprietor to dine there. Now Sheriff Jones, who had long set his heart on destruction of this "hotbed of abolitionism," took charge. No company in the forces numbering perhaps 750 bore the Union flag, but a banner, inscribed on one side "Southern Rights" and on the other "South Carolina," was raised over the *Herald of Freedom* office. Jones's men demolished the offices of both newspapers, broke up the type, and tossed it into the river. Having completed this work, encouraged by a grand jury and a sheriff, the enraged ruffians turned their cannon on the stone hotel. It resisted shot and kegs of powder ignited to blow it up; and after ransacking it, and taking the stock of wines

* Lawrence is the county seat of Douglas County.

and liquors, the mob burned the hotel. Before departing, they set fire to Governor Robinson's house and pillaged various other houses.

They dispersed, some of them returning to Kansas City where the correspondent of the London *Times* "first came in contact with the Missouri patriots," as he sarcastically put it. "I had just arrived in Kansas City, and shall never forget the appearance of the lawless mob that poured into the place, inflamed with drink, glutted with the indulgence of the vilest passions, displaying with loud boasts the 'plunder' they had taken from the inhabitants. . . ." They were, he went on, "Men, for the most part of large frame, with red flannel shirts and immense boots worn outside their trousers, their faces unwashed and unshaven . . . wearing the most savage looks, and giving utterance to the most horrible imprecations and blasphemies; armed, moreover, to the teeth with rifles and revolvers, cutlasses and bowie-knives. . . ."

Such was the Sack of Lawrence. Only one man was killed, and he a proslavery man struck by a brick falling from the Free State Hotel. The men of Lawrence made no effort to resist, and doubtless would not have offered resistance even had their leader, Robinson, not been under arrest. But the attack on Lawrence, exaggerated in the eastern press, occurring simultaneously with the assault upon Sumner, shook the North. Proslavery men had ridden roughshod over law and order. The chief justice of the territory and his grand jury had fomented this outrage, the sheriff of Douglas County had perpetrated it, and the U. S. marshal had been present while it was committed. President Pierce, anxiously awaiting the Democratic convention that was soon to assemble, although apprised of the motley crew forming as a posse, had not intervened. "If there is to be armed resistance to the laws of the country and the constitutional rights of the south, it might as well occur at this time and in Kansas as elsewhere," he is supposed to have said.

The muddle of territorial government in Kansas combined with the dichotomy in American values exposed in northern and southern responses to the brutal caning of Sumner attested to the deterioration of the American republic. One week after the Sumner affair, which he had known about in advance and approved, Congressman Lawrence Keitt of South Carolina wrote from Washington: "The Kansas fight has just occurred and the times are stirring. Everybody here feels as if we are upon a volcano."

If Washington was a volcano, Kansas was a tinderbox that was soon aflame, and the match was applied by a northern antislavery man—John Brown. His irresponsible deed was the act of a man with insanity in his ancestry and failure in his own past, a man possessed by abolitionist fanaticism, and imbued with the spirit of violence epidemic in frontier Kansas. The son of an abolitionist, he had been a wanderer and a ne'er-do-well, suspected of dishonest practices, befriended by the abolitionist Gerrit Smith. He once kept a station on the Underground Railroad, and he believed in violence. With five of his sons—he fathered 20 children—he migrated to Kansas in 1855, where he figured in the Wakarusa War.

His cramped mental processes were seamed with a strong vein of religiosity. He believed in an Old Testament God of vengeance and somehow came to regard himself as God's instrument. The success of the proslavery forces in Kansas profoundly disturbed him; and he was not without outside encouragement. Father Giddings wrote him from Washington in mid-March: "The death of the first man by the troops will involve every free State in your own path. It will light up the fires of

Civil War through out the North, and we shall stand or fall with you." [15]

The Sack of Lawrence aroused Brown, now fifty-six years of age, perhaps, as his son Salmon later said, "to cause a restraining fear" among the Border Ruffians. Whatever his motive, on the night of Saturday, May 24, with four of his sons and two other men, John Brown and his unholy band deliberately murdered in cold blood five proslavery men near Dutch Henry's crossing, where the California trail crossed Pottawatomie Creek. The bodies were brutally mutilated, one man's skull was split open in two places.

The John Brown legend began. To some men he became the liberator of Kansas, and escaping punishment now, he went on to wreak havoc at Harper's Ferry in 1859, leading to his execution and martyrdom. But it is plain that, although his soul was touched with abolitionist fervor, his mind was tainted. He was a criminal deserving of execration instead of exaltation, whose crime inaugurated guerrilla war in Kansas lasting until autumn. Unhappily, this horrifying act, coming on the heels of the Sack of Lawrence and the assault upon Sumner, transpired on the eve of the great national party conventions.

6

The territories should be kept open
for free white people

From the start of his Administration Pierce
had hoped to distinguish himself by his conduct of foreign relations. A bold course, he
believed, would acquire additional territory
for the United States, augment foreign commerce, enhance American prestige, and uphold the Monroe Doctrine. Moreover, it
would distract attention from domestic discord. His hope had not been fulfilled.

A note of desperation entered Pierce's
calculations, for as Marcy in July, 1854,
wrote to the American minister in France:
"To tell you an unwelcome truth, the Nebraska question has sadly shattered our
party in all the free states and deprived it of
that strength which was needed & could
have been much more profitably used for the
acquisition of Cuba."

Meeting on Marcy's instructions, three
American diplomats, John Y. Mason, minis-
ter to France, James Buchanan, minister to
Great Britain, and Pierre Soulé, minister to
Spain, drafted a confidential dispatch, com-
monly called the "Ostend Manifesto." Not

The chapter title is quoted from a speech made by
Abraham Lincoln at Kalamazoo, Michigan, in 1856.

released to the press until March of 1855, it recommended that the United States offer Spain "a price for
Cuba, far beyond its present value. . . ." If Spain should
refuse, the dispatch continued in startling language,
"then, by every law, human and Divine, we shall be justified in wresting it from Spain, if we possess the
power. . . ." The opposition newspapers made the
worst of this gasconade when it was released, *The New-
York Weekly Tribune* branding it the "Manifesto of the
Brigands." Many northerners were confident the Administration meant to acquire slavekeeping Cuba, no matter
what the means.

The document aroused feeling both North and South,
and played its part in the Presidential campaign of 1856.
It figured in the Republican platform as we shall see, and
it enhanced the availability of James Buchanan in the
eyes of southern Democrats.

Pierce's decisive and spirited foreign policy—contrasting with his Kansas policy—did not bring him re-nomina-
tion. Indeed, as Democratic delegates assembled in
Cincinnati, his chances of succeeding himself were dim.
Kansas was to be the dominant issue of the campaign of
1856. And Pierce's Kansas policy had disenchanted many
northern Democrats. Without northern supporters, notwithstanding Pierce's popularity in the South, the party
could not win. The President's former secretary wrote on
May 29, Pierce "is in rather bad odor, and will stink worse
yet before the 4th of next March. The Kansas outrages
are all imputable to him, and if he is not called to answer for them here, 'In Hell they'll roast him like a
herring.'"

The party's logical choice would seem to have been the
proponent of its central tenet, popular sovereignty, Stephen A. Douglas. However, Douglas labored under two
disabilities; first, he held his main strength in the North-

west, and second, Kansas was howling like a cyclone. What the party needed was a nominee who approved repeal of the Missouri Compromise, favored popular sovereignty, and yet had not been involved in the controversy over Kansas. He should also enjoy broad strength among northern voters, particularly in crucial Pennsylvania, a swing state, where the iron interests were an important consideration.

The man with these qualifications was James Buchanan, who had been out of the country as minister to the Court of St. James's. Long in public service, now sixty-five years of age, a Pennsylvanian, he had the support of the iron interests. In response to the urging of Senator John Slidell of Louisiana, who was organizing his forces, Buchanan publicized his acceptance of the Kansas-Nebraska Act's principles "as a finality," and declared, "had I been a member of Congress I should have voted for the Kansas Bill. . . ." [1] Four Senators, Slidell, Bright of Indiana, Judah P. Benjamin of Louisiana and James A. Bayard of Delaware, repaired to the convention city in order to coordinate the Buchanan movement. On Friday night before the convention Bright committed the Indiana delegation to Buchanan.

Kansas, then, was to dictate the Democratic nomination. The party, in choosing Cincinnati, "the Queen City," had gone farther west than ever before, and at the same time had selected a site with a southern flavor, immediately across the Ohio River from slavery. The convention opened Monday June 2, feeling the impact of the Sack of Lawrence and the assault on Sumner. The veteran editor of the Washington *Globe*, John C. Rives, astutely told John C. Breckinridge, "I think the principal reasons why Buck is a little ahead of the pack, are 1st He starts with Penna in his pocket, and 2nd He is not mixed up with the repeal of the Missouri Compromise, the settlement of

Kansas, &c &c." "It seems to me this morning that old Buck is the choice of most of the Democrats about here & he deserves to win." [2]

At the first session the delegates noisily feuded over seating rival groups from Missouri and New York. Meantime Buchanan's managers began to unfold their strategy: it embraced naming a Buchaneer as permanent chairman, admitting all contesting delegations, thus dividing their strength, and adopting the platform first. To conciliate Douglas the platform would include a popular-sovereignty plank; and to diminish his chances, Bright as dispenser of patronage in the Northwest would make promises to Douglas's weaker backers, while the Little Giant's stronger supporters would be reminded of his youth and availability in 1860.

The strategy was executed; and on Wednesday morning the platform was adopted before nominations were made, differing from the procedure of Baltimore in 1852 and making a bad precedent for 1860. The heart of the platform was in the portion on slavery in the territories. The convention affirmed that the principles found in the Kansas-Nebraska Act embody "the only sound and safe solution of the Slavery question." With regard to the immediate, pressing issue, the delegates unanimously asserted:

"That we recognize the right of the people of all the Territories including Kansas and Nebraska, acting through the legally and fairly expressed will of the majority of the actual residents, and whenever the number of their inhabitants justifies it, to form a Constitution, with or without domestic Slavery, and be admitted into the Union upon terms of perfect equality with the other States." The party pledged itself to execute the Fugitive Slave Law and to resist renewal of agitation of the slavery question. It denounced the Know Nothing political crusade for its illiberal spirit.

With regard to other matters of domestic policy, the Democracy avowed anew its faith in a limited national government, and declared the Federal government could not charter a national bank, enact a protective tariff, or assist in internal improvements. A resolution favoring a public road between the Atlantic and the Pacific incurred so much opposition it was laid on the table. In contrast with the conciliatory and negative quality of the domestic planks, the foreign-policy planks boldly asserted the role of the United States as a world leader of free trade and watchdog of the Western Hemisphere, and blustered about the commanding interest of the United States in Central America.

The delegates then turned to finding a champion for their dogmas. Four men were nominated: Pierce, Douglas, Buchanan, and Cass. On the first ballot Buchanan led, with 103 votes from the North and 32 from slave states, including all the votes from Virginia and Louisiana—a nucleus of southern strength—for which Governor Wise and Senator Slidell were responsible. All through the day, through fourteen ballots, Buchanan kept first place, Pierce second, and Douglas third. The next morning, following negotiations between Douglas and Pierce supporters, Pierce withdrew; but even so Douglas stood second. After the sixteenth ballot, William A. Richardson, Douglas's floor manager, rose and read aloud to a hushed convention a letter in which the Little Giant withdrew his name because he feared "an embittered state of feeling is being engendered in the convention," and because he would "let no personal considerations disturb the harmony of the party or endanger the triumph of our principles."

Their work completed, the weary delegates adjourned, having adopted a creed—popular sovereignty—and chosen a candidate—Buchanan—to present to the country in its time of peril. Although their party was the only truly national party, the convention had revealed sectional stresses in making the platform and in designating a nominee. It had failed to renominate its titular head, Pierce, who had forfeited respect in the North, or to nominate its tutelary genius, Douglas, who had suffered from the struggle in Kansas. It had gladly endorsed Douglas's policies, and lukewarmly Pierce's, but it had turned to a neutral figure to advance them. It had endured dissension among rival delegations and upon nonslavery aspects of the platform; it had passed through prolonged balloting before the candidate of availability triumphed on the seventeenth ballot. It had chosen the best possible nominee to bring party victory: an aging conservative, strong in Pennsylvania, appealing to moderates North and South, respectful of slavery's interests yet himself from a free state. It had, finally, balanced the ticket with the nomination of youthful John C. Breckinridge of slaveholding Kentucky for the Vice-Presidency.

The Democratic platform was out of touch with reality. It spoke righteously of "the right of the people of all the Territories" to act "through the legally and fairly expressed will of the majority of the actual residents" in forming a constitution, yet the party, when clothed with full power, had permitted a flagrant violation of these principles in Kansas. It made the issue of slavery in the territories—clearly the great national question, shaking the Union to its center—a local matter, except for Federal aid in returning fugitives.

Its political philosophy was negative, if not retrogressive. It exalted a weak central government, "one of limited power," a "Union of States," and affirmed the Virginia and Kentucky Resolutions as "one of the main foundations" of the Democratic Party's political creed. It took no cognizance of the rapid change in the nation from an agricultural to an industrial economy. It failed to appreciate the transportation, commercial, and industrial revolutions the American republic was undergoing. It discounted the onrushing nationalism, burgeoning industrialism, and enlarging freedom that were hallmarks of the history of the nineteenth century.

Particularism and agrarianism formed the central planks of the platform. Much of it was repeated word for word from earlier platforms. Much of it harked back to Jacksonian Democracy; and in turn much of Jacksonian Democracy—nostalgic for a lost Arcadia that never was —had been out of touch with reality in Old Hickory's time.

The Democratic candidate, James Buchanan, after graduating from Dickinson College, had practiced law, and entered politics as a Federalist. He served in both state and national legislatures, as U. S. minister to Russia, as Secretary of State under Polk, and as U. S. minister to Great Britain. What were his views on slavery? As a Congressman in 1826 he had said, "Slavery is a great moral evil. . . . It is, however, one of those moral evils, from which it is impossible to escape, without the introduction of evils infinitely greater." To this view of the practical impossibility he coupled the belief of the constitutional impossibility of ending slavery. The Founding Fathers left jurisdiction over it to the states, and "The Constitution of the United States never would have been called into existence if the question had not been left to the States themselves." Violate this fundamental compact, and the "Union will be dissolved and incalculable evils will come from its ashes. . . ." As a United

States Senator he had voted for a bill to exclude abolitionist literature from the mails; and he had taken a middle position in the "gag" controversy, upholding the right of petition while favoring immediate rejection of the abolitionist memorials.

Buchanan was an ardent expansionist, favoring acquisition of Texas in 1844 as well as Cuba in 1854. He answered antislavery men who opposed acquisition with the diffusionist theory; annexation of Texas, he thought, might "be the means of limiting, not enlarging, the dominion of slavery." Moreover, recognizing the prevalent racialism, he argued that in Texas slaves would flee to Mexico, and there "mingle with a race where no prejudice exists against their color."

Like many of his contemporaries, Buchanan realized how racial difference complicated the American problem of emancipation. "It is true," he wrote in his 1865 apologia, "that other countries enjoyed facilities for emancipation which we do not possess. In them the slaves were of the same color and race with the rest of the community, and in becoming freemen they soon mingled with the general mass on equal terms with their former masters."

Buchanan had long abhorred abolitionists, believing they had retarded emancipation by the South and that they threatened the preservation of the Union. "Before this unfortunate agitation commenced," he claimed in 1838, "a very large and growing party existed in several of the slave States in favor of the gradual abolition of slavery; and now not a voice is heard there in support of such a measure. The Abolitionists have postponed the emancipation of the slaves in three or four States of this Union for at least half a century." If they continued to pursue their mad course, they would "cover the land with blood." "The Union is now in danger, and I wish to proclaim the fact," he solemnly warned.

As a young man he had at first opposed the Missouri Compromise, favoring exclusion of slavery from Missouri; but he later became the compromise's vigorous defender, holding it almost as sacred as a Constitutional provision. Not in public life at the time of the Compromise of 1850, he had steadfastly adhered to extending the Missouri Compromise line, disliking popular sovereignty as a doctrine that would invite territorial warfare.

Now in 1856 James Buchanan was the standard-bearer of popular sovereignty. It was a Delphic doctrine, an oracle interpreted one way in the South, another in the North. In part that was the beauty of the doctrine, its ambiguity making it acceptable to both sections. Many southerners understood popular sovereignty to mean that the inhabitants of a territory would decide about slavery at the time of statehood. Until then slavery was secure in a territory. This interpretation made the operation of popular sovereignty consistent with Calhoun's common-property doctrine. Many northerners understood the phrase to mean that the inhabitants of a territory could decide about slavery at the time of territorial organization. This second interpretation, sometimes known as "squatter sovereignty," conflicted with the southern view that a territorial legislature could not prohibit slavery.

Buchanan's own interpretation remained something of a mystery, even after he had accepted the nomination. As Governor Wise wrote him in distress, "There is a single phrase in your letter of acceptance which seems to signify that you concede the power to the people in a Territory, whilst in the territorial stage, to prohibit Slavery—in other words, which expresses Squatter Sov-

ereignty doctrine." Although the letter referred to statehood as the time of decision, "an old Calhoun clique . . .
are already slyly hinting that I, as well as you, am
intending to betray the South on the Kansas doctrine." [3]
Buchanan in reply declined to go beyond his original
letter, and it was not until his inauguration that the
ambiguity was removed.

The Democratic Party was a well-established organization. It currently held power in all the branches of the
Federal government—executive, Senate, Supreme Court,
and officeholders—except for the House of Representatives. It traced its ancestry to Jefferson and Madison,
albeit it had been reconstituted in the age of Jackson as a
part of what historians call "the second American party
system." The Whig Party—its traditional foe—lay mori-
bund; and in 1856 the Democrats faced a stripling
opponent—the Republican Party. Consolidation of the
state Republican organizations in 1856 inaugurated the
third American party system. To the story of the formation of this antislavery axis we must now turn.

It will be remembered that anti-Nebraska politicians
had begun to plan a national political organization in
December, 1855. In mid-January, 1856, a group of Republican state chairmen issued a call, inviting "the
Republicans of the Union" to meet informally at Pittsburgh on George Washington's birthday, 1856, to perfect
a national organization and to provide for a national
nominating convention.

Representatives of twenty-four states, sixteen free and
eight slave, came to Pittsburgh in response to this call.
They were a congeries of faiths: Free Soilers like Joshua
Giddings and his son-in-law George W. Julian, abolitionists like the editor of *The National Era,* Gamaliel Bailey,

anti-Nebraska Democrats, Know Nothings, Whigs and Republicans. The old Jacksonian Democrat Francis P. Blair was named chairman. "Think of an anti Slavery Convention being presided over by a slaveholder!" moaned the abolitionist Lewis Tappan.

In the search for unified opposition to the Administration's Kansas policy, moderation prevailed. The convention created a national Republican Party by forming a National Executive Committee. It was headed by Edwin D. Morgan, the New York State chairman, a wealthy merchant closely associated with the Seward-Weed machine. The first Republican national chairman, energetic and upright, evinced such marked political skill that he held the post in all for twelve years and as Civil War governor of New York and U. S. Senator found a high place for himself in public life. Morgan's committee was authorized to arrange for a nominating convention in Philadelphia on June 17—Bunker Hill day.

Besides organizing party machinery and providing for the Philadelphia convention, the Pittsburgh representatives issued an address "to the people of the United States." It asserted that the government was being employed to advance the interests of slavery and that popular sovereignty was without constitutional warrant. On the general issue of slavery in the territories, the Republicans demanded repeal of laws reopening to slavery territories once free, and pledged resistance by every constitutional means to slavery in the territories. In this mildly worded pledge the delegates fell short of the defiant "no more slave territory" cry of the Free Soilers of '48, and stopped short of the position the Republican Party would take, as we shall see, in June. Abolitionists including Gerrit Smith, Lewis Tappan, and Frederick Douglass, disappointed in the Pittsburgh convention, with its opposition to extension of slavery but not to slavery, endorsed a call for a mass convention at Syracuse in May to nominate "thorough Abolition Candidates."

On the special issue of dual government in Kansas, the delegates favored immediate admission of Kansas as a free state. Finally, they announced their purpose to overthrow the "weak and faithless" national Administration.[4]

The Pittsburgh gathering left to the national committee the task of arranging for the Philadelphia convention. It would be a mistake to suppose that northerners of an antislavery persuasion rushed to join the new Republican Party. For months after the Pittsburgh proceedings there were men of that persuasion who variously wanted to re-form the Democratic Party, revive the Whig Party, or shape the Republican Party to their own views.

Alive to this feeling the committee in sending out its call for the nominating convention shunned the word "Republican" and, carefully selecting the ground to stand on, invited delegates from persons "who are opposed to the repeal of the Missouri Compromise, to the policy of the present administration, to the extension of Slavery into the Territories, in favor of the admission of Kansas as a Free State, and of restoring the action of the Federal Government to the principles of Washington and Jefferson. . . ."

During the first six months of 1856 events played into the hands of the new party's fathers. First came the election of Banks as Republican speaker in company with Pierce's fumbling of the Kansas problem. The call for the Philadelphia convention, as Morgan said, "was broad to meet the views of many who voted for Banks but who are not yet enrolled as Republicans." [5] In March the Republican Party was organized in Rhode Island and Connecticut. In May the consanguinity of Bleeding Kansas and 'bleeding Sumner' was exploited to organize voters as Republicans. During the month Pierce vetoed three river-and-harbor bills. By the time of the Philadelphia meeting the Republican Party was a rising power.

The first Republican national convention met in Musical Fund Hall, Philadelphia, on Tuesday, June 17, while Kansas was enkindled in guerrilla war. The assembly had the air of a revival meeting, as the ardent delegates gathered, intent on saving the soul of Kansas and redeeming the republic from the slave power. Radicals mingled with moderates, and veteran politicians with freshmen. There was a conspicuous absence of men like Bright and Slidell who had so adroitly pulled wires in the Cincinnati convention. There was, again, a conspicuous absence of delegates from the South; only four border slave states were represented. "The Philadelphia black republican convention . . . can, in no proper sense, be regarded as a national convention, but, in the strictest sense of that term, it was *sectional* and geographical," observed the Washington *Union*. "The few *exotics* from Maryland, Virginia, and Kentucky, who appeared there as delegates, have no constituencies at home."

Chairman Morgan, after bringing the delegates to order, in a brief address sounded a patriotic note, keynoting the question, "whether the people of the United States are to be . . . forever chained to the present policy of the extension of human slavery," and pleading, "let us avoid all extremes. . . ." On the second day David Wilmot, as chairman of the platform committee, made his report. It was fitting that this venerable Free Soiler should report the platform. He was the father of the Wilmot Proviso—the proposal to have Congress exclude slavery from the Mexican Cession—which was the germ of the Republican Party. His interest had not been in the Negro but in keeping the territory free for white men. Back in 1847 he had told Congress: "I plead the cause and the rights of white freemen. I would preserve to free white labor a fair country, a rich inheritance, where the sons of toil, of my own race and color, can live without the disgrace which association with negro slavery brings upon free labor."

The issue of slavery in the Federal territories had called the Republican Party into being. This issue from now through the disastrous party split of 1860 would separate men into rival political parties. The Republican national platform of 1856 went beyond the Pittsburgh statement and far beyond repeal—the Republican creed of 1854–55. It denied the authority of both Congress and a territorial legislature to give legal existence to slavery in a territory. Constitutional authority for this position it found in the due-process clause; to establish slavery would be a deprivation of liberty without due process of law. Ironically, as we shall see, the Supreme Court of the United States would use this same clause in the Dred Scott case to protect slavery in the territories. To prohibit slavery would be a deprivation of slave property without due process of law, it stated.

The role of Congress was not merely negative, being without power to establish slavery, or permissive in the exercise of power. The Constitution conferred upon Congress sovereign power over the territories and was mandatory; "it is both the right and the duty of Congress" to prohibit slavery in the territories. Concerning the immediate problem, the platform, after reciting the wrongs of Kansas and threatening "condign punishment to those responsible," advocated the immediate admission of Kansas as a state under the Topeka constitution.

The short platform, less than half the length of the Cincinnati document, condemned the Ostend Circular as "the highwayman's plea, that 'might makes right,'" urged immediate Federal aid to a railroad to the Pacific Ocean by the most central route, and asserted Congressional appropriations for river-and-harbor improvements were constitutional and justified.

Who could lead the new party to victory? For several months politicians and press had been sifting out possible candidates. Chase, who had done much to create the party, had been eliminated as too radical on slavery. Seward suffered from the same handicap; moreover he himself was not persuaded the party could win in 1856. Like the Democrats, the Republicans needed a man not closely associated with the Kansas strife. The daring explorer, young Colonel John C. Frémont, met the party's special needs more than any other available man.

"The Pathfinder," aged forty-three, whose exploits in surveying the West were household knowledge, was a romantic figure, who had courted and married the brilliant Jessie Benton, daughter of the Missouri leader. Speaker Banks boomed him for the nomination, and in a letter to Governor Robinson of Kansas confided, "We think he is a safe man, and that he can be elected." [6] A letter from Frémont to Robinson soon appeared in the press, criticizing Pierce's February proclamation and assuring the freestate governor of his support. Frémont, a former Democrat, in late April announced his firm opposition to the extension of slavery, thereby embracing the central dogma of the Republican Party. By this time Frémont had only one rival—Supreme Court Justice John McLean. The elderly McLean, long in public life, appealed to conservatives and persons who distrusted the young romantic explorer. Abraham Lincoln, among others, preferred McLean to Frémont; "his nomination would save every Whig." Thaddeus Stevens of Pennsylvania thought McLean was the only man who could save his state.

In making their nomination in 1856 the Democrats had sought to prevent dissension; the Republicans, in contrast, sought to unite their disparate elements. Only two names were placed in nomination—Frémont and McLean—and on an informal ballot Frémont led 359 to 196. He was unanimously designated the Republican nominee on a formal ballot. William L. Dayton of New Jersey, a former Whig, became his running mate. The antislavery Know Nothings, the "North Americans," endorsed Frémont and with some reluctance Dayton, because they had hoped to name the Vice-President. A fusion of antislavery forces had been achieved. Leaving direction of the campaign in Morgan's hands, the convention adjourned.

The heart of the new platform was its slavery resolutions. They were moderate—the outcome of a search for a northern consensus. Historians have written freely of extremists, radicals, and fanatics during this period, but in point of fact these elements were almost nonexistent. John Brown is the exception that proves the rule. The resolutions were disappointing to abolitionists, for they did not attack slavery in the states or in the District of Columbia, the Fugitive Slave Law, or the interstate slave trade. They did not propose to move against the slave codes by which southern states kept their bondsmen under a special set of laws, or to elevate the lot of the Negro, nor did they proclaim that the black man was created equal with the white. "It is not so much in reference to the welfare of the Negro that we are here," Lyman Trumbull of Illinois told the convention, "but it is for the protection of the rights of the laboring whites, for the protection of ourselves and our liberties."

The Hartford *Courant* endorsed this sentiment when it observed, "The Republicans mean to preserve all of this country that they can from *the pestilential presence of the black man.*" Garrison charged, "The Republican party has only a geographical aversion to slavery. Its morality . . . is bounded by 36 deg. 30 min. North latitude. It is a complexional party, exclusively for white men, not for all men, white or black." And during the campaign the New York *Evening Post* warned that if slavery were introduced into the territories, "The white farmer will take his place by the negro field-hand. . . ." In a rhetorical passage of a speech made at Kalamazoo, Lincoln asked, "Have we no interest in the free Territories of the United States—that they should be kept open for the homes of free white people?"

"The Republican 'Platform' had no room for the slave or the free man of color; of course I could not stand upon it," exclaimed the abolitionist Lewis Tappan in disgust. In dismay a small band of abolitionists held in vain a convention to effect northern secession from the Union.

The Republicans had dealt only with the limited and immediate issue—slavery in the territories, particularly in Kansas. Their demand for immediate admission of Kansas under the Topeka constitution was unwise, for Kansas lacked the requisite population for statehood and the Topeka movement had been the work of an irregular faction. Notwithstanding the general moderation of the platform, many southerners were terrified, because for the first time in American annals a major party had placed itself in opposition to slavery interests. "We have an abiding conviction that it is impossible for the Union to last," said *The Charleston Mercury*. "As soon as the element of slavery entered into the politics of the Union, its doom was sealed. The South has the simple alternative of separating herself from the Union or being destroyed by it."

The platform was not primarily an economic blueprint, though it has erroneously been interpreted that way. The economic planks were progressive and with them a modern, commercial America could be shaped. Just as the Democratic and Republican platforms differed in their views of the country's economic future, they differed sharply in their views of the Federal Union. State rights dominated the first document; nationalism was conspicuous in, if it did not dominate, the second. The Republican platform construed the Constitution broadly, conferring upon Congress the duty to prohibit slavery in the territories and permission to aid a transcontinental railroad and to appropriate money for internal improvements. At the same time, however, it respected state rights, especially with regard to slavery in the States, and like the Democratic document spoke of the "Union of the States" (not the people). Neither of the two parties was radical, despite the provocation of the times. Neither offered the voter assurance of a just settlement of the Kansas question.

Nor did either party, in its concern for availability, offer the voter a strong candidate: Frémont had not been picked because of his record as a statesman, but, as a Republican strategist told Banks, "as a *veiled prophet* he will have followers from the romance of his life and position. . . ." The Pathfinder's political experience was meagre and undistinguished. Greeley, who had mounted the Frémont bandwagon only days before the nomination, had lamented in mid-May: "All would be well if F. [Frémont] were not the merest baby in politics. He don't [*sic*] know the ABC's." An astute political analyst rejoiced to Buchanan: "The prospect is bright, rendered the more so, it seems to me, by the very extraordinary nomination of the Republican Party—a nomination, in the language of Webster—not fit to be made. . . ." [7] Young, inexperienced, impulsive, without marked talent for public affairs, of vague political, constitutional, social, and economic views, the explorer of the Rockies was not equipped to guide the nation through the critical period of the next Presidential term.

The campaign of 1856 was a three-way race. The American Party nominated a former President of the United States, Millard Fillmore, who accepted leadership of the nativist movement, in order among other reasons, to use the seemingly patriotic party as a means to promote national unity. The American platform contained a vaguely worded resolution that seemed to endorse popular sovereignty. Continuing prosouthern dominance of the party caused North Americans to adhere to Republicanism. Whiggery was not yet dead, and although a group of Whig Congressmen early in the year had disfavored holding a national convention, a saving remnant met at Baltimore in mid-September and lamely concurred in the American Party nominations. The brief platform appealed for national unity, recognizing "that civil war is raging, and that the Union is in peril," and deploring its two rival parties, "one claiming only to represent sixteen Northern States, and the other appealing mainly to the passions and prejudices of the Southern States. . . ." It was silent on slavery issues, and acceded to Fillmore's candidacy as representative of neither sectional party. In retrospect it is clear the party system in 1856 had failed to devise a program or designate a leader adequate to cope with the Kansas issue.

Congress stayed in session while the Democrats and Republicans formulated their positions on Kansas. Five days after the Republican convention adjourned, the astute Toombs offered the Senate a way out of the Kansas quandary. His measure was perhaps the highest act of statesmanship on Bleeding Kansas that the times produced. An old Whig, he loved the Union, and he believed "the election of Fremont would be an end of the Union, and ought to be. The object of Fremont's friends is the conquest of the South." Toombs's Union was a confederation of sovereign, equal states that were entitled under the Constitution to protection of slavery in the territories. It was a Union that must maintain permanently a biracial society, because the African is "inferior, intellectually, to the white race." In a lecture delivered to a large audience at the Tremont Temple in Boston in January, with eyes alight and long, black hair brushed back, he had audaciously expounded upon two points: the common-property doctrine and the racial inferiority of Negroes. He later denied the notorious report that he would "call the roll of his slaves at the base of Bunker Hill Monument."

The Toombs bill aimed to vindicate the principle of popular sovereignty. It was a long-delayed attempt on the part of the Administration to provide Federal supervision of the process and to ascertain the will of the majority in Kansas. The bill provided for a census of inhabitants, for registration as voters of all adult, white males who were bona fide residents, and for election of delegates to a constitutional convention which would assemble in December. These steps were to be taken under the supervision of five commissioners appointed by the President and confirmed by the Senate. Election day was to be in November when Missourians and persons in adjoining states would be busy balloting at home. To meet Republican objections in the Senate the bill was amended to afford time for freestate men who had been driven from the territory to return and register and to nullify some of the more obnoxious territorial laws.

The Toombs bill differed markedly from the Douglas measure of the preceding March. It provided for Federal supervision of the state-making process; it set aside many of the "bogus" laws; it contemplated early admission of Kansas without waiting for the population that would entitle it to a representative in Congress under a constitution reflecting the will of the inhabitants. The bill, in implementing popular sovereignty, paradoxically repudiated in part the doctrine of Congressional non-intervention. Congress would intervene to guard the integrity of the ballot box and to repeal certain laws of the Shawnee legislature. Toombs had made a resourceful effort to resolve the Kansas issue, which to his alarm had given birth to a new sectional antislavery party that imperiled his party, his section, and the Union.

Though the bill was named for Toombs, Stephens privately claimed it was his measure. It soon became an Administration measure; a party Senate caucus on June 26 "resolved to put the bill on its passage early," [8] and Douglas, reporting it four days later, gave notice he would ask for a final vote the day after next. Pierce, somewhat resentful that his party had not renominated him, came around to support it, and offered assurances he would impartially select the Federal commissioners provided by the bill.

The free soiler Hale admitted that the bill was fair and reasonable, a "devil-tempered concession," which the rabid partisan Greeley found unforgivable. Seward conceded "it gives an equal chance to the people of Kansas to choose between freedom and slavery." But it was this very equality of opportunity to which the "higher law" Senator objected. "I recognize no equality, in moral right or political expedience, between slavery and freedom. I hold the one to be decidedly good, and the other to be positively bad," he declaimed. Seward remained enamored of his proposal for the immediate admission of Kansas under the Topeka constitution. After two long days of debate, the bill passed the Senate at 8 A.M., July 3, by a party vote of 33–12.

It was another matter to get House approval. Later

that same day the House, with its Republican plurality, passed the bill, 99–97, to admit Kansas under the Topeka constitution, Negro exclusion clause and all. The Toombs bill was scarcely considered. There is little doubt that partisanship explains the House's course of action. The bill would probably have been acceptable a year—perhaps months—earlier. However it is to be remembered that a blundering Kansas policy had modified the Republican position from demanding repeal of the Kansas-Nebraska Act to demanding prohibition of slavery in the territories. The Republican Party had committed itself at Philadelphia. To accept the Toombs bill meant repudiation of the party's central tenet.

Each party meant to make political capital of the bill. Passage would strengthen Buchanan, failure Frémont. As the chairman of the national democratic resident committee, Congressman Charles J. Faulkner, wrote Buchanan: "With such a bill, we should soon put an end to Black Republican agitation & secure an easy triumph." But he despaired of being able to push it through the House. As to the tactic of Frémont's supporters, Senator William Bigler told Buchanan, "the republicans do not want peace in Kansas until after the election." The upshot of this substitution of political craft for statecraft was the failure of the House to vote upon the measure.[9]

With Republican aid the Toombs bill could have been enacted. In that event, if it had been fairly executed (as the Kansas-Nebraska Act hitherto had not been), the Kansas question would have been resolved. But there appeared no disposition to share in a bipartisan policy. The Toombs bill was in part a Democratic device, born of the tempest of Bleeding Kansas and Black Republicanism, to bail out the party in this Presidential election year. Obstruction was in part a Republican ruse to keep the new party alive and to steer it to victory in November. But along with lamenting the failure of the bill, one should recognize that the freestate men in Kansas opposed it and that a major party opposed to the spread of human bondage was long overdue in libertarian America.

The Republican members of the Congressional committee to investigate affairs in Kansas reported to the House on July 1. Weeks of taking evidence in Lecompton, Lawrence, and Leavenworth resulted in these conclusions: all elections held under territorial law had been carried by "organized invasions from the State of Missouri"; the Shawnee legislature was an "illegally constituted body"; neither Whitfield nor Reeder had been elected under valid law; "in the present condition of the Territory, a fair election cannot be held without a new census, a stringent and well-guarded election law, the selection of impartial Judges, and the presence of United States troops at every place of election." Finally, Howard and Sherman judged, the Topeka constitution "embodies the will of a majority of the people." The report might well have served to promote the Toombs bill, and so might the minority report that Oliver made on July 11. From the latter the Congress learned the horrible details of John Brown's massacre.

But nothing availed. The session witnessed the utter bankruptcy of Bleeding Kansas politics. The House refused to seat either Whitfield or Reeder as territorial delegate. It failed to enact an army appropriation bill after Sherman had tacked on an amendment virtually prohibiting use of Federal troops to enforce the Shawnee legislature's laws. On August 8 it adjourned. The Douglas bill for the ultimate admission of Kansas was dead. The Seward bill for the immediate admission of free Kansas was dead. The Toombs bill for the early admission of Kansas by fair process of law was dead.

Kansas Territory did not have a lawful delegate to Congress. The army bill had not been passed, disarming the country. And Kansas was ablaze with guerrilla war.

Pierce, who was capable of occasional vigor, summoned Congress into special session, to meet within three days. For a week the two chambers struggled with one another, until on August 30 the Representatives approved the army bill without Sherman's amendment. House approval was no credit to the Republicans, who were immovable. A few Americans abandoned the game of politics in order to provide for the common defense, and the bill passed 101 to 98.

Eighteen fifty-six was the summer of Kansas discontent. The Sack of Lawrence and "Old Brown's" massacre on the Pottawatomie had instituted frontier warfare. Shooting affrays became common, and armed bands wandered the territory, fighting, pillaging, burning. The bumbling governor, Shannon, issued a proclamation June 4, commanding armed combinations that were resisting the laws to disband, and later in the month he departed on an official mission to St. Louis. Before leaving he directed Colonel E. V. Sumner to disperse the Topeka legislature, if it should reassemble on July 4. At noon on that patriotic day, as they were convening, the members of the freestate legislature were dispersed by Federal forces, at the point of bayonets but without violence and with little protest. Soon, however, the northern press reported the incident of "despotism" in Kansas to an indignant public. The Pierce Administration was embarrassed as well as further censured.

With Governor Robinson in prison and Reeder in the East, leadership of the freestate cause fell into the hands of Jim Lane. As the flow of emigrants from eastern free states continued, Missourians, who had the most to lose from a free Kansas, began a blockade of the Missouri River. Northern interest in the Kansas aid movement quickened. A national body to aid freestate settlers was organized in July, with headquarters in Chicago. During its half year of existence it distributed $120,000 in cash and quantities of clothing, provisions, and arms.

If Missourians were fearful of a free Kansas, Iowans were hopeful of that prospect. They cooperated with Lane in establishing the "Lane Trail" through their state as a means of circumventing the blockade. The trail was not much used until August, when Lane led companies of emigrants, called "Lane's Army of the North," into the territory. He soon had organized the freestate militia, and was attacking proslavery strongholds. Now Shannon intervened, and on Sunday August 18 he negotiated a second treaty that effected a momentary truce in the August war. Three days later he learned Pierce had removed him and had appointed John W. Geary as the new governor.

The ablest of the Kansas territorial governors, Geary enjoyed an impressive presence and background. A native of Pennsylvania, he had served as an officer in the Mexican War, wherein he had led an attack on Chapultepec and had been promoted colonel. Polk had made him postmaster of San Francisco and he had become the city's first mayor. He stood six feet five and a half inches tall, a military figure, who carried himself with precision. Energetic and resourceful in handling men, he had the habit of acting with promptitude and judgment. Pierce had promised him full military support to quell anarchy in Kansas.

On his arrival in the territory on September 9 he discovered that the rival factions had been warring all the more wildly because they believed the army appropriation would not pass and Federal troops would be withdrawn.

But the bill had passed, and Geary's first move was to disband the proslavery militia. He next intercepted a Missouri army of 2,500 men, led by Atchison and others and dissuaded its leaders from committing another sack of Lawrence, inducing them to retire. Arrests of guerrillas, both freestate and proslavery, followed; and the courts, warned by Geary's deeds and words of reproof, abated their proslavery bias. By late September the decisive, thirty-seven-year-old governor had effected the pacification of Kansas.

Perhaps two hundred lives were lost in the territory between November 1, 1855, and December 1, 1856. The loss of property was estimated to be not less than $2 million. Bleeding Kansas gave the Republicans their campaign material, and the Frémont press made the most of the disorder. Each Republican state election victory of the summer was hailed as a "shriek for freedom." Thomas H. Gladstone's dispatch to *The Times* of London on October 11, vividly describing the violence and vulgarity of the Border Ruffians, was exploited by the freesoil press with telling effect. Greeley singled out the Kansas iniquity as the campaign's cardinal theme, and in the pages of the *Tribune* he hammered away at the twin themes of freeing Kansas from the slaveholders and admitting it as a free state under the Topeka constitution. The most influential Democratic newspaper, *The New York Herald*, defected to Frémont.

Seward gave the campaign its keynote in a speech called "Political Parties of the Day." The former Whig spoke of the political realignment of the past two or three years, which he attributed to slavery. He then asked rhetorically, "What shall I discourse upon?" The American Revolution? The Constitution? "The tariff, National Bank and internal improvements, and the controversies of the Whigs and Democrats? No," he answered, "they are past and gone.

"What then, of Kansas," he inquired, "the extension of slavery in the territories of the United States? Ah yes, that is the theme . . . and nothing else."

Yet something else was involved, for nearly all Americans seemed to realize that the Union was in peril. "A flame is kindled in Kansas," John Bell told the Senate, "which threatens to extend beyond the borders and sweep over the whole country." "The development of each day makes it clearer and clearer that the preservation of the Union depends on the triumph of the democratic party," affirmed the Washington *Union* in early July.

The nation's leaders, past, present, and future, dwelt on the danger of disunion, although their understanding of its nature differed. Fillmore said little of nativism in his speeches and much of nationalism. The election of a sectional, Republican ticket would send the South into secession. "And let me also add," he warned, "that when this Union is dissolved, it will not be divided into two republics . . . but be broken into fragments, and at war with each other." The great constitutional lawyer, Rufus Choate, an old-line Whig, declared in a public letter the victory of the Republican Party would establish, in southern eyes, an alien, hostile government, "its mission to inaugurate freedom and put down the oligarchy. . . ." "In these circumstances, I vote for Mr. Buchanan."

Buchanan himself believed that upon his success hinged the fate of the Union. He stressed the national character of the Democratic Party in his acceptance letter. It was no mere stratagem, as his correspondence reveals; in a "private and confidential" letter to Henry A. Wise he asserted: "A crisis has now arrived in the affairs of the Republic, seriously endangering the Union.

In fifteen states there can be no Frémont electoral ticket. The sectional party has been distinctly formed; & the battle of union or disunion must be fought by the Democratic party of the free states, after having heartily adopted the principles endorsed by the South on the subject of slavery."

By autumn Buchanan's concern had deepened—"My letters from the South are alarming." His correspondent, Governor Wise, summoned a meeting of southern governors, before the Presidential election, to consult upon means to protect the slaveholding states. He believed Frémont's election would bring about a dissolution of the confederacy, and declared that the day after that event, he could "arm and equip 50,000 men . . . ready for revolution."

Ex-President John Tyler concurred in ex-President Fillmore's dark reading of the meaning of a Frémont victory. "It is quite sensibly felt by all," he said, "that the success of the Black Republicans would be the knell of the Union." President Pierce told the Democratic Vice-Presidential candidate, "I consider the continuance of the Union as directly involved in the contest." [10] And future President Abraham Lincoln asserted in a speech at Kalamazoo, "They tell us that the Union is in danger." But he minimized the possibility, and appealed to Democrats to adhere to the Republican stand on Kansas.

In the South press and politicians saw in Frémont's election a menace to both national harmony and race relations. The editor of the New Orleans *Daily Crescent* gave an answer when he asserted that the coming election would demonstrate whether the northern people preferred "niggers . . . [and] a false, wretched, miserable and resultless philanthropy, to their own race and color and the Union and all its countless blessings." R. M. T. Hunter, leader of the "Southern Rights" faction of the Democratic party in Virginia, in a speech before the Democratic mass meeting of Poughkeepsie held on October 1, explained the southern outlook on slavery. The institution, he said, was a practical solution of a more serious race problem. Destroy slavery, he went on, and race would continue to keep the Negro in economic servitude. Racialism was the heart of the matter.

For their part the Republicans either deprecated talk of imminent disunion as Democratic bluster, or exploited it as proof positive that slavery must be contained if the Union was to survive. A founder of the Republican Party in Massachusetts, and a future Secretary of the Treasury, George Boutwell, wrote Banks, "There is no occasion for despair. The North is determined. Slavery is an old hulk, and whenever struck between wind & water will surely go down with all on board. The sooner slaveowners make terms, and abandon the idea of extending the 'peculiar institution,' the better for them. This government is not strong enough to stand the shock of slavery extension, nor is there any government that is."[11]

The citizen's decision about how to vote in 1856, therefore, could not rest alone on Kansas—the question that had called up the larger issue of disunion. Many northern voters, even those of an antislavery persuasion, were constrained to cast a ballot for Buchanan or Fillmore—each of whom depicted himself as a national candidate —instead of Frémont, the sectional candidate, in order to preserve the Union. Old Thomas Hart Benton, whose adamantine opposition to the spread of slavery into the Nebraska country had figured in the origins of the crisis, and who was Frémont's father-in-law, could not vote for a sectional ticket. He urged fellow Missourians to support Buchanan, the nominee of peace and tranquillity.

Nor was it easy to see the issues clearly. The nation's press was rabidly partisan long before the phrase "yellow journalism" was invented; and the voice of the demagogue was loud in the land. Myths became current which historians have been long in dispelling. Let us recreate some of these.

"The slave Power" had, "as part and parcel of an atrocious plot," broken a sacred pledge and repealed the Missouri Compromise. An "unnatural emigration" to distant Kansas had been organized by New England abolitionists, who formed an immense corporation with $5 million. Emigrant-aid societies had paid the passage of thousands of antislavery settlers and had fiendishly equipped them with Sharps rifles and munitions of war. In retaliation, Border Ruffians from Missouri had invaded the territory in vast numbers to elect a "bogus legislature," which proceeded to pass "bogus laws." At the same time the wicked Pierce Administration was plotting to steal slaveholding Cuba from Spain, as the Ostend Manifesto proved. In response to these developments, the Black Republican party was organized, headed by such abolitionists as Chase, Sumner, and Seward. The nation was disgraced or sanctified when "Bully Brooks" thrashed "Bleeding Sumner." Simultaneously, proslavery ruffians, masked as officers of the law, perpetrated the "Sack of Lawrence," followed by "Osawatomie Brown's" laudable or lamentable deed. Champions of rights, southern or northern, were now struggling in Bleeding Kansas. Meanwhile the Black Republicans were intent on electing the abolitionist Frémont President and freeing the slaves. Or, meanwhile the Slavocracy was intent on electing the "doughfaced" Old Buck President and spreading slavery into Central America and Cuba. Such were the perfervid notions of a complex period held in varying degree by some contemporary Americans. The rhetoric obscured the root issue—the future of race relations in America.

Throughout the South in the fall, panic about slave insurrections spread. Wild allegations of an extensive slave plot, set for Christmas Day, billowed through the slaveholding states from Delaware to Texas. For generations southerners had been haunted by a sense of insecurity about their biracial society. Tales of earlier insurrections and plots now rose like specters: Toussaint's in Santo Domingo, Gabriel's in Richmond, Vesey's in Charleston, and Turner's in Southampton County, Virginia. Apprehensively, men armed, formed patrols, and whipped, shot, and hanged suspected plotters. A large number of slave crimes was reported. *The New-York Tribune* attributed the slave restlessness to the Kansas issue: "These last suppressed insurrections grew out of the discussions on Kansas." The Richmond *Enquirer* said the reports of plans for a revolt admonished the South of the calamities of a Frémont victory. Thinking men of the North, it adjured, should understand how Black Republican success would usher in "unspeakable calamities—calamities which will fall with peculiar severity upon the very race for which the people of the North affect so much sympathy." Hysteria and panic were companions to the exaggerations and distortions of the political campaign.

Besides the public meetings for Kansas, political rallies, and the secular press there were other agencies of the campaign. The intelligentsia took part as they had never done before. Emerson who was an alternate delegate to the Republican national nominating convention, Longfellow who gave up a trip to Europe to vote for Frémont, Bryant who took the stump for the Republican nominee, Whittier who wrote campaign poetry for the Pathfinder—all contributed to give the Frémont cause an intellectual tone. The historian George Bancroft, an ardent Democrat who had served as Polk's Secretary of the

Navy and had voted for Pierce, defected from his party. "This cruel attempt to conquer Kansas into slavery," he said, "is the worst thing ever projected in our history." And Longfellow wrote to Sumner: "Well, one good result of all this is, that at length Freedom and Slavery stand face to face in the field as never before."

Speeches, pamphlets, and handbills jetted forth as in a mill race. Republicans broadcast copies of Sumner's "Crime Against Kansas," while Democrats distributed 500,000 copies of a document detailing the Black Republican destruction of the Toombs bill. The Negro editor, Frederick Douglass, at first opposed the Republican Party, favoring a true abolition ticket headed by Gerrit Smith. However, in midsummer Smith's name was removed from the head of his paper's columns and Frémont's inserted. Douglass explained to his readers he had switched because Frémont's election would "prevent the establishment of slavery in Kansas, overthrow Slave Rule in the Republic" and "give ascendency to Northern civilization over the bludgeon and blood-hound civilization of the South. . . ."

In financing their canvass the Democrats enjoyed advantages over the Republicans; they were an established party, controlled the Federal patronage, had a nationalistic appeal, and possessed men of substance like August Belmont, American agent for the Rothschilds. For the Republicans Morgan did heroic work among New York financial interests and others; his papers reveal that by election day the Republican national committee had raised $44,285.64. The two parties vied with one another in what has been termed "the Wall Street War." The Democrats raised more, how much it is impossible to say. But astute Thurlow Weed thought the Democratic margin was $50,000 for Pennsylvania alone, a substantial sum for the times.

The politicians' assessment of the canvass began with the certitude that Buchanan would carry the South. A solid South would give him 112 of 149 electoral votes necessary to elect. In addition he must carry his home state of Pennsylvania and find 10 more electoral votes in the remaining four doubtful northern states: either Indiana or Illinois, or California and New Jersey together. Frémont, on the other hand, could count on 114 electoral votes. In addition he must carry Pennsylvania and find 8 more electoral votes.

Everyone agreed Pennsylvania was absolutely crucial to victory. The poet Whittier sang:

> O State prayer-founded! never hung
> Such choice upon a people's tongue,
>   Such power to bless or ban,
> As that which makes thy whisper Fate
> For which on thee the centuries wait,
>   And destinies of man!

Geary's timely pacification of Kansas aided the Democratic cause. Speakers and propaganda assailed the Pennsylvania electorate. "We feel deeply sensible of the importance of carrying Pennsylvania at the October election," Buchanan wrote his running mate. "The State has never been so well & so judiciously organized & the machinery is working with powerful effect." [12] The outcome in the Keystone State on October 14 was a comfortable Democratic victory.

On the same day Indiana voted. Jim Lane returned to lend his remarkable eloquence to picturing the freesoil cause in Kansas. The race issue figured in the campaign, as girls in white dresses marched with banners reading, "Fathers, save us from nigger husbands!" The anti-Nebraska element eschewed the name Republican and called itself the People's Party. It defended itself against charges of abolitionism and insisted, as George W. Julian said, "at the most we only opposed the *extension* of slavery which the Old Whig and Democratic parties did years ago, whilst we were decidedly opposed to marrying the negro or setting them free among us." Like Pennsylvania, Indiana plumped for the Democracy, the People's Party failing to do as well as in 1854.

Pennsylvania and Indiana had been political weathercocks. Democrats rejoiced in the result and anticipated victory in the November balloting. "The downfall of Black Republicanism and Know-Nothingism" exulted the Administration organ. Voters, stimulated by the existing contest, turned out in unprecedented numbers to name the next president. The total vote jumped by 900,-000 votes over the 1852 figure, compared with an increase of only 270,000 between 1848 and 1852. The three-way race ended in Buchanan's election. A close analysis of the vote is revealing.

To begin with, Buchanan was a minority victor. He had polled only 45 per cent of the popular vote, while Fillmore polled 22 per cent, and Frémont 33 per cent. The most striking trait in the voting pattern was sectionalism. Buchanan carried all the South except Maryland; Frémont carried all the North except five states: Pennsylvania, Indiana, Illinois, New Jersey, and California. Fillmore carried only one state, Maryland, but his showing in the five northern Buchanan states was large enough, if added to the Frémont vote, to have cost Buchanan three of these states: Illinois, New Jersey, and California.

Frémont's name had not been on the ticket in eleven slave states. But the real line of division was an imaginary one at the 41st parallel of latitude. North of the line the Democrats carried scarcely a county; here was the Republican stronghold.

The transformation of New England was thoroughgoing. In 1852 Pierce had carried the region except for Massachusetts; now in 1856 Frémont carried every state, actually winning all but four of sixty-seven counties. Although the American Party had swept Massachusetts in 1855, it ran a poor third in 1856. In the Middle Atlantic States the notable upset occurred in New York, once a stronghold of the Democracy and recently strong in the American faith. The candidacy of native-son Fillmore cut into Democratic strength and gave the state to the Republicans. In Pennsylvania Buchanan's margin over the combined vote for Frémont and Fillmore was but 1,014.

As startling as the shift of New England was the swing of the Northwest. Formerly the political ally of the South, the states of the Upper Mississippi Valley (now comprising Ohio, Indiana, Illinois, Michigan, Wisconsin, and Iowa) in the two previous Presidential elections had given all their electoral vote to the Democracy. The opening of the Nebraska country to slave competition and the antagonism of the Democratic Administration to river-and-harbor measures had their effect. Four of the states went Republican, Ohio to remain a GOP preserve until 1912, and the Republican Party replacing the Democratic as the major party in Michigan and Wisconsin. Although Indiana gave the Democratic Party a good majority, Illinois gave Buchanan a plurality of only 9,368 over Frémont. The American vote was substantial, and the Democrats benefited from the reluctance of old Whigs, living in central Illinois, to embrace the Republican Party. The entire Northwest seemed within Republican reach in 1860, with the right platform and the right candidate.

Frémont's name was on the ticket in only four slave states: Delaware, Virginia, Maryland, and Kentucky. His aggregate vote in the South was 1,194. Elsewhere in the region a two-party system prevailed, the American

Party replacing the Whigs. Kentucky and Tennessee, states once staunchly Whig, went to Buchanan; and Georgia decisively arrayed herself in the Democratic column. Only in Louisiana, where the Americans claimed 48.3 per cent of the popular vote, did the opposition come close to success. The decay of the Whig Party in the slave states was outwardly visible. From its eminence in 1848, when it had swept eight of the fourteen states that chose electors by popular vote (all but South Carolina did), it sank low, carrying only Maryland.

In the campaign of 1856 the American Party underplayed anti-Catholicism and emphasized antiforeignism, alleging that aliens corrupted American politics. But to many southern voters it was a party of patriotism, deserving its name, devoted to preserving the Union. On the premise that it was the truly national party, many former Whigs in the South welcomed the American alternative to Democracy.

So far as the South is concerned, it has been pointed out, "The Democratic Party scored its largest victory that it was to receive in the South prior to the Civil War, and more and more Southerners were identifying themselves and their sections with the Democrats. . . ." It has also been maintained that, "The Americans fared far less well in the slave states than the Whigs had in any of their campaigns. . . ." While this second assertion may be true in terms of the electoral vote, it is not true in terms of the popular vote. The American total in the slave states in 1856 was the largest ever received by a party opposed to the Democrats.* And Whiggery was not dead; it would reappear in the Constitutional Union party of 1860 and remain a force in southern history through the election of 1876.

* This conclusion and portions of the foregoing analysis are adapted from the election returns in W. Dean Burnham's *Presidential Ballots, 1836–92* and in *Political Textbook for 1860*.

Historians have traditionally said, with some exception, that the German-Americans voted for Frémont, augmenting Republican strength especially in the West. Ethnic and religious loyalties counted heavily. Although there was some shifting of the German vote from the Democratic Party, it seems that only German Lutherans tended to switch parties, while German Catholics remained Democratic.

Except for New England, and Pittsburgh, Cleveland, and Chicago, Buchanan carried the principal urban counties of the nation. The Democratic machine was strong in the cities. The new Republican Party was strong in rural America. The voting pattern of 1856 belies the notion that the party then rested on the commercial and financial interests of America. Nor does it buttress the belief that the party was aggressive in wishing to impose the yoke of industrial capitalism on the agricultural South. The large northern cities, housing commerce and industry—Boston, New York, Philadelphia, and Cincinnati—preferred Buchanan to Frémont. Baltimore gave Fillmore almost a two-to-one majority over Buchanan, and little or no vote to Frémont.

The election of 1856, in retrospect, was ominous for the future. Obviously the republic was being sundered by the Kansas question. Nonetheless, the campaign, with its available candidates and moderate platforms, underscored the essential conservatism of the nation. All three candidates were northerners; none attacked the institution of slavery. Buchanan, experienced, ripe in years, moderate, represented the closest approximation to a consensus which the troubled republic could make.

The election was prophetic, too, of the fate of parties. The American Party could not again be a force in the North; it was essentially a party of transition in a time of party reformation. The Republican Party had shown itself a lusty infant; only months old in November, it had nearly grasped victory. A slight shift in votes in Pennsylvania and Illinois would have turned the trick. As for the Democratic Party, now, more than ever before, it was in thrall to the slave states. And what no one yet knew, the tide had turned; Buchanan's election was the last proslavery victory.

The election ostensibly gave the Democrats the power to govern the Union. By the time the Thirty-fifth Congress would assemble, the Democrats would fully control both houses and the Presidency as well as the Supreme Court. Could a party whose center of gravity lay in slaveholding states resolve the Kansas question in the light of the national interest? Was the aged prosouthern President capable of the energetic and impartial leadership requisite to cope with the crisis of the Union?

"Mr. Buchanan and the Northern Democracy are dependent upon the South," observed a Virginia judge in writing to Senator Hunter. "If we can succeed in Kansas, keep down the Tariff, shake off our Commercial dependence upon the North and add a little more slave territory, we may yet live free men under the Stars and Strips [sic]."

And from Boston, Edward Everett, who had voted for Fillmore as the candidate of the "patriotic whig party," counseled Buchanan on the eve of the inauguration: "broken down as the democratic party is in a majority of the free states and greatly enfeebled in the rest, its continued ascendancy will depend mainly upon its pursuing a policy, which conservative whigs can conscientiously support." [13]

The Democratic Party, assailed by sectionalism, stood on trial.

7

Slavery, or social subordination, must be the common law

The rigid American constitutional system left Franklin Pierce, cast aside by his own party, four months of authority between Buchanan's election and inauguration. It also imposed on him the duty to make an annual report on the state of the Union. Pierce's last annual message, to the final lame-duck session of the Thirty-fourth Congress, was self-justifying. He scolded his critics and claimed credit for success in his endeavors, and most of all, he left painfully clear the infirmity of his public philosophy and the erring understanding he brought to the events of his administration.

If Pierce had been discarded, his party had been restored to power. In his message the President lectured like a schoolmaster on the principles sanctioned by the election. The people, he said, had asserted the constitutional equality of the states; they had affirmed the equality of all citizens of the United States; they had proclaimed their devotion to the Union superior to local or sectional controversies; and, finally, they

The chapter title is quoted from the Richmond *Enquirer* (1857).

had condemned the organization of mere geographical political parties.

He followed this curious interpretation of the election with an assault upon the Republican Party, organized, he charged, by persons pretending to seek to prevent only the spread of slavery, but really "inflamed with desire to change the domestic institutions of existing states." Their object was to work a revolution in race relations. It could not be effected peacefully; "the only path to its accomplishment," he warned, "is through burning cities, and ravaged fields, and slaughtered populations. . . ." Their party had attempted "to usurp the control of the Government of the United States."

How had the country reached this consummation? It was, he charged, through a series of acts of indirect aggression. The first act was "strenuous agitation" by northern citizens of the question of Negro emancipation in the southern states. The second evil step was northern obstruction of the Fugitive Slave Law, and the third was the imposition of a line restricting slavery in the Louisiana Territory. Happily, it could now be seen clearly that Congress did not have the power to impose this restriction, denying equality to the sovereign states. "All the repeal [of the Missouri Compromise] did," Pierce contended, "was to relieve the statute book of an objectionable enactment, unconstitutional in effect and injurious in terms to a large portion of the States."

Turning to the Kansas problem he charged that the "revolutionary disorder" there had been instigated by certain members of the Congress that had passed the Kansas-Nebraska law. As chief executive he had had no authority to interfere in the elections with their "imputed irregularities." It was somehow—and he did not explain how—left to the people of the United States to be the "all-sufficient guardians of their own rights." If the

President interposed in elections, "to see to their freedom, to canvass their votes, or to pass upon their legality . . . the Government might be republican in form, but it would be a monarchy in fact. . . ." Kansas was now at peace, and he hoped steps would be taken either by the Shawnee legislature or by Congress to assure the territory's citizens their rights under the Constitution.

Pierce's message succinctly summarized a sad regime in American history. His views on the nature of the Union may be set in antithesis to those of Abraham Lincoln, which were founded on popular (not state) sovereignty and faith in the libertarian and equalitarian principles of the Declaration of Independence (not in the abstract rights of sovereign states).

Lincoln, speaking at a Republican banquet in Chicago, humorously remarked of Pierce's message, "Like a rejected lover making merry at the wedding of his rival, the President felicitated himself hugely over the late Presidential election." Growing more grave, he observed that Pierce had credited the "people" with this trumph of good principles, but the President forgets that the "people" who voted for Buchanan are a minority by about 400,000 votes. Turning philosophical, he mused that the American government rests on public opinion, which always has one "central idea." That idea until recently had been "the equality of all men." "The late Presidential election," he went on, "was a struggle by one party to discard that central idea and to substitute for it the opposite idea that slavery is right in the abstract."

Pierce's denigration of a major political party in a state message was deplorable. His reading of the election returns was sophistical, his insensitivity of antislavery sentiment was cold-hearted. His interpretation of repeal of the Missouri Compromise was unhistorical. His sanction of the Shawnee government in Kansas and his disclaimer of responsibility to intervene fixed his reputation in history as a do-little, if not do-nothing, President.

Pierce had hailed prematurely the pacification of Kansas. Geary's quelling of insurrection had not resolved the fundamental conflict between proslavery and freestate forces. It was an uneasy peace; and Kansas again was aboil with activity. On November 17, 1856—more than two years after the territory was opened—the first public lands went on sale in Leavenworth. Settlers, speculators, and onlookers thronged the town in numbers estimated at three to four thousand; the boarding houses and hotels could not accommodate the crowds. The Leavenworth *Weekly Herald* reported that some $5 million had been brought for land purchases and loans. Much of the land sold that day passed speedily into the hands of speculators or was mortgaged to them at interest charges ranging from 25 to 40 per cent. Following this first sale there were three more in June and July of 1857, while rival factions were tilting at one another for control of the territory.

The freestate men would never accept the Shawnee government and its laws. Time was on their side, as every spring emigration enlarged their strength. Certain proslavery men, led by John Calhoun, the surveyor general of the land office and boss of several hundred Federal employees (not to be confused with the Senator), discerned in Geary's probity and power a barrier to their purposes. A showdown between the governor and the proslavery faction occurred in the opening weeks of 1857.

In a remarkable "confidential" letter to Pierce, Geary revealed his understanding of what had happened in Kansas territory since passage of the organic act in 1854. Geary first made it plain that no man more "heartily despises the contracted creed of the abolitionists than

I do." He believed their doctrines to have a "pernicious tendency." However, unlike Pierce he did not attribute the blame for the Kansas strife to abolitionists and emigrant-aid societies, but to proslavery men who had determined to make Kansas a slave state "at all hazards." They made this determination before emigrant-aid societies began to attract public attention. Geary censured unnamed persons in high quarters, overzealous men on the Missouri border, and various Federal officials in the territory. Pierce, he said, was not culpable; he had been betrayed by the "criminal complicity of public officials."

Geary reported a plot of a thousand Missourians to invade the territory in February and seize possession of the Shawnee Reserve lands. The Federal Indian agent lived there; and Calhoun was spending time there. With the President's support, "I can and will . . . make Kansas a Model State," Geary promised.[1] The honest, impartial governor, whose "wisdom and energy" the President had praised in the annual message, richly deserved Pierce's sustaining hand.

Before writing this letter Geary had asked Pierce to remove Judge Lecompte, whose charge to a grand jury had incited the assault upon Lawrence, Clarke, the Federal Indian agent who had committed murder, and Donaldson, the marshal who had been present during the Sack of Lawrence. Pierce dismissed Clarke and accepted Donaldson's resignation, without naming a successor, leaving Donaldson in office. He nominated a new Federal judge, but neglected to send Lecompte a letter of dismissal. Lecompte vigorously defended himself and assailed Geary in a thirty-five-page letter; the Senate refused to confirm the new nomination; Pierce ignored Geary's reply; and in mid-January the political situation in Kansas rapidly deteriorated.

When the proslavery legislature met in Lecompton on

January 12, Geary recommended a course of action that would base the government upon the will of the majority. He urged in particular repeal of the "bogus laws" that had earned such notoriety for the territory. The lawmakers should strive, he said, to implement the principles of self-government contained in the organic act.

However, the legislators had determined to make Kansas a slave state; and they were, moreover, apprehensive of the imminent spring migration. They ignored almost all of the governor's recommendations, and brazenly provided for a rigged constitutional convention. County officers were to take a census of free, adult male citizens residing in the territory. Only persons resident in the territory on March 15 were permitted to vote in June for delegates to the convention. The residence requirement would eliminate the new settlers, mostly freestate. From first to last, proslavery officials would supervise the electoral procedure. What was most obnoxious to friends of a free state was the legislature's failure to require submission of the completed constitution for popular ratification. Ratification of constitutions was rooted in American political practice reaching back to the Massachusetts constitution of 1780. And although the practice had not been invariable, clearly a constitution framed in frontier Kansas would be controversial. If government was to be by consent of the governed, a constitution for Kansas demanded ratification by the people.

Geary slapped his veto on the convention bill. He assigned cogent reasons for refusing to approve: the measure was premature for a territory with no more than thirty thousand inhabitants; it put the statemaking process under one party; and it did not authorize popular ratification. The Lecompton lawmakers speedily overrode the veto. Geary's life was in danger. He had earlier been defied, insulted, and even spat upon. Now, ruffians

armed with bowie knives and revolvers were openly talk-
ing assassination. The proslavery commander at Fort
Leavenworth, a friend of Pierce, declined to furnish
Geary with the additional dragoons that the governor requested. At this juncture Secretary of State Marcy asked
Geary to explain some discrepancies between his charges
and Judge Lecompte's letter. Discouraged by his en-
counters with the legislature, the Federal troop commander, and the Administration in Washington, on
March 4, 1857—the day Buchanan took office—Geary
resigned.

Geary hastened east in order to alert the nation to the
new crisis in Kansas. In a widely read press interview he
condemned "the felon legislature," and called for "prompt
and vigorious intervention" by the President. The territory
had lost its ablest governor to date. The proslavery minority held sway in Kansas. And James Buchanan faced
the problem of making popular sovereignty work.

Militancy among proslavery elements in the South
matched the militancy of the proslavery party in Kansas.
The election's outcome emboldened southern activists.
The Richmond *Enquirer* announced that the danger of
dissolution of the Union was past; for the election was
another striking evidence of the growing popularity of
Negro slavery, and slavery is "the strongest bond and
cement of our Union." Not long after, the same newspaper was proclaiming, "The Extension of Slavery the
Policy of the South."

The Democratic victory exerted a heady effect upon
Governor James H. Adams of South Carolina. Stormy pet-
rel of secession, the Palmetto State, it was agreed by
leaders of all factions, would have withdrawn from the
Union in the event of Frémont's triumph. Adams in November called for the reopening of the foreign slave trade.
He argued that revival of the traffic, prohibited since

1808, was essential to economic development, to restoring the South to equality in the Federal government; and, in a society of "unequal races," it had civilized and christianized the African, and it had "exalted the white race to higher hopes and purposes." Slavery, he brashly asserted, "has vindicated its claim to the approbation of an enlightened humanity."

Adams had ventured beyond majority sentiment in the South. The legislature referred his proposal to special committees, by whom it was put aside. There was still much Unionist feeling in the state, which was struggling between nationalism and sectionalism. A leader of the South Carolina national Democrats, James L. Orr, sponsored a resolution in the national House of Representatives, declaring that it was "inexpedient, unwise, and contrary to the settled policy of the United States, to repeal the laws prohibiting the African slave trade." Orr hoped to unite the Democratic party, North and South, behind his resolution. He did not quite succeed; of the 191 votes, 8 opposed his resolution, all Deep South Democrats, including Preston Brooks and Lawrence Keitt of South Carolina. Elsewhere in the South the proposal to revive the African slave trade met limited success. Some newspapers took it up; and delegates from three states at a southern commercial convention held in Savannah advocated it, but the convention refused to make an appeal to Congress.

The expansive tendency of slavery seemed manifest, to alarmed northerners, in the activities of the filibusters (i.e., private individuals who made war against the Spanish colonies). William Walker's slave republic in Nicaragua found favor in the South. General John A. Quitman of Mississippi, formerly a Democratic Congressman, who was fated to die from poison presumably placed in his food at a banquet in Washington during Buchanan's inauguration, was at this time reported to be recruiting for a filibustering expedition to Nicaragua. The United States had just elected one of the authors of the Ostend Manifesto as its President. Moreover, Buchanan seemed under the influence of Senator John Slidell of Louisiana, who was seeking the annexation of Cuba as well as abrogation of the Treaty of 1842 by which the United States had agreed to cooperate with Great Britain in a patrol of the African slave-trading coast.

The United States Congress was again the scene of turbulence. Pierce's ill-conceived message provoked angry replies. Oregon's territorial delegate, Joseph Lane, impatiently waiting for Congress to act on Oregon's demand for statehood, told a friend, "Nothing has been done but talk about niggers, niggers, and when this is to end no one can tell." Congressmen quarreled over interpreting the doctrine of popular sovereignty, upon which Buchanan had come to power. Members of the President-elect's party differed sharply over the Douglas and Calhoun interpretations: slavery could be decided upon by a territorial government; no! it could be decided only at statehood.

In the United States Senate, Henry Wilson and Thomas Jefferson Rusk of Texas, who had assumed command at the battle of San Jacinto after General Sam Houston was wounded, had a bitter exchange. Rusk branded the Frémont Republicans as rapacious politicians bent on securing the patronage of the government and trampling underfoot the sacred compact binding the nation together. Wilson, who in the heat of the campaign had delivered the famous characterization of southerners as "lords of the lash," now retorted to Rusk: "The Senator from Texas may sneer, and others may sneer, at 'bleeding Kansas'; but . . . We have resolved . . . that if by any lawful effort, any personal sacrifice, Kansas can be saved to freedom, it shall be saved in spite of your present administration, or anything that your incoming administration can do."

Northern emotions had been chafed raw by the year's events. The treatment audiences accorded to the South's most illustrious writer, William Gilmore Simms, was one sign of this sensitivity. Simms had embarked on a lecture tour of northern states in the fall, and soon sadly found he had to cancel his engagements "in consequence," as he told the Troy Young Men's Association, "of the singular odium which attends my progress as a South Carolinian, and the gross abuse which has already assailed myself, personally, and my performances."

Kansas was without a governor, and its recognized legislature, contemptuous of democratic procedures, was scheming to ram through a proslavery constitution. Its chief Federal judge and its land commissioner were suspect. The Kansas issue, quieted by Geary in time to assist Buchanan at the polls, had erupted again, furthered by Geary in his description of the "felon legislature." Certain aggressive southern leaders were gilding "the peculiar institution" with virtue, championing its extension to other lands, and calling for its increase through fresh importations. Dual construction of popular sovereignty's meaning boded ill for Democratic party unity. Settlers moving west in their wagons in anticipation of spring planting intensified the problem of providing fair and lawful government for Kansas. The Republicans' determination to see Kansas become a free state complicated the problem.

Buchanan's faction-rent party presented him with a problem similar to Pierce's in naming a Cabinet. Pierce had sought party harmony by including all factions. Buchanan sought party harmony by ruling out extremists, thereby forming a Cabinet that would in his view be conservative and national. The outcome was an undistinguished group of Presidential advisers inferior to Pierce's Cabinet. The most competent man was the new Secretary of the Treasury, Howell Cobb, the Georgia Unionist, esteemed by northern Whigs. The most prominent man was the new Secretary of State, Lewis Cass, who had lost his Senate seat to the Republican Zachariah Chandler. Now seventy-four years of age, lethargic, indolent, and a notorious Anglophobe, Cass was best known for his career in domestic politics, although he had served as minister to France from 1836 to 1842. He was chosen as a symbol of Buchanan's policy: a party regular, father of popular sovereignty, former Presidential candidate, a staunch nationalist. The remaining cabinet members were undistinguished: John B. Floyd of Virginia, Jacob Thompson of Mississippi, Aaron V. Brown of Tennessee, Isaac Toucey of Connecticut, and Jeremiah S. Black of Pennsylvania. In all, Buchanan's "national" Cabinet contained three northerners and four southerners. New England had one representative, the Old Northwest one, and Buchanan's home state one; New York was not represented because of the factional split in its Democratic organization. Virginia had one representative, Tennessee one, and the Lower South three. Buchanan had paid his obligation to the section that had made him President. Could such a company of advisers, lacking in vision and statecraft, weighted in favor of the South, help engineer a satisfactory national solution to the exigent Kansas question?

Much depended upon the chief executive's own vision and statecraft. Could he rise above the dissensions in his party, transcend the stormy present, comprehend the evolutionary forces at work in America, and head the nation toward the future? The prospects were dim. He

was entering the evening of a life climaxed by his elevation to the Presidency. His career in politics had been
long, marked by party regularity and respectability, save
in signing of the Ostend Manifesto. He was a striking
figure, tall, a trifle ponderous, white-haired, habitually
wearing a high cloth collar with a flowing white necker-
chief, his wry neck tilting his head to one side. As a
lawyer, he had earned a competence, and he resided not
far from Lancaster, a bachelor—the squire of Wheat-
land. Soft-spoken and pliable, he owed his worst fault to
a chronic irresolution. The decisive Polk, under whom he
had served as Secretary of State, observed, "it is one of
his weaknesses that he takes on and magnifies small
matters into great and undeserved importance." On Inaugural Day Longfellow melancholically recorded, "The
reign of Buchanan and the rest begins to-day. A poor
piece of business at best. Before long we shall have a
sad state of things."

Buchanan's political philosophy may be gleaned from
his pre-Presidential career and his inaugural address.
His conception of the Union resembled Calhoun's; indeed,
as a Senator he had voted for Calhoun's celebrated resolutions of December 27, 1837, including the compact-
theory of the Union. In his inaugural he asserted that
the Federal Constitution is a grant from the states to
Congress of certain specific powers; and he went on to
say that long experience and observation "have convinced
me that a strict construction of the powers of the Government is the only true, as well as the only safe, theory
of the Constitution." On the question of Federal aid to a
transportation connection with the Pacific coast, he was
willing to construe the war-making power broadly
enough to embrace "construction of a military road" (he
did not say railroad). With respect to another exigent
political issue—the homestead question—he said the

cardinal public-land policy is "to reserve these lands, as much as may be, for actual settlers . . . at moderate prices."

By implication he equated the Union with the Constitution, a fixed, legal entity, made of parchment and not of a shared past. Unlike John Marshall, Daniel Webster, and Abraham Lincoln, he did not base the nation upon the people but upon the states; and unlike his successor he did not discern that "A nation may be said to consist of its territory, its people, and its laws." He loved the Union, albeit it was a Union whose center of gravity lay in the South. He feared disunion, which he thought might come about not through the agency of southern extremists but through the agency of antislavery agitators. Deference to the South was the price of Union.

To him emancipation was not the wave of the future. Slavery might continue indefinitely and expand. For twenty years, he pointed out, agitation of the question of slavery in the territories had been "productive of no positive good," while it had been "the prolific source of great evils. . . ." The agitation should be suppressed, for, since the recent legislation of Congress (the Kansas-Nebraska Act), it "is without any legitimate object." The Calhoun resolutions of 1837 had included a denunciation of northern interference with acquisition of lands where slavery might expand. During the Mexican War, which he defended in his inaugural, Buchanan had favored taking more territory than the United States eventually did take. His interest in Cuba was pronounced, and in the inaugural he spoke of further extending our possessions.

On the immediate issue of Kansas he made several points. Taking note of the difference of opinion in his party with regard to the time when the people of a territory shall decide the issue of slavery, he dismissed it as "a matter of but little practical importance." "Besides," he continued, "it is a judicial question, which legitimately belongs to the Supreme Court of the United States, before whom it is now pending, and will, it is understood, be speedily and finally settled." Once the court had ruled, the question would be settled, and the nation could pass on to other questions of more pressing and practical importance. There was no other question about slavery, because every one agreed the Constitution protected it in the states. Time is a great corrective, and the issue, if the agitators could be suppressed, would soon pass away and be nearly forgotten.

So far as his own interpretation of popular sovereignty was concerned, he had always believed the people of a territory should decide at statehood. Calhoun again!

A Jacksonian Democrat, he did not share Jackson's view of strong Presidential power. Indeed, during the secession crisis of 1860–61, Buchanan's critics were to wail, "Oh, for an hour of Andrew Jackson!" Buchanan did not look upon his office as a post of leadership but one of Administration. He would not initiate policy but execute it; he would not suggest laws but enforce them. In him the American creed of antigovernmentalism had its perfect exemplar: he regarded himself as a limited leader of a limited government, charged with the limited program of his laissez-faire, state-rights party. The maintenance of the *status quo,* if not negativism, in domestic affairs was his central thought.

Such was the purblind outlook of the incoming chief executive, called upon to administer the republic during a critical period.

The new President had said that the issue of slavery in the territories was a judicial question. He had alluded to a case pending before the Supreme Court, and, apparently speaking with inside knowledge, remarked that the question "will, it is understood, be speedily and finally settled." It was a long-standing issue. Douglas's report attached to the Nebraska bill had declared that " 'all cases involving title to slaves,' and 'questions of personal freedom,' are referred to the adjudication of the local tribunals, with the right of appeal to the Supreme Court of the United States." The question whether Congress had the authority to prohibit slavery in the territories had divided men into political parties. The question whether a territory had the authority to prohibit slavery during the territorial stage or not until statehood was dividing Democrats into factions. Beyond these particular questions with their partisan overtones was the more general constitutional question of the locus of sovereignty in the American political system: did it lie with the central government or with the states? And beyond this reposed the question of the future of slavery in the republic.

The case before the court, then, involved both partisan and contitutional considerations. The plaintiff, Dred Scott, had been born a Negro slave in Virginia, and later had been taken to Missouri. Purchased by an army surgeon, he had accompanied his master into the northern part of the Louisiana Territory, from which slavery had been "forever prohibited" by the Missouri Compromise, and then had returned to Missouri. In 1846, encouraged by white people, the illiterate Scott placed his cross on a court petition, asking for his freedom on the ground that his residence in the territory north of 36°30′ had made him a free man. He was at first freed and then on appeal re-enslaved. His case moved upward through state and Federal courts while the nation was quarreling about the constitutionality of Congressional action over slavery in the territories.

Dred Scott's appeal to the Supreme Court of the United States was argued in February, 1856. In May the chief justice announced the court would hear a reargument of the case in December. One may suppose that the tribunal, recognizing the political character of the case, postponed its decision until after the heated Presidential election. Between the two hearings a sectional party had been organized on the principle that Congress has the right and duty to prohibit slavery in the territories and Buchanan had been elected on the principle of popular sovereignty. The Supreme Court heard the reargument December 15–18, and handed down its landmark decision on March 6—two days after Buchanan's anticipatory remarks, which he based on a confidential letter from his old friend, Supreme Court Justice John Catron of Tennessee.

Roger B. Taney, the eighty-year-old chief justice, had been born into a wealthy slave-owning Maryland tobacco family. At first a Federalist, he later had supported Andrew Jackson for President, and he had served in Jackson's cabinet before being appointed John Marshall's successor in 1836. Taney possessed acumen, learning, and idealism. His decisions had moved the court away from Marshall's nationalism to an emphasis upon federalism, viz., the division of powers between central and state governments. An economic liberal, he had upheld the rights of the community against monopoly. He had freed his own slaves and as a devout Catholic he daily prayed to God. Yet he lacked breadth and a national outlook, and he was not alive to the nineteenth century's evolutionary thrust that was making obsolete his narrow constitutionalism, his agrarianism, and his sectionalism.

On March 6, 1857, as he read his extended opinion in the case of Dred Scott v. Sanford, he appeared almost unearthly. His parchment skin was yellow, his nervous fingers bony, his face deeply lined, his voice thin and high. Although each of the nine justices wrote a separate opinion, Taney's is usually cited for the majority. The most discussed by contemporaries and historians, it is what is meant by "the Dred Scott decision."

The decision comprised three significant legal questions: (1) whether Dred Scott was a citizen of the State of Missouri and therefore entitled to bring suit in a Federal court; (2) whether his residence on free soil had given him a title to freedom that was still valid when he returned to the slave State of Missouri; and (3) whether the Missouri Compromise, which had made his temporary place of residence free soil, was constitutional.

On the first question Taney ruled that Dred Scott could not sue, because he was not a citizen of Missouri, "and not entitled as such to sue in its courts." Therefore, he said, the Federal courts had no jurisdiction. The chief justice gave as one reason why Scott was not a citizen that he was a Negro. And no Negro, not even a freeman, could be a citizen under the Constitution, because evidence showed that in 1787 the states excluded Negroes from citizenship, as slave codes and servile status proved. Racial differences lay at the root of this, the judge observed, for in 1787 Negroes had been regarded as "beings of an inferior order, and altogether unfit to associate with the white race, either socially or politically; and so far inferior that they had no rights which the white man was bound to respect."

Taney was wrong in saying that the states had excluded Negroes from citizenship, because some had extended political rights to Negroes; and his remark that Negroes had no rights the white man was bound to respect was torn out of context by critics, who forgot he had only said that this was true in 1787. Even so, the judge's point was marred by bad history and harsh judgment. To this reason for denying citizenship Taney added the point that Scott was not a citizen because he was a slave. The Declaration of Independence, with its phrase "all men are created equal," was not intended to embrace "the enslaved African race."

Taney might have stopped here, as Justice Nelson did. Scott had no right to sue because he was not a citizen, and therefore there was no case. Seven years before, in a similar situation, the court had refused to hear a suit, holding that the decision of the state court was final. However, seven years of convulsive history had passed, and Taney, quite rightly as we have said, proceeded to examine the question whether residence on free soil had emancipated Scott. Here he held that Scott's status was determined by the law of the state in which he lived when the question was raised. The Federal court had no jurisdiction, and Missouri law, interpreted by Missouri state courts, prevailed.

It was the third question that contained political dynamite. Did Congress have power to outlaw slavery in the territories? In examining the source of Federal authority over the territories, Taney declared the authority did not stem from the power to make all needful rules and regulations respecting the territories, but rather from the powers to create new states and to acquire territory by treaty. It followed, therefore, he said, that the Federal government had no general sovereignty over the territories; its authority was connected only with the right to acquire territories and prepare them for statehood. The Federal government did not have a general police power over the territories; it could not infringe upon rights of person or of property. Coming down to the heart of the matter, Taney ruled that an act of Congress excluding slavery from the territories deprived owners of slave property without due process of law—in violation of the Fifth Amendment. The Missouri Compromise was unconstitutional.

Taney's decision was weakened by the disunity of a court that wrote nine separate opinions, by the faultiness of his reasoning, by the dubiety of the history he invoked, and by the strength of the dissents. Only three judges agreed that no Negro of slave ancestry could be a citizen, while two affirmed he could; six asserted a slave's temporary residence had not made him free on his return to Missouri, while two disagreed; five declared that the Missouri Compromise was unconstitutional under the Fifth Amendment, one under the Louisiana Purchase treaty, and two declared that the Missouri Compromise was constitutional.

In his dissent, Curtis showed that in 1787 Negroes had been citizens in five northern states and held the right to vote. He pointed out that by the treaty of 1848 with Mexico the United States had given citizenship to persons of color. Besides dissenting on the question of Negro citizenship, Curtis dissented on the question of Congressional power over slavery. He argued that the constitutional grant of authority to Congress to make "all needful rules and regulations" respecting a territory clothed Congress with the power to prohibit slavery. Arguing from history, he demonstrated that Congress in eight instances had excluded slavery from the territories. The national legislature had repeatedly exercised the constitutional power to contain slavery; the Missouri Compromise had been within its power to govern.

It is, of course, a myth to consider the Supreme Court of the United States as a distinguished group of nine Solons, individually and impartially pondering the Constitution, the Founding Fathers' intentions, and legal precedents in order to disclose to the nation *the* meaning of the law of the land. But the myth is suggestive of expectations not fulfilled. Indeed, a sense of outrage filled many northern hearts.

"Poor betrayed, imbruted America," mourned Emerson. Friends of the Negro saw that the true purport was that no man of African descent, slave or free, could claim any rights or protection under the Constitution. Frederick Douglass condemned in a speech "This infamous decision of the Slaveholding wing of the Supreme Court. . . ." "Such a decision cannot stand," he intoned. The Ohio legislature angrily resolved that Taney had taken occasion "to promulgate extrajudicially certain doctrines concerning slavery, no less contradictory to well-known facts of history, than repugnant to the plain provisions of the Constitution, and subversive to the rights of free men and free states." Taney's seemingly callous assertion (really a statement of what he thought true in 1787) that "negroes had no rights which the white man was bound to respect" was at once a shock to reformers, an impetus to partisans, and a guideline to Federal officials. Following the decision the commissioner of the general land office declared that as Negroes were not citizens, they were ineligible for pre-emption benefits (squatters' rights). The State Department invoked the ruling as a justification for refusing passports to Negroes, although it previously had granted passports to men of color.

A "monstrous" idea, thundered *The North American Review*, of the ruling that no person descended from imported African slaves, "however remote, and however minute" his portion of African blood, could be a citizen of the United States. In rebuttal it argued that in effect the Constitution recognizes a general citizenship acquired in the states by birth, and this extends to "*all* the children of the 'sovereign people. . . .' " It scorned Taney's racialism and held aloft for ridicule Daniel's concurring view of the Negro's status in 1787, when the Virginian wrote: "The African was not deemed politically a person. He was regarded and owned, in every state, as property merely." The states were incompetent, after the Constitution had been adopted, to change a status created by the Constitution, the state-righter reasoned. The *Review* condemned "such groundless assumptions, false premises, and sophistical conclusions."

Old Judge Taney had administered the oath of office to Buchanan. Before the new President read his inaugural address he and the chief justice chatted briefly. A few minutes later Buchanan announced the Supreme Court was expected soon to rule on the question of slavery in the territories. Bystanders swore Taney had told Buchanan how the court would decide. Partisans, including Seward and Lincoln, took up the charge of a conspiracy. Seward in a speech in the Senate charged the ceremony had been "desecrated by a coalition between the executive and judicial departments, to undermine the national legislature and the liberties of the people." The unfounded charge so infuriated Taney that much later he confided to his biographer that, had Seward been elected President in 1860, he would have refused to administer the oath of office. Privately, Taney likened the war "being waged upon me" to the controversy over his removal of deposits in the Jackson Administration. Purblindly, he believed his judicial ruling would be approved by the "sober judgment of the country. . . ." And confidentially, he hoped the Democratic Party would unite behind Administration policy. Lincoln, for his part, implicated Douglas, Pierce, Taney, and Buchanan in a vast plot to make slavery national. "We find it impossible not to believe," he prosecuted his charge, "that Stephen, and Franklin and Roger and James all understood one another from the beginning, and all worked upon a common plan or draft drawn up before the first blow was struck."

The author of repeal of the Kansas-Nebraska Act welcomed high judicial sanction of his deec repeal had been abrogation of a law null and void at the time it had been enacted. Douglas commended the court for making a broad decision, going beyond the technical issue of court jurisdiction, and praised Taney and his *confreres*. The nation must accept the decision; "whoever resists . . . aims a deadly blow to our whole republican system of government." However, he could not fail to recognize the apparent incompatibility between popular sovereignty and the court's principle that slaves were property protected by the Constitution. To this he made an adroit reconciliation, of which we shall hear more: an owner's right to a slave in a territory, while immune to a Congressional denial, "remains a barren and a worthless right, unless sustained, protected, and enforced by appropriate police regulations. . . ." Unless the people of a territory wished to protect slavery, it could not exist. Popular sovereignty was preserved.

Douglas expounded these views in a speech at Springfield, Illinois, given at the request of the Federal grand jury, on June 12, 1857. Historians have noted that part of the address concerned the constitutional issue; however, in their preoccupation with political developments that often mask social phenomena, they have tended to neglect the significant part devoted to racial inequality. Douglas sounded the depths of the slavery question until he touched its bottom—race prejudice.

"We are told by a certain political organization that that decision is cruel—is inhuman and infamous, and should neither be respected nor obeyed," he remarked, alluding to Republican critics of the case. The Little Giant was full of confidence, forceful, speaking extemporaneously and deliberately. The Hall of Representatives could not hold the throng that came to hear him; the governor of Illinois presided; and "the Hon. A. Lincoln" was in attendance, as a Democratic reporter sarcastically noted.

Douglas amplified Taney's racialist presuppositions. The fathers of the Constitution, he asserted, "understood that great natural law which declares that amalgamation between superior and inferior races brings their posterity down to the lower level of the inferior, but never elevates them to the high level of the superior race." Race mixing in Latin America proved his point. He asked the Mexican War veterans in his audience whether their experience in Mexico hadn't confirmed the "proposition that amalgamation is degradation, demoralization, disease and death?"

"Is it true," he demanded, "that the negro is our equal and our brother?" He gave the answer to "immense Applause"; "the history of the times clearly show that our fathers did not regard the African race as any kin to them, and determined so to lay the foundation of society and government that they could never be kin to their posterity."

When he closed, his hearers gave him three hearty and enthusiastic cheers. The speech was widely reprinted, in the press and in pamphlet form. The Democratic Party press carried editorials of approval. The speech was a bid for the Presidency, both friends and foes said. "It has produced a very deep sensation," observed the Washington *Union*.

The portion on white supremacy was of great immediate consequence. Race equality became the issue of the next campaign. If the exigencies of the gathering crisis had caused many southerners to shift from seeing slavery as an abstract evil to regarding it as a positive good, so now the racialist sanctions of the Supreme Court and the Little Giant caused many northern Democrats to accept slavery as appropriate for an inferior race. The racialist argument, a political backlash to antislavery agitation, became prominent in northern Democratic literature after publication of the Dred Scott decision.

The abolitionist editor Sherman M. Booth, who had flouted the Fugitive Slave Law, now accused the Democratic Party of demagoguism on race. In an editorial attack he charged: "Hereafter that party['s] catch words are to be 'negro equality,' 'amalgamation,' etc. etc." During the last campaign, he continued, the party's platform had been "the humbug of 'Squatter Sovereignty.' The Supreme Court has just made that doctrine inconvenient, and "the Democratic party is to be arrayed on another humbug platform of opposition to negro equality, amalgamation, etc." The end in view, he cried, was perpetuation of human bondage.

A fortnight after Douglas's speech, Lincoln spoke in the same hall, which was only "comfortably filled." Carrying an armload of books for references, he entered a little after eight thirty at night, and explained he was there partly because "some of you" had asked him to speak, and partly because he wanted to answer Douglas. He took up Douglas's intimation that Republicans resisted the decision. "We think the Dred Scott decision is erroneous," he declared. "We know that the court that made it, has often overruled its own decisions, and we shall do what we can to have it overrule this. We offer no *resistance* to it." The Republicans had good cause to try to overrule it, he said, in view of the disagreement among the judges, the apparent partisan bias of the court, and the flouting of both practice and historical fact by the court.

Lincoln observed that the condition of the Negro race was worse now than in 1787. Two states had taken the right to vote away from the Negro, and no state had extended it since the days of the Revolution. Since then voluntary emancipation had been placed under restraints; and state constitutions had withheld from legislatures the power to abolish slavery. In 1787 Congress had the power to prohibit slavery in the territories; now it does not.

Lincoln's racialist views differed from Douglas's less in their biological basis than in their political aspect. He shared Douglas's horror of race mixing. He acknowledged that nearly all white people have "a natural disgust" at the idea of indiscriminate amalgamation of whites and blacks. He believed, and he thought a very large proportion of Republicans did too, that separation of the races was the only perfect preventive of race mixing. It was not Republican policy of opposing slavery but southern policy of encouraging slavery that favored mixing of blood: "Slavery is the greatest source of amalgamation. . . ."

Douglas, Lincoln charged, was trying to exploit the white man's disgust of amalgamation for his own benefit and fasten the odium on the Republicans. "He therefore clings to this hope, as a drowning man to the last plank." Douglas had lugged in the idea from opposition to the Dred Scott decision, and had moved on to argue that Republicans wanted to sleep with and marry Negroes. Lincoln rejected the impeachment.

"Now I protest against that counterfeit logic which concludes that, because I do not want a black woman for a *slave* I must necessarily want her for a *wife*." In some respects she was not his equal, he asserted. "But in her natural right to eat the bread she earns with her own hands without asking leave of anyone else, she is my equal, and the equal of all others."

Lincoln pointed out that he differed from Douglas in interpreting the intention of the authors of the Declaration of Independence. Douglas and Taney believed that the authors did not intend to include Negroes. If the Declaration did not at first place all white men on a basis of equality, Lincoln argued that the authors meant to declare a right which would be unfolded gradually. The Declaration, moreover, did not state that men were created equal in all respects—not in color, intellect, and so on—but in certain respects, i.e., the inalienable rights to life, liberty, and the pursuit of happiness. The authors "meant to set up a standard maxim for free society . . . constantly labored for. . . ."

The Republicans hold that the Negro is a man, that slavery is wrong, and that it ought not to spread. The best way to prevent race amalgamation is to separate the races. For instance, if whites and blacks "never get together in Kansas, they will never mix blood in Kansas." If separation is ever to be effective, it must be done by colonization. But it would be very hard to return Negroes to Africa so long as the spread of slavery made Negoes a source of profit in America. "It will be ever hard to find many men who will send a slave to Liberia, and pay his passage while they can send him to a new country, Kansas for instance, and sell him for fifteen hundred dollars, and the rise."

In the two Springfield speeches prompted by the Dred Scott decision, Douglas and Lincoln had said nearly all they were to say in the more celebrated Lincoln-Douglas debates of the following year. Douglas had stated, in his remarks about slavery's dependence upon the police power in the territories, what later was called his "Freeport Doctrine." The two men had laid down their essential arguments about the Constitution, the Declaration, slavery, and the Negro. The 1858 debates have glamour because of the clash on the stump of two men aspiring for high political favor, and because we know of the future eminence of Lincoln. But it was Dred Scott's case that first drew forth a nearly full expression of their competing ideas.

The speeches revealed differing uses of racialist

premises. Douglas employed his belief in the Negro's inferiority to justify slavery, popular sovereignty, and opposition to seeming Republican equalitarianism. He invoked racial amalgamation as the dread outcome of Republican policy. Lincoln employed his belief in the Negro's inferiority to justify containment of slavery, national prohibition to expansion, and opposition to popular sovereignty. He invoked racial amalgamation as the dread outcome of Democratic policy. The two Illinois leaders differed most markedly in applying the Declaration of Independence to black men. The one would uphold the *status quo*; the other would strive to attain the ideal "that all men are created equal" in certain rights.

The New-York Tribune was deriving the fullest partisan value from the case. Greeley attacked it as "entitled to just so much moral weight as would be the judgment of a majority of those congregated in any Washington barroom." The decision made slavery national, and he expected soon, "Mr. Toombs can call the roll of his chattels on the slope of Bunker Hill."

Northern condemnation of the decision was bitter and widespread. Not only freesoilers, ministers, and editors were stirred to anger, but gentle citizens lost their tempers. The chief justice was vilified. Six months after the ruling, a leading citizen of New York shouted across the railroad station to a friend (with ladies present) that Roger B. Taney was "a son of a bitch." The New York legislature adopted two resolutions reading that the state would not permit slavery within her borders in any form, and that the Supreme Court, having identified itself with a sectional and aggressive party, had impaired the confidence and respect of the people of New York. The Supreme Court as an institution stood discredited; and it did not regain its prestige until after Reconstruction.

Southern response to the decision and its Republican reception underscored the widening sectional chasm. Alexander H. Stephens, who had striven to bring about the decision, rejoiced that the constitutional questions which had long agitated the nation, as "doubtful and mooted," had been settled. The extension of slavery no longer was impeded by law: "There is not now a spot of the public territory of the United States, over which the national flag floats, where slavery is excluded by law of Congress. . . ." But that was not sufficient. The United States must expand, into Mexico, Central America, and especially Cuba. However, he told an Augusta, Georgia, audience, "you may not expect to see many of the territories come into the Union as slave States, unless we have an increase of African stock." He stopped short of actually advocating reopening the slave trade. Stephens endorsed Taney's racialist preconceptions: "Subordination is the normal condition of the Negro." This was a divine principle, ignored by abolitionists, he said. "The wickedest of all follies, and the absurdest of all crusades, are those which attempt to make things equal which God in his wisdom has made unequal." The Dred Scott decision "was fully up to the demands of the South"; by it the right of expansion—"the great practical object had in view"—was amply secured.

Jefferson Davis in his massive two-volume history of the Confederacy lauded Taney as "a man eminent as a lawyer, great as a statesman, and stainless in moral reputation." He asserted, not quite accurately, that seven of nine judges had concurred in the three major points of an elaborate and exhaustive opinion. But northern agitators had later flouted and denounced "the ultimate authority in the interpretation of constitutional questions."

The Democratic Senate of the United States ordered

printed twenty thousand copies of the decision for use as a campaign document. The decision was a political windfall. "What are you going to do about it?" Democrats taunted Republicans. The South calmly accepted the decision as its due. The court had rendered the only correct opinion.

The South appeared not to notice, however, that Taney's ruling did not rest on Calhounist premises. Taney had not used the common-property doctrine, viz., that the territories are the common property of the states and are therefore immune to Congressional interference. He had used the Fifth Amendment to the Constitution, finding a sanction in the Federal Constitution and not in a mere interpretation of the Union as an agent of the States.

What the South did notice, with apprehension, was the North's furor about the ruling. Influential elements of the northern press, pulpit, and political leadership condemned the opinion. It reopened the controversy over personal-liberty laws, as northern states sought to assure basic rights to free Negroes. The outcome of the case had betrayed the hopes of Douglas, Taney, and Buchanan for a judicial healing of the painful territorial question. Time would show the ruling to be, not a vindication of repeal of the Missouri Compromise and of Taney's legal judgment, but a Pyrrhic victory for the South. It contributed not only the separation of the sections but to the disruption of the Democratic Party—the strongest security the South enjoyed in the Union. Most grievous of all, the opinion's failure of judicial statesmanship, added to the political failures of Congress and the administrative failures of two Presidents, contributed to the coming of the Civil War.

8

The constitution with slavery

A narrative about the impact of Bleeding Kansas upon the national polity must center for the year 1857 on the issue of the pro-slavery Lecompton constitution. That instrument raised the question whether Kansas was to enter the Union under a notorious, undemocratic frame of government, or whether the strife-torn territory was to pass through a fair application of popular sovereignty under the Kansas-Nebraska Act. The responsibility resting upon the new President and his party was vast. Looking back at the times, Jefferson Davis pointed out, "The strife in Kansas and throughout the country continued during nearly the whole of Mr. Buchanan's Administration, finally culminating in a disruption of the Union."

The same party that had passed the Act now was in power. It had taken the principle of popular sovereignty to the electorate in 1856, and it had been restored to authority. It had recognized in its platform the right of the people of territories, "acting through the legally and fairly expressed will

The chapter title is the key phrase in the Lecompton state constitution of Kansas (1857).

of the majority of the actual residents," to frame a constitution with or without slavery. It had stated the time for framing a constitution to be "whenever the number of their inhabitants justifies it." It had assigned the Presidential office to a man who personally disapproved of the Act, but who publicly had endorsed it. Would the Democracy, a party divided on sectional lines, fulfill its commitment?

James Buchanan's correspondents in the weeks before he assumed office apprised him of the dimensions of his task. Governor Geary described the bullying and conspiring by proslavery leaders determined to make Kansas a slave state in disregard of popular sovereignty. From Fort Leavenworth the Federal army commander General Smith, writing in a similar vein, told how Atchison and Stringfellow had said to him they were resolved to make slavery a Kansas institution, without regard to the Democratic Party. He went on to say, "In speaking of their views & plans, they used the same arguments & even words employed by Butler, Mason & Hunter in debate, showing the connexion & communication between them & all that party." Sage George Bancroft, who could not make himself vote for Buchanan, advised, "I trust it will fall to your lot to bring Kansas into the Union as a free state and with the general acquiescence of the South. That is the only great healing measure, which can restore the country permanently to tranquillity. . . ." And editor James Gordon Bennett, whose New York *Herald* had favored Frémont, had no hope at all for the future; *"after you will come the Deluge,"* he grieved.[1]

On the day Buchanan became President Governor Geary resigned. His successor had to be chosen. Two governments continued to exist in Kansas Territory, at Topeka and Lecompton. The irregular Topeka government unsuccessfully had sought through Republican auspices to be admitted to the Union the previous year. Now the recognized Lecompton government (successor to Shawnee) had set in motion machinery to make Kansas a slave state.

Buchanan's initial Kansas policy comprised three elements: a fair settlement, a quick settlement, and a Democratic state. To forward his policy he chose Robert J. Walker as the new governor. It was a good beginning, for Walker was an eminent public figure, the possessor of experience in politics and intellectual power. A native of Pennsylvania he had graduated first in his class from the University of Pennsylvania. In 1825 he married a great-granddaughter of Benjamin Franklin, and the following year he moved to Mississippi to practice law.

Mississippi sent him to the U. S. Senate in 1835, a Jacksonian Democrat. A politician of expansion, he labored for the annexation of Texas and helped maneuver the nomination of the "dark horse" Polk in 1844. Polk appointed him Secretary of the Treasury, and in office he wrote a notable Treasury report, espousing free-trade principles that were put into partial practice by the Walker Tariff of 1846. Since leaving office he had been living in Washington, practicing law and speculating in land. Following Buchanan's election he had been a leading candidate for Secretary of State, but some southerners had objected. His appointment as governor of Kansas Territory won the concurrence of all Democratic factions.

Walker was reluctant to accept the post in Kansas, "the grave of governors." Both Buchanan and Douglas importuned him to take the position. When he agreed, the Washington *Union* exclaimed with pleasure, "The country will be equally surprised and delighted . . . while Mr. Walker will be everywhere regarded as making great personal sacrifices. . . . We cannot disguise our profound conviction that this proceeding . . . will end in the early adjustment of all disputes in Kansas. . . ." A tiny figure, he stood scarcely five feet two inches tall and weighed barely one hundred pounds. A contemporary described him as "a mere whiffet of a man, stooping and diminutive, with a wheezy voice and expressionless face." Never healthy, he may have been an epileptic. What he lacked in size he made up in mental and physical energy. What moved him was a desire for material wealth and the political limelight. He may have taken the governorship as a stepping stone to the Presidency. It is certain he had a grandiose plan for the economic development of Kansas.

To make emphatic where he stood with the Administration, Walker wrote to Buchanan: "I understand that you and all your Cabinet cordially concur in the opinion expressed by me, that the actual *bona fide* residents of the Territory, by a fair and regular vote, unaffected by fraud or violence, must be permitted in adopting their State Constitution to decide for themselves what shall be their social institutions." An expounder of the theory that the solution for the slavery issue was diffusion, he did not however expect slavery to flourish in Kansas. During the campaign of 1856, Walker wrote a pamphlet predicting Kansas must surely become a free state; geographical factors and emigration made freedom inevitable. A million copies of his pamphlet, containing the remark, "I do not believe Kansas will become a slave State," were broadcast across the country. An ardent Democrat, he hoped to make Kansas a western bastion of Democracy. Above all he valued the Union; and during the Civil War he would do yeoman service in selling Union bonds in Europe.

If Buchanan's appointment of Walker had been a sign of good intentions toward the Kansas problem, his orders to General Harney to take charge of the fifteen hundred troops in the territory and to maintain order were a second good sign. On his way west, Walker talked with Douglas in Chicago.

"You must go, Bob," the Little Giant urged him. "I feel intensely on this. The whole success of the Kansas-Nebraska Act in that territory is to a great extent dependent on your consenting to go. I beg it of you." The author of the Act and the agent of its execution discussed how to make popular sovereignty prevail in Kansas, and together they went over Walker's inaugural message.

In late May Walker arrived on the frontier, and on the twenty-sixth delivered his inaugural message in the slatternly territorial capital at Lecompton. A significant statement of policy with respect to the Kansas imbroglio, it had been drafted with assistance from Buchanan and Douglas. The governor gave assurances that the impending election of delegates to the constitutional convention would be free from fraud and violence; and he urged the freestate men to take part in voting. Acknowledging that he had no power to dictate to the convention, he went on to observe that unless the constitution was submitted to popular ratification, it "will and ought to be rejected by Congress."

The governor described a glowing prospect for the economic growth of Kansas. The Federal government would grant land liberally, and with this largesse the state could construct railroads and prosper. So fair a future should not be marred by a senseless quarrel over slavery. Kansas was unsuited by climate for the peculiar institution; an "isothermal" line, drawn by the thermometer, not politics, regulated the system of labor. Although slavery was unprofitable in Kansas, still the development of a free Kansas would benefit the South, as it would foster the growth of the southwest Indian territory, which would become a slave state. Kansans therefore should not abstain from the constitution-making process.

Walker appealed to race sensibilities, in a mistaken understanding of the freestate position. "Is the sable African alone entitled to your sympathy and consideration, even if he were happier as a freeman than as a slave, either here, or in St. Domingo, or the British West Indies, or Spanish America, where the emancipated slave has receded to barbarism, and approaches the lowest point in the descending scale of moral, physical and intellectual degradation?"

He ended with the warning "that in no contingency will Congress admit Kansas as a slave state or free state, unless a majority of the people shall first have fairly and freely decided this question for themselves by a direct vote on the adoption of the Constitution, excluding all fraud or violence."

Walker had hoped to persuade his hearers that slavery had no chance in Kansas and that Kansas should press on to statehood with its advantages. He told Buchanan shortly after he made his address that the territory probably contained no more than two hundred slaves in an estimated population of 24,000. His political strategy aimed at uniting the national Democrats and bringing Kansas into the Union as a free, Democratic state.

He was confronted, however, not only by freestate men who had supported Frémont, but also by a determined band of proslavery men. This last group looked for leadership to John Calhoun, the surveyor general, whom Buchanan continued in office along with Judge Lecompte.

A sordid incident occurring after the inauguration portended trouble. The frontier capital held a banquet in Walker's honor. In a series of postprandial toasts the turn came for Calhoun's clerk Maclean to offer one. A rough frontier type, prosouthern in sympathy, who towered over the shriveled figure in the seat of honor, he publicly insulted and challenged the new governor, "this pygmy" sent from Washington. Kansas had broken governors before and could do it again. Walker could tell Buchanan her people cared little for Presidents. The toast that was a tirade broke up the banquet.

Resolutely, Walker set out to head off rash, independent action by the freestate men. He urged them to take part in the October election of the third territorial legislature, where suffrage was not limited by the unsatisfactory census. Speaking before the freestate "legislature" at Topeka on June 6, he pledged that if the constitutional convention failed to provide a popular vote on its work, "I will join you, fellow citizens, in opposition to their course. And I doubt not that one much higher than I, the chief magistrate of the Union, will join you." Walker scored a fair measure of success in this portion of his policy. The Topeka assembly did not enact a separate law code, as he had feared, and seemed disposed to participate in the coming balloting. It did not, however, abandon its separate political identity.

Walker had stirred up a hornet's nest in Washington and in the South. His insistence upon popular ratification seemed to many persons to be executive interference with the convention's business. His prophecy of slavery's fate seemed to show partiality. And his enlistment of himself upon the side of the freestate element, should the convention not submit the constitution to popular ratification, seemed to evince partisanship.

The Lower South was aroused. Under whose authority was Walker speaking? Secretary Cobb told Stephens that Buchanan did not want Walker or any official to use his position to affect the decision on the slavery question. Stephens was outraged by Walker's words that raised "the devil all over the South." But his outrage struck some observers as odd, since he had recently "voted for that clause in the Minnesota bill requiring that the Constitution shall be submitted to the people." The two Georgians maintained a vigil on the state making in Kansas. The Democratic state convention in Georgia denounced Walker's inaugural message and demanded his removal.

The Democratic state convention in Walker's home state of Mississippi adopted similar resolutions, and branded the address an unjust discrimination against the South and a dictatorial intermeddling with the Kansas convention's duties. The Senate of Alabama condemned Walker. The Richmond *South*, organ of Senator R. M. T. Hunter, accused Walker of delivering Kansas into the hands of the abolitionists. The fire-eating editor, Roger A. Pryor, refused to publish a moderate article, accepted by the Richmond *Enquirer,* observing: "It is said that it [Walker's course] will result in making Kansas a free state. If so, it must be by a fair vote; and to make it a slave state by any other process would not only disease the cause of the South, but would inevitably, in the end, fail of its purpose." In South Carolina, center of secession, the attack upon Walker began before his inaugural, and continued throughout the year 1857. Critics associated Buchanan with Walker's treachery, asking, why, if Buchanan disapproved Walker's policies, did he keep him in office? The profound dissatisfaction over the Administration's Kansas policy threatened to disrupt the Democratic Party.

On June 15 the election of delegates for the constitutional convention took place. Territorial law had left the census and registry of voters under proslavery officials. Their work was defective and discriminatory, omitting many freestate voters. Beyond this, in apportioning delegates the territory was gerrymandered in favor of the proslavery element. On election day out of 9,250 registered voters, only about 2,200 çast ballots. Proslavery men were elected to the Lecompton constitutional convention.

"The black Republicans would not vote," Walker told Buchanan, "and the free-State Democrats were kept from voting by the fear that the constitution would not be submitted by the convention, and that by voting they committed themselves to the proceeding of the convention." [2]

Sherman Booth, the abolitionist editor, underscored Buchanan's great opportunity to resolve the Kansas question by a display of executive leadership. Buchanan's stand on popular ratification had become a test of Presidential leadership in a new phase of the continuing territorial crisis. "Buchanan has now a fair chance to establish himself in the confidence and affection of the whole people," Booth observed. "If he possesses and chooses to manifest a little of the Jackson characteristic, by insisting firmly on submitting the constitution to the whole voting population, he will commend himself to a large majority of the whole nation, and we think, bring peace so far as that Territory is concerned. He stands where Pierce once did, with his opportunities and difficulties. Will he prove equal to the emergency, or fall as Pierce did?" he posed the issue.

Buchanan sought at first to deal firmly with the developing crisis. He caused the Washington *Union* to run an editorial defending Walker and asserting that the people of Kansas ought to vote on their constitution. In a private letter to Walker he sustained the governor. "On the question of submitting the constitution to the bona fide residents of Kansas, I am willing to stand or fall. It is the principle of the Kansas-Nebraska Bill, the principle of Popular Sovereignty, and the principle at the founda-

tion of all popular government." The President said he
thought, if the principle was applied, "The strictures of
the Georgia and Mississippi conventions will then pass
away and be speedily forgotten."

Douglas encouraged Walker to insist upon popular
ratification. In a lengthy missive from Chicago he attributed the southern outbreak to dissatisfaction about Cabinet choices and patronage, and said Kansas was a
pretext and Walker the scapegoat. "I have never hesi-
tated to express the opinion that the constitution ought
to be referred to the people for ratification," he assured
the Kansas magistrate.[3]

The freestate element in the territory might take heart
from the Great Migration occurring in 1857. The inrush
of settlers had started earlier than ever; a large number,
halted by winter the previous fall, had recommenced
their march with the first fair weather. They came west
in their white-covered Conestoga wagons, carryalls, bug-
gies, clumsy oxcarts, and on foot. *The Herald of Freedom*
conjectured they were arriving at the rate of a thousand
a day in April. Railroads were offering cheap rates from
the East to their terminals in Chicago and St. Louis, and
assuring settlers easy transportation for the remainder
of the journey west. "Our hotels are full of strangers,
and the public conveyances are crowded with passen-
gers," observed the Lawrence *Republican* in late June.
"We notice more females among the late arrivals than
earlier in the season." The pioneers thronged through
Kansas City, Lawrence, and Topeka, and established
Emporia, which mushroomed as the territory's third
largest town. The Emporia *Kansas News* of August 15
observed, "Four months ago there was not a house where
Emporia now stands. . . . Now . . . as far as the eye

can reach in every direction, every quarter-section is occupied."

Promoters and speculators appeared among the pioneers. Not only was northern capital invested in great
abundance, but southern capital too in surprising
amounts. Quarrels over claims were common; and differences were often settled by vigilante claim associations. The scenes at land sales smacked of the frontier.
A freestate party leader told of attending a sale at Paoli.
"There we met Govs. Walker, Bigler, Shannon, & Stanton
[acting governor before Walker's arrival]. I was in the
crowd at that meeting where the bowie knives and revolvers looked their prettiest into neighbors faces and I
immediately put myself in the best attitude of self-defense . . . by drawing my broken-bladed jackknife and
'keeping a civil tongue in my head.' " Dr. Charles Robinson, upon inventorying his estate in early October,
concluded he was worth $44,000. After one more busi-
ness venture, he told his wife, "I intend to fix what I
have so as to get a good income from it & then get *quiet*
with my good wife." [4] Land conflicts were a fruitful
source of difficulty.

Most of the pioneers were aspiring farmers, looking
for farmland and a home. They were on their way up in
the world. They came unassisted by emigrant-aid societies. The large majority were freesoilers but not abolitionists. Sharing the nearly universal aversion to Negroes,
they found the territorial government in 1857 in the
hands of a proslavery minority, hellbent on entrenching
an alien institution. The delegate election was rigged;
the forthcoming constitutional convention was rigged.
What redress would they find from Washington?

Dr. Robinson's sister wrote a poem, of which freestate
papers frequently reprinted one stanza:

Far Kansas is a dreadfyl land
Where factions wild conspire
To whelm our country in disgrace,
And *set the world on fire*!

The Topeka movement revived in the spring and by midsummer took a militant turn. Apprehending a fresh Missouri invasion at the October territorial election, a Topeka convention authorized Jim Lane to form volunteer companies to protect the ballot box. Walker, anticipating freestate efforts to overthrow the territorial government, appealed to Washington for two thousand troops. Buchanan, unwell, was away, and Secretary of State Lewis Cass took charge of successive Cabinet meetings. The majority of the Cabinet members suspected Walker "was trying to make a record for the future." [5] Perhaps five of the seven members favored admitting Kansas as a slave state. It was suggested the tiny enigmatical governor was forwarding his own political aspirations, that he exaggerated the danger in Kansas, and that he wanted to fasten blame for failure on someone else. In Buchanan's absence his Cabinet turned against Walker. With the Lower South rumbling in protest and with the majority of his Cabinet in opposition to Walker, Buchanan's position had become delicate.

The October election was a turning point in the history of territorial Kansas. At the general election a new legislature, a delegate to Congress, and county officers were to be named. Walker and Lane urged freestate men to participate; and the governor arranged to have soldiers guard those polls where danger was anticipated. It was expected the vote would decide the slavery question. The Lecompton constitutional convention met and adjourned, pending the result of the voting.

At first it appeared the proslavery party would continue to control lawmaking in the territory. But that party had once again compounded its politics with fraud. Oxford precinct, a village of six houses, sent in a return purporting to record 1,628 votes for eleven proslavery delegates. The official return was "a roll of paper, forty or fifty feet long, containing names as thickly as they could be written," the territorial secretary, Stanton, later said. Inspection revealed the names had been copied from an old Cincinnati directory! Proslavery men perpetreated a similar fraud in McGee County, largely inhabited by Cherokee Indians. Following an on-the-spot investigation, Walker by proclamations threw out the forgeries and certified the election of freestate candidates. His forceful executive act aroused the resentment of the proslavery party. The revelation of frauds angered the freestate party. Walker by his honesty had destroyed his own hopes of forging a majority moderate party. His proclamations thoroughly documented the spurious franchise, and the nation again swayed with excitement over Kansas. For the first time the freestate party had won a recognized election. It would control both houses of the legislature and would be represented in Congress by a freestate delegate.

The success of the freestaters became known when the delegates to the Lecompton convention began work in late October. Upon this unrepresentative body, made up of men of "ordinary respectability," lay the fate of Kansas, of the Buchanan Administration, of the Democratic Party, and ultimately, perhaps, of the nation. Of the sixty delegates only forty-three took part in the convention that might create the sixteenth slave state. The eastern press was well represented, as the nation watched attentively the proceedings in the picturesque prairie hamlet.

Much of the document was conventional, providing for customary forms and function of state government. Nor was the clause in the bill of rights excluding free Negroes unusual. It was the slavery article to which free-staters took hot exception. Baldly declaring the right of property in slaves higher than any constitutional sanction and inviolable, it forbade the legislature to emancipate slaves without the consent of the owner and without paying him. It prohibited amendment for seven years, apparently to safeguard the slavery provisions.

What was egregiously outrageous about the constitution was the disingenuous plan for ratification. The question of submission to the electorate had been a thorny one. Extreme proslavery men, with encouragement from the southern press and Senator R. M. T. Hunter, favored bypassing the electorate and transmitting the document directly to Congress. Yet in that heated hour it was necessary to afford some kind of referendum. The notion of submitting to voters only the question of slavery occurred to various men; and John Calhoun, president of the convention, was led by an article in the Douglas organ, the Chicago *Times,* to believe that his friend, the author of the Kansas-Nebraska Act, favored the scheme.

Support, of a kind, for evading the Kansas electorate came from the Cabinet in Washington. That little dynamo, Alexander H. Stephens, had continued his confidential correspondence with Secretary Cobb. It is well to remember here the behind-the-scenes role of Stephens in this whole Kansas question. Little Aleck had driven the Kansas-Nebraska bill through the House by an adroit parliamentary maneuver; he had claimed to be the real author of the Toombs bill, which did not provide for ratification of a constitution; and he had unconscionably exerted his influence over Justice Wayne to effect a proslavery ruling in the Dred Scott case (see Appendix,

p. 275). State-righter, proslavery expansionist, and racialist, a statesman of warped vision, he appears as a strategist of the southern cause. Now he suggested to Cobb that the best strategy for the Lecompton convention was to "say nothing in the constitution about slavery and submit it to the qualified voters under the constitution, and to require a new registration of voters so as to require all who vote for it to recognize the existing government." These maneuvers would maintain slavery.

Cobb wrote to a member of the Lecompton convention about the plan. He also talked with Secretary of the Interior Jacob Thompson of Mississippi about the problem. The two Cabinet members from the Deep South, who desired to see Kansas become a slave state, instructed a land-office clerk to go to Lecompton and make their views known. Thompson told the clerk they were in favor of popular ratification, but "I am not prepared to take ground against the admission of Kansas if a proslavery constitution should be made and sent directly to Congress. . . ." In Kansas the clerk conferred with Calhoun and others.

The upshot of the submission controversy was to allow the white male inhabitants a choice between "Constitution with slavery" or "Constitution with no slavery." If a majority voted for "Constitution with no slavery," slavery would no longer exist in Kansas, "except that the right of property in slaves now in this Territory shall in no manner be interfered with. . . ." Either choice would approve the constitution and make Kansas a slave state. As bad as any feature of the convention's handiwork was the decree that the rigged referendum would be under the supervision of John Calhoun, bypassing Governor Walker who had earlier demonstrated he would reject fraudulent ballots.

Cries of "the Lecompton swindle" filled the antislavery

press. Thoughtful citizens wondered whether the President of a nation that prided itself upon free institutions would accept Lecompton. Would the father of the Kansas-Nebraska Act, Stephen A. Douglas, embrace this maimed child? Would the Congress of the United States give its assent to a government that flouted the consent of the governed?

The struggle for Kansas had occurred during good times. Prosperity scaled new heights in the months before the Lecompton convention. But by the time Congress took up consideration of the Lecompton constitution panic had spread over the nation.

The nation had built ahead of its requirements. In late summer a leading bank in New York closed, dealing a blow to popular confidence in New York banks. New York had long since become the financial heart of the nation, the metropolis where country banks maintained deposits. Now withdrawals commenced, and New York banks were forced to call in their loans. A severe banking crisis ensued. It did not endure long, but a depression lasted on into 1859–60, as business failures piled up and capital investment shrank.

Unemployment was widespread, especially in eastern cities. The idle were largely dependent upon charity. Men held "hunger meetings," marched and demonstrated and published their demands for relief and work. Hard times aggravated class tensions. In terms of the new Republican Party two meaningful results flowed from the panic of 1857. Some persons blamed it upon the low tariff which, it was said, exposed American labor and manufacturers to foreign competition. The Republican Party incorporated a protective tariff plank in its 1860 platform. Land reformers renewed their efforts to secure a homestead law. In 1860 Congress approved a law reducing the

cost of public land to actual settlers to 25 cents per acre.
James Buchanan blindly vetoed it, remarking that the
honest poor man desires no charity. The bill, he unfeel-
ingly declared, would go far to demoralize the people and
repress the noble spirit of independence. The Republican
Party incorporated a homestead plank in its 1860 platform.

Hard times aggravated sectional tensions. The depression, mainly affecting capital investment in industry,
commerce, manufacturing, and banking, left the staple-
growing South largely unaffected. The two economies
stood in contrast. Where many northerners saw a need for
government action on tariff and homestead measures,
many southerners saw a proof that their institutions
were sound and indeed superior to the North's. Cotton
crops remained abundant, exports rose, and prices of
slaves soared. "The wealth of the South is permanent
and real," boasted *DeBow's Review*, organ of the Deep
South, "that of the North fugitive and fictitious."

"Pernicious social theories," to borrow Buchanan's
phrase, threatened the North, while laissez-faire, state
rights, slave labor, a low tariff, and a purchase basis for
public lands seemed confirmed as the true policy for the
agricultural South.

Nowhere was the heady effect of the seeming contrast
between the southern and northern economies reflected
better than in a notorious speech given by Senator James
H. Hammond of South Carolina, successor to Butler. An
affluent publisher, nullifier, expansionist, and proslavery
propagandist, he hotly defended slavery in his speech.
Every social system, he said, must have a class "requiring but a low order of intelligence and but little skill."
They are the "mudsills of society." In the North these
were manual laborers and operatives. In the South, "Our
slaves are black, of another, inferior race. The *status* in

which we have placed them is an elevation."

The South, Hammond continued, provided the bulk of the nation's exports. The North and England alike depended upon her. Turning defiant, he cried, "No, sir, you dare not make war on cotton. No power on earth dares make war upon it. Cotton is king." Historians have often quoted Hammond's phrase "Cotton is king," pointing out its economic, political, and diplomatic connotations; but they have slighted Hammond's racialism—the main premise of his regal assertion. In an interesting epistle to the editor of the London *Spectator,* written in 1856, Hammond had explained the racial basis of slavery in the United States. Had the editor ever really known slavery? the southerner had inquired. "You speak of African slavery as if it were the slavery of . . . [Anglo-Saxon or Celt]. . . . But it is not & you are wholly wrong. . . . Nowhere and at no time has the African ever attained so high a status . . . as in the condition of American SLAVERY," he boasted.

To Hammond's harsh theory of the relation between capital and labor Lincoln replied more than a year later. "Labor is prior to, and independent of, capital . . . in fact capital is the fruit of labor, and could never have existed if labor had not first existed . . . labor is the superior—greatly the superior—of capital." Every man, he characteristically declared, is entitled to the bread his head and hands earn.

The panic of 1857 was accompanied by a revival of religious piety. While the stock market was crashing in September, special daily prayer meetings began to be conducted in New York City. A "Great Awakening" set in. As the winter of 1857–58 spread distress, the religious movement extended throughout the country.

In the South the revival manifested itself in a questioning of mammon and an intensification of distrust of

Yankee money getting. God was demonstrating the superiority of southern society over northern. The South's duty lay in saving the nation from corruption or, failing this, in withdrawing from a polluted polity. It was in this atmosphere of economic recession and religious resurgence—each phenomenon sharpening sectional tensions—that the Federal government would consider the Lecompton constitution.

In early summer it was still a question which party would control the next Congress. There was no uniform day of election, and the Democrats lacked seven seats to be assured a majority in the house. Most of the remaining Congressional elections were to be in the South, where the American Party formed the opposition to the Democrats. The national council of Americans met in Louisville on June 2, reaffirmed the 1856 platform and left plans of organization to the party in each state.

The August elections could be decisive, as five slaveholding states were to ballot. The contest in Missouri, neighbor to Kansas, was fraught with special interest, because a freesoil candidate, James S. Rollins, was running for governor on the position that he would let climate settle the future of slavery. He believed the northern latitude of Missouri would lead slaveholders to cooperate in abolishing the peculiar institution. Earlier in the year an emancipationist had been elected mayor of St. Louis. What would be the bearing of Missouri's voting upon the future of Kansas?

The final result was a Democratic sweep, with a net gain of 10 seats, clinching organization of the House. States once Whig showed a decline in American strength; in Kentucky the Democratic delegation gained 4 seats; in North Carolina only one American won; in Tennessee only two Americans were named to the state's 10 seats. In Missouri, apparently owing to vote-stealing, Rollins lost to a Democrat by only about 300 votes; the Democratic nominees for Congress won.

Other elections revealed the temper of the voters. Three southern states, Tennessee, Alabama, and Texas, elected Democratic governors, and the party scored a full success in California. Iowa voters adopted a new constitution, rejecting a clause permitting Negroes to vote, which was balloted upon separately. The constitutional convention in Minnesota Territory withheld suffrage from Negroes but extended it to Indians and persons of mixed white and Indian blood who had adopted the customs and habits of civilization.

Events in Kansas afforded not only a background for the state elections, but also often the issue. Southerners exploited Governor Walker's inaugural speech and policies. They expressed fear of a northern invasion, on learning that Eli Thayer of the New England Emigrant Aid Company was planning a free-labor emigration to the South. They were apprehensive about the fate of the Middle Border, where Kansas might be lost to slavery and Missouri might emancipate her bondsmen.

The October elections bolstered Democratic strength. Mississippi was swept by the Democrats, who won every House seat; and Georgia, formerly a Whig bastion, sent two Americans and six Democrats to Washington. In Buchanan's home state of Pennsylvania the voters elected a Democrat as governor and placed his party in decided control of the legislature. The outcome of the gubernatorial contest in Ohio remained in doubt for several days after the election, until it appeared that Chase had been re-elected by a plurality of 1,503—one of the thinnest margins in the state's history. The Democrats, however, captured both branches of the legislature. The Democrats in November carried the state of New York, where the financial panic had cost the Republicans votes. The

Democrats also won a preponderance of seats in the New Jersey legislature and showed impressive strength in Minnesota. Iowa seemed almost an isolated Republican stronghold outside of New England; in this state the Republicans elected a governor and a majority of the legislature.

Whatever the impact of Kansas upon American politics, however influential the Lecompton question may have been, the end of the year showed plainly that the Democratic Party was the one great national party. Its appeal seemed to know no sectional lines. It would claim 118 votes in the new House of Representatives as against 92 Republicans, and 26 Americans. These figures, in comparison with the previous Congress, gave the Democrats a gain of 35 votes, the Republicans a loss of 16, and the Americans a loss of 5. In the Senate the Republicans had risen to 20 votes, a gain of 5, and the Democrats had dropped to 36, a loss of 4. The American members had grown to 8, a rise of 3. On the eve of the thirty-fifth Congress, which was to take up the fateful Lecompton constitution, the Democratic Party controlled the Congress, the Supreme Court, and the Presidency. As the one great national party, possessing the three branches of American government, it held the dread responsibility of insuring domestic tranquillity and maintaining the Federal Union.

9

What a mockery is all this sympathy with the Negro

"We shall hear no more of Bleeding Kansas," Buchanan had asserted sanguinely in November, 1856. Kansas, he expected, would "slide gracefully into the Union."

If the President could have looked at Senator Douglas's incoming mail in late 1857, he then could have judged the northern temper about Lecompton. Douglas's correspondents in great volume, as many as twenty to thirty a day, and with great vehemence, urged submission either of the entire Lecompton constitution or a new constitution to the Kansas voters.

"The latest news from Kansas comes upon us like a firebell in the night," the great Mississippi River engineer, James B. Eads, wrote from Iowa. "The democracy of this Union stand pledged not only to the people of Kansas, that they should vote upon their own Constitution; but that the strong arm of the General Government would protect them in the right." Another Iowa correspondent, who formerly had been a United States fugitive-slave commissioner in Pennsylvania,

The chapter title is quoted from a speech in the United States Senate (1858) by Albert G. Brown.

wrote that to make the Lecompton constitution law without ratification by the people is "monstrous."

An Illinois newspaper publisher told the Little Giant
that "it would be madness for the administration or Congress to sustain" the Lecompton convention. A Terre
Haute, Indiana, judge wrote, "The Kansas convention
has done all it could to destroy the party." The eminent
historian George Bancroft rehearsed the precedents for
a popular referendum, from Massachusetts in 1777–78
to the recent Minnesota enabling act, and wisely observed: "The plan to cheat the people of Kansas of their
right is unstatesmanlike. Anybody who studies history,
or human nature, must know that it will leave any administration that should attempt it, helpless in Congress,
& hopeless with posterity." Douglas's friend James W.
Sheahan, editor of the Chicago *Times*, warned, "Every
Democratic paper in Illinois is out in denunciation of
Calhoun's convention. They all insist on sending the constitution back. . . . To admit Kansas as a slave state
would be destructive of everything in Illinois. We could
never recover from it." [1]

The President of course was not unaware of the gathering storm. The press was full of lightning and thunder.
Sherman Booth raged against the "Felon Constitution of
Kansas." "If this constitution is attempted to be forced
upon the people of Kansas, it will lead to violence," he
forecast. George Bancroft wrote him too: "I entreat you,
as one who most sincerely wished honor and success to
your Administration, not to endorse the Lecompton Constitution." Governor Walker came to Washington, and
after a long friendly talk with Buchanan, met with the
hostile Cabinet and gave an emphatic statement of his
views.

But the die already seemed cast. The Administration
organ, the Washington *Union*, published on November

17 an endorsement of the Lecompton constitution. The article had been written by the Attorney General, Jeremiah Black, who on showing it to Buchanan secured approval, and then on his own—and to Buchanan's distress —highhandedly deleted the portion praising Walker.

Black's arbitrary action signified the Cabinet attitude toward the malleable, aged executive. The story has been told that the Secretary of the Treasury was once asked why he seemed worried. "Oh, it's nothing much," he answered, "only Buck is opposing the Administration." The Cabinet exerted powerful pressure on Buchanan. Black, Cobb, and Thompson had told Walker they intended to exterminate opposition in Kansas. Jefferson Davis, who had stepped from Pierce's Cabinet to a seat in the Senate, along with other leaders threatened to lead a revolt if Walker were not forced to resign. The Alabama and Georgia legislatures resolved in favor of secession if Lecompton were not accepted.

Buchanan, then, was in the middle of a divided Democratic Party, with angry northerners looking to Douglas for leadership in opposing Lecompton, and hot-blooded southerners looking to Buchanan for leadership in accepting the proslavery constitution. The President made his decision, and in advance of transmitting his first annual message to Congress released the Kansas section to the press. He would urge Congress to approve the constitution.

Buchanan, ineptly, had not consulted Douglas, and had incorrectly supposed the Calhoun compromise had Douglas's support. Whatever the reason, whether because the principle of popular sovereignty was being flouted or because his Senate seat was threatened in the impending Illinois election, Douglas in a fury went to the White House. There was a stormy interview, Douglas threatening to denounce the forthcoming message and

Buchanan threatening to destroy politically any Democrat who differed with him. Buchanan reminded his visitor how President Andrew Jackson had similarly dealt with party disloyalty. The Little Giant, tossing his black mane, looked up into the frigid face of tall, white-haired "Old Obliquity." "Mr. President," he shot back, "I wish you to remember that General Jackson is dead."

Why had Buchanan embraced Lecompton? The southern influence upon him was great, and southerners defiantly talked disunion. To the aged, backward-looking President the price of union was conciliation of the minority South. Congressman William P. Miles of South Carolina told Senator Hammond that Buchanan was "frightened into repudiating Walker and was bent upon conciliating Alabama, Georgia, and Mississippi in particular and the Southern people generally." And the Pennsylvania publisher, John W. Forney, told a Congressional investigating committee that Buchanan "changed his course because certain Southern states had threatened that if he did not abandon Walker and Stanton they would be compelled either to secede from the Union or take up arms against him."

Southern threats, seen through the prism that distorted Buchanan's nationalism, afford one explanation of Buchanan's course. A second explanation, advanced by his sympathetic biographer, Philip S. Klein, is that he was a legalist. The Lecompton constitution had been drafted by procedures that technically seemed quite legal. From this point of view, if the people of Kansas chose not to vote in elections, that was their business; not all state constitutions in the past had been submitted to popular vote; the slavery provisions could be changed after Kansas became a state; and Buchanan had never promised that, if provision was not made for submission, he would oppose the constitution.

Whatever Buchanan's apologists may say, it is clear that the President betrayed his party pledge, his territorial governor, and the cause of national unity, in taking up Lecompton. Lecompton did not rest, in the platform's phrase, "upon the legally and fairly expressed will of the majority of the actual residents." Buchanan's sanction of Lecompton did not square with his forthright reassurance to Walker: "On the question of submitting the Constitution to the bona fide residents of Kansas, I am willing to stand or fall." Nor, with the prospect of a northern rising led by Douglas, did his sanction bode well for party or national harmony.

"It may be" the historian Don Fehrenbacher has judged, "that the most important single decision of the 1850's was Buchanan's decision to endorse the work of the Lecompton convention." "The role that Buchanan did play may be counted one of the signal failures of American statesmanship," Allan Nevins has observed. "Seldom in American history has a chief magistrate made a greater error, or missed a larger opportunity."

As the venerable N. P. Tallmadge, former Senator from New York, remarked to Douglas: "No President ever had such an opportunity for a brilliant *debut* for his administration, as Mr. Buchanan had on this question [of popular sovereignty]. Instead of seizing hold of it, he has run counter also to the Kansas act, to the Cincinnati platform, to his Inaugural, to his instructions to Governor Walker, to his Manifesto to the Connecticut clergymen [in which in August he had spoken of submission], and, in short, to every thing he has said on this subject or the principle involved in it." "Persevere, then, in the course you have taken," he exhorted Douglas. "The whole people are with you." [2]

As members of the Thirty-fifth Congress foregathered

in Washington, the immediate issue facing House Democrats was electing a speaker. The Administration favored James L. Orr, the South Carolina moderate, who had visited Kansas and had supported Governor Walker's regime. A graduate of the University of Virginia, energetic at thirty-five years of age, endowed with patience, common sense, and a ringing voice, he was an admirable choice. The southern anti-Walker group marked him for defeat, but the upshot of the intraparty struggle was an administration victory.

The Senate named as president pro tem Benjamin Fitzpatrick, an Alabama Democrat, over Hannibal Hamlin of Maine, who was destined to be Lincoln's first Vice-President, by a vote of 28 to 19—an index of party strength in that body. New members on the Democratic side included James H. Hammond of South Carolina, Jefferson Davis of Mississippi, Andrew Johnson, the "Mechanic Governor" of Tennessee, and on the Republican side Zachariah Chandler, Cass's aggressive successor from Michigan, Preston King, who had led the Democratic defection in New York in 1854, and Simon Cameron of Pennsylvania, who had left the Democratic Party at the time of the Kansas-Nebraska Act and who would become Lincoln's first Secretary of War. The Democratic majorities in the two branches of Congress doubtless had emboldened Buchanan to approve Lecompton. The Senate, despite the new faces that marked a transition to a new era, was safely in Administration hands. The House, despite the Democratic majority, was precarious because of sectional differences.

The Lecomptonites had counted on Buchanan's sanction of their constitution. They were not disappointed when the Annual Message was delivered on December 8. The President stamped his approval on the circumstances under which the document had been drafted.

The law providing for electing delegates was "in the main fair"; the territorial legislature under whose authority they were acting had been recognized by Congress; forty-three of fifty delegates had signed the constitution; and at the pending election every citizen would have an opportunity to express his opinion.

So far as his instructions to Governor Walker were concerned, Buchanan said his only desire had been to let the people of Kansas have a vote without fraud or violence on the question of slavery. The Kansas-Nebraska Act required only a popular vote on the slavery issue. He strongly implied a hope Lecompton would be approved. If after statehood Kansas wanted to abolish slavery, no human power could prevent her. But in the territorial stage to abolish slavery would be confiscation of property, in violation of the Supreme Court's recent ruling.

Kansas, he complained, "has for some years occupied too much of the public attention." Once she is admitted, he declared astigmatically, "the excitement beyond her own limits will speedily pass away. . . ." Most of what Buchanan said was specious, sophistical, and short-sighted. The making of the Lecompton constitution was indefensible on any grounds of justice; the interpretation of the Kansas-Nebraska Act was inaccurate, as this constitution gave no alternative to slavery; and the notion that excitement about slavery would vanish upon the admission of Kansas was chimerical.

The next day Douglas rose in the Senate to reply. It was a dramatic hour as the author of the Kansas-Nebraska Act and foremost northern Democrat made his awaited attack upon the Administration. The Senate galleries were thronged as they had not been since Daniel Webster made his Seventh of March speech during the crisis of 1850. Adéle Cutts Douglas, a young, comely bride, twenty years her husband's junior, a Washington belle said to be the most attractive woman in Washington, sat in the front row.

The Little Giant, after observing that the President had not explicitly endorsed the constitution or asked Congress to endorse it, but had merely referred it to Congress, made his case point by point. To begin with, he stoutly disagreed with the President's assertion that his Nebraska bill required submission of only the slavery issue. He asserted the national Administration, the territorial administration, and the people of the territory had understood that the constitution would be submitted, until the October defeat of the proslavery party.

What was the choice now open? "All men must vote for the constitution, whether they like it or not, in order to be permitted to vote for or against Slavery." That was as fair an election as the one attributed to Napoleon, when he told his soldiers: " 'If you vote for Napoleon, all is well; vote against him, and you are to be instantly shot!' " How do the Lecomptonites explain their refusal to allow men to vote against the constitution? "They say, if they had allowed a negative vote, the constitution would have been voted down by an overwhelming majority; and hence the fellows shall not be allowed to vote at all. [Laughter]"

Had his Nebraska measure been reduced to despotism? "Is that the mode in which I am called upon to carry out the principle of self-government and popular sovereignty in the territories—to force a constitution on the people against their will . . . ?" The doctrine that left people perfectly free to form and regulate their institutions was at issue. "It is none of my business which way the Slavery clause is decided. I care not whether it is voted down or up," he asserted in a sentence that antislavery men were to fling back at him—out of context.

In his final passage he referred to the political risk

he was running. "I have no fear of any party associations being severed. I should regret any social or political estrangement even, temporarily, but if it must be, if I can't act with you, and preserve my faith and honor, I will stand on the great principle of Popular Sovereignty. . . ." He demanded a new constitutional convention, and proposed to revive the Toombs bill, with a submission clause added.

Douglas's masterful speech drove a deep wedge among Democrats, pleased Republicans, thrilled northerners, and alarmed southerners. Legend to the contrary, it was because of his opposition to the Lecompton constitution, and not because of his famous "Freeport doctrine" of 1858 that Douglas lost standing in the South. "Douglas came out against the administration stronger than I supposed he would, and his course has greatly alarmed the party," Senator Wade told his wife. "The President and the South are greatly alarmed at the attitude of affairs. It created a great sensation when this fight began. I called it a *Slave Insurrection*, it goes by that name." A Pennsylvania correspondent wrote Justice John McLean that the Administration stood in great danger of being defeated on Lecompton. "Mr. Buchanan had better be governed by moderate council [*sic*] and permit the Lecompton constitution to be thrown into some dark corner among the owls and bats." The Hartford editor Gideon Welles gave Douglas his sense of gratification; Lecompton "is more arbitrary and more centralizing, than any measure ever proposed since the adoption of the federal constitution." "I have not met a single Democrat who does not entirely support you. . . ." wrote John W. Forney, the Philadelphia editor, to Douglas. "If you have lost some friends in the South you have gained thousands in the North." [3]

Meanwhile turbulent Kansas politics had taken a new

turn. Concerned about the prospect of violence in the rigged referendum, F. P. Stanton, acting governor while Walker was in Washington, summoned the recently elected freestate legislature into extra session. This move by the obscure Stanton was one of the most statesman-like acts of the whole Kansas controversy. Coming at a time of impending collision on the prairie, it kept the peace and enabled popular sovereignty to operate. The legislature met on December 7, and in response to Stanton's urging passed an act to submit the entire Lecompton constitution to a fair vote on January 4, the day appointed by the Lecompton constitution for election of state officers under that constitution.

Buchanan promptly removed Stanton and named James W. Denver in his place. Walker thereupon resigned in a long letter to Secretary of State Cass. The President's policies toward Kansas, he said, "admonish me that, as governor of that territory, it will no longer be in my power to preserve the peace or promote the public welfare." He reminded Cass how the Administration had entreated him to take the post. "I accepted . . . on the express condition that I should advocate the submission of the constitution to the vote of the people for ratification or rejection." "The slavery question," he went on, "as a practical issue, had disappeared from Kansas long before my arrival there, and the question of self-government had been substituted in its place. For Congress to force Lecompton on Kansas would be to substitute the will of a small minority in place of the will of an overwhelming majority," he warned in his letter, which the freesoil press published.

The referendum arranged by the Lecompton convention took place on December 21. The vote "for the constitution with slavery" was 6,266; the vote "for the constitution without slavery" was 567. Freestate men had

boycotted the obnoxious choice. An investigating committee later judged at least 2,720 votes were fraudulent.

The Buchanan Administration acquiesced in the legislature's decree of another referendum on January 4. Denver (for whom Colorado's capital city is named), a veteran
of the Mexican War and a former Democratic Congressman, acted impartially and decisively, indifferent to
threats against his life. The vote "For the constitution
with slavery" was 138; the vote "For the constitution without slavery" was 24; and the vote "Against the constitution" was a thumping 10,226. By a majority of over
10,000, and with few votes in favor, Kansans had turned
down Lecompton. Proslavery men had stupidly perpetrated fresh forgeries—called the "candle-box fraud"—in
the legislative election. An investigating committee, sus-
picious of certain figures reported for election of state
officers, found the returns secreted in a candle box buried
under a woodpile near Calhoun's office. In place of the
original number of 43 votes, a forged list of 379 proslavery votes had been substituted. Calhoun was arrested,
but released on a writ of habeas corpus by a proslavery
judge.

Acting Governor Denver advised Buchanan that the
freestate men had elected their slate of officers and that
Kansans had expressed their will on the Lecompton constitution in the only valid vote upon it. Denver had joined
his predecessors, appointees of proslavery Presidents,
in sustaining the freestate cause. We may note, in ap-
praising the respective merits of the parties in Kansas,
that successive territorial governors found the freestate
adherents had the superior claims to respect for law and
to representing the majority of the inhabitants. Galusha
Grow, Wilmot's successor in Congress, during debate on
the English bill, declared, "Four Governors have returned
from that Territory, all telling the same story to the

American people; that is, that the rights of the people of Kansas have all been trampled in the dust. . . ." Reeder, after his removal, had become a freestate leader; Shannon, failing as peacemaker, had resigned; Geary resigned for lack of Presidential support from Pierce; and Walker resigned for lack of Presidential support from Buchanan. A sorry record of relations between the Presidents and their Kansas governors.

The new referendum plainly showed that the Lecompton constitution must be discarded if Kansas was to have a government resting on the consent of the governed. But in view of Buchanan's commitment it seemed unlikely that he would accept Denver's counsel.

While Congress girt itself for the struggle on Kansas's organic law, the nation labored with excitement. The Administration press, led by the kept Washington *Union*, attacked Douglas as a traitor to his party. Republicans eyed Douglas in varying lights, some rejoicing that he had broken with the Administration, others regarding him suspiciously. Sumner, for one, told Chase, "Our experience of Douglas, I think, would prevent any strong confidence in his labors for the good cause." He thought the Illinois Senator was pursuing the only course that could re-elect him.[4]

The curious choice extended to Kansas voters incurred ridicule. One editor remarked it was an illustration of the old jest, "I will take the turkey and you the buzzard, or you take the buzzard and I will take the turkey." Voices raised in ardent protest were numerous. The state legislatures of Ohio, Iowa, Michigan, Wisconsin, Massachusetts, Connecticut, and Rhode Island denounced the constitution and endorsed Douglas. A Democratic convention in Kansas memorialized Congress in protest against admission under the document. The Nebraska territorial legislature joined in the denunciation.

What was happening in pivotal Indiana is suggestive. The "Lecompton fraud" threatened to divide the Democratic Party. At the Democratic state convention on January 8, 1858, Senator Bright, who supported Buchanan and Lecompton, beat down resolutions endorsing Douglas. Under Bright's domination the Hoosier convention endorsed the Dred Scott decision and accused the Republicans of fostering "the loathsome doctrine of 'negro equality.'" Douglas Democrats countered by calling a mass meeting on February 22, where they passed resolutions endorsing the Little Giant and upholding the right of the people of Kansas to vote on their constitution. As for the opposition party in the state, the fact that it now officially dared call itself Republican further suggests how party differences were sharpening. The Republican state platform in 1858 made no concessions to the Know Nothings, and for the first time incorporated a homestead plank.

Buchanan found backing not only in the Administration press but also in the legislatures of Alabama, Tennessee, and Texas, in the Democratic state convention in Pennsylvania, and in a meeting of Democratic editors in New York. A legislative caucus in Virginia sustained him, but Governor Henry A. Wise, Hunter's rival, wrote a vigorous protest to be read at an anti-Lecompton meeting in Philadelphia. The fire-eating Senator Albert G. Brown of Mississippi blustered, "we mean neither to be defrauded of our rights in the name of the Union nor to surrender them for the shadow when the substance has been wrested from us."

The strain told on the aged executive. Stephens, who was counseling him on Kansas policy, observed, "He is run down and worn out with office-seekers, and the cares which the consideration of public affairs has brought upon him. He is now quite feeble and wan. I was struck with his physical appearance; he appears to me to be failing in bodily health."

On February 2 Buchanan transmitted to Congress a copy of the Lecompton constitution, which he had received from Calhoun, and a special message recommending immediate admission of Kansas under the controverted document.

Buchanan had embraced Lecompton despite his knowing that a month earlier 10,000 Kansans had voted against the constitution, that fewer than 4,000 favored it in the December referendum, and that frauds had marred both elections. He had received Denver's advice to reject, which he dismissed, saying he was sorry he had not gotten the advice earlier, but as he had already written a special message favoring Lecompton and had shown it to several Senators, he could not withdraw it!

Buchanan opened his special message with a condemnation of the Topeka government, which he called revolutionary, treasonable, and a usurpation. He then recounted the history of the making of Lecompton, arguing that the convention was lawfully constituted. As to submission, the delegates "did not think proper to submit the whole of this constitution to a popular vote, but they did submit," he went on inaccurately, "the question whether Kansas should be a free or a slave State to the people." "The only remedy," he asserted helplessly, lies in the people's "power to change their constitution or their laws to their own pleasure." When he had instructed Walker in general terms about submission, "I had no object in view except the all-absorbing question of slavery," he declared.

With respect to the January 4 election, it was held

after the territory had been prepared for admission into the Union as a sovereign state, and therefore when no authority existed in the legislature; it involved the "strange inconsistency" of persons voting against the constitution yet at the same time recognizing it by voting under its provisions; and finally, "I have yet received no official information of the result of this election."

Turning from this legalistic outlook he urged the expediency of immediate admission. Domestic peace will be the happy consequence; if the majority of the people wish to abolish slavery, there is no mode more speedy than prompt admission. "Kansas once admitted into the Union, the excitement becomes localized and will soon die away for want of outside aliment."

Freestate partisans were particularly outraged by a passage referring to the Dred Scott decision and by his theory of the Union. "It has been solemnly adjudged by the highest judicial tribunal . . . that slavery exists in Kansas by virtue of the Constitution of the United States. Kansas is therefore at this moment as much a slave State as Georgia or South Carolina. Without this the equality of the sovereign States composing the Union would be violated and the use and enjoyment of a territory acquired by the common treasure of all the States would be closed against the people and the property of nearly half the members of the Confederacy."

In closing he linked prompt admission to salvation of the nation. Speedy admission might dissipate the dark and ominous clouds now hanging over the Union, whereas if Kansas should be rejected, "I greatly fear these clouds will become darker and more ominous than any which have ever yet threatened the Constitution and the Union."

Why, we must ask, had Buchanan rejected the plainest evidence proving that popular sovereignty had been trampled on in Kansas? His sympathetic biographer,

Philip S. Klein, asserts the President believed that political questions should be settled by law and practical politics and not by moral principles; that the personality clashes between Douglas and Buchanan were irreconcilable; that the President aspired to earn a "historical" reputation by settling the problem of slavery in the territories and at the same time preserving the Union and letting slavery die a natural death "by the silent operation of economic and moral forces"; that he derived a spiteful satisfaction in seeing Douglas's dogma turn out to be a catastrophe; and finally, that he believed he had the votes in Congress to pass the enabling act.

Very little of this explanation reflects credit upon Buchanan's statesmanship. The best that can be said for the President may be found in his private correspondence. In a "confidential" letter to Denver he said, "The defeat of the bill would alarm the fears of the country for the Union, reduce the value of property and injuriously interfere with our reviving trade." Above all, it would seem, he believed Lecompton would placate Georgia, Alabama, and Mississippi, preserve the Union, and end for all time the problem of slavery in America.

What were his alternatives? He could, first of all, have returned the constitution to Kansas with his insistence upon a fair referendum, under Federal supervision. Second, he could have insisted upon a wholly new constitution, based from first to last upon the consent of the governed. And finally, and perhaps ideally, he could have required Kansas to wait for statehood until it had the population necessary for a Congressman; meanwhile the freestate legislature, chosen in October, would control the territory.

For four years Kansas had been a recurring menace to the American republic. Scarcely had the rumblings

over Walker's policies abated with his resignation than
new thunder came from the Lower South over Lecompton. Governor Joseph E. Brown of Georgia asserted that if
Congress rejected Kansas it would become his "imperative duty to call a convention which . . . [would] determine the status of Georgia with reference to the Union."
The governor of Alabama, John A. Winston, pronounced
that the Union was not the paramount good to Alabama
or to the South; and the state senate directed his successor to call an election for delegates to a convention
that would consider the means to protect Alabama's
rights. To many in Mississippi, which had officially condemned Walker, dissolution of the Union seemed imminent. The South Carolina press, with few exceptions,
kept up a running diatribe against Douglas; even the
moderate Benjamin F. Perry urged, "By keeping the
South united we may with that minority be able to maintain our equality in the Union or independence out of
it." "I trust that our southern representatives will leave in
a body when Kansas is rejected," a friend told Stephens.[5]

Tempers rose in Congress as well as in the country.
When the veteran Free Soiler Galusha A. Grow of Pennsylvania stepped over to the Democratic side of the
House, Keitt of South Carolina shouted: "Go back to your
side of the House, you Black Republican puppy!" Grow
shot back a jeering defiance of "nigger drivers." Grow, the
father of the future homestead law, and Keitt, who would
keep the territories open to slavery, grappled with one
another, Grow knocking Keitt to the floor. Stephens wrote
his brother: "Last night we had a battle-royal in the
House. Thirty men at least were engaged in the fisticuff.
Fortunately, no weapons were used. . . . Nobody was
hurt or even scratched, I believe; but bad feeling was
produced by it. It was the first sectional fight ever had on
the floor, I think; and if any weapons had been on hand it

would probably have been a bloody one. All things here are tending to bring my mind to conclusion that the Union cannot or will not last long."

Fisticuffs in Congress. Secessionist threats in the South. What was at issue in the Lecompton controversy? To Buchanan, as we have seen, the issue was the Union, endangered by the militancy of the Deep South. To Walker and Douglas, the issue was not primarily the Union, but self-government for Kansas and Democratic politics. Both men aimed at creating a Democratic state and Douglas aimed at keeping his Senate seat. To Republicans, the issue comprised their native principle of nonextension of slavery and a chance to split the Democratic Party, discredit the Administration, add a free state, and win ensuing elections. In late March representatives of the Republican state committees met in Washington to exploit Lecompton. Speakers were sent to Kansas to influence the next territorial election; and Republican Congressional speeches were franked by the tens of thousands. With Lecompton defeated, "our triumph in the next Presidential election is *assured*," declared a group of Republican Congressmen.[6]

To southerners, the issue embraced the principle of nonintervention in the territories, which was a point of pride and self-respect, the necessity to maintain the Democratic Party as the bulwark of southern rights, and a chance to add a slave state and win ensuing elections. To most Kansans, the issue was the right to devise their own government.

Behind these issues, and others that might be itemized, lay the inexorable specter of race. In mid-January Congressman Francis P. Blair, Jr., of Missouri, elected as a Democrat but now a Black Republican, introduced a resolution proposing a committee to inquire into the expediency of colonizing freed Negroes in the Central

American states. In order to fulfill the Republican purpose of preventing the extension of slavery on the North American continent, "we might," he said in explaining his proposal, "plant those countries with a class of men who are worse than useless to us."

"Mr. Chairman," Blair went on, "it is evident to every man of thought that the freed blacks hold a place in this country which cannot be maintained. Those who have fled to the North are most unwelcome visitors. The strong repugnance of the free white laborer to be yoked with the negro refugee breeds an enmity between the races, which must end in the expulsion of the latter. . . . In spite of all that reason or religion can urge, nature has put a badge upon the African, making amalgamation revolting to our race."

Colonization of Negroes, he thought, would be a sensible alternative to the Administration's Kansas policy. Northerners and southerners could support such a plan. Although Blair thought the colonization scheme was "the finest theme with which to get at the hearts of the people . . ." nothing came of his resolution.

Three weeks later the South's leading statesman, Jefferson Davis, spoke on the Lecompton question. The southern states "present a new problem, one not stated by those who wrote on it in the earlier period of our history. It is the problem of a semi-tropical climate. . . . A race suited to our labor exists there. Why should we care whether they go into other territories or not? Simply because of the war that is made against our institutions; simply because of the want of security which results from the action of our opponents in the Northern States. . . . You have made it a political war. We are on the defensive. How far are you to push us?" he cried.

The pre-eminent Republican spokesman, William H. Seward, in early March made a speech on Kansas, of which the national chairman, Morgan, distributed fifty thousand copies. Seward interpreted the Republican purpose to exclude slavery from the territories in terms of advantage to the white race. "Free labor has been obstructed in Kansas," he asserted. "The white man needs this continent to labor upon." After discoursing upon the past continental expansion of Americans, the speaker declaimed, "Mr. President, this expansion of the empire of free white men is to be conducted through the process of admitting new States, and not otherwise."

Senator Albert G. Brown of Mississippi took a large part in the Lecompton debates. He favored adoption of the Lecompton constitution and expounded the doctrine of Congressional nonintervention. "Just let the negroes alone," he told the Senate. "Just get all your northern friends to attend to local matters which concern you," he adjured a northern member to whom he was replying, "and let us down South attend to our own local affairs." He defended racialism with the state-rights argument ("I put the rights of the States above the Union") and jeered at the contrast between northern humanitarian pretensions and practice: "What a mockery is all this sympathy with the negro . . . and yet northern gentlemen will no more allow him to go into their States than they would allow a pestilence to come in if they could prevent it."

A key figure in Congressional consideration of Lecompton, as we shall see, was the Democratic representative from Indiana, William H. English. A resident of southern Indiana, he was a Douglas partisan. English told the House in 1860 in Indiana, "We believe that the negroes are inferior by nature, and that whenever they are brought in contact with the white man, they will, in some form or other, be subject to his superior intelligence and will."

The famous Copperhead leader of the Civil War era,

Clement L. Vallandigham, speaking in the House of Representatives on May 22, 1858, decried the notion of equality for the Negro, "the descendant of a servile and degraded race." He forebodingly observed, "And when this government shall be broken up, and the fanaticism of the age shall have culminated in the North in red Republicanism and negro equality, and the South shall have driven out her free negroes upon you, and you shall have stolen away her slaves, then your troubles with this race, which has already plagued America for a century, will but have begun. . . ." No wise people, he warned, would ever encourage attempts to raise such a race to social and political equality.

Southerners like Davis, Brown, and Hammond, whose "Cotton is King" speech was delivered in the course of the Lecompton debate, and northerners like English and Vallandigham agreed that slavery was the best social arrangement for the inferior Negro. A politician from a border slave state, like Blair, believed colonization was the best solution to the race problem. Northerners like Seward and the freesoilers believed exclusion of Negroes from the Federal territories widened economic opportunity for the white man in an expanding nation. A rare Congressman like Hale might be skeptical of the black man's supposed inferiority and speak well of the northern freedman—"industrious, patient, exhibiting very many amiable and excellent traits of character." An impassioned southerner like Toombs more than offset Hale's moderation, when he sneered at northern objections to a constitution in Congress "when there is a 'nigger' in it."

The distinguished historian, James G. Randall, branded the men of the midcentury a "blundering generation." They were indeed blundering because they were a flawed generation—flawed by their belief in the African's innate inferiority. The element of race was integral to the Kansas crisis. It permeated the debates and confined the horizons of the statesmen charged with resolving the crisis.

Buchanan's special message renewed the dialogue over Lecompton. Douglas was determined to stand firm. "If the Party is divided by this course it will not be my fault," he wrote a friend. In a letter to the Great Democratic Anti-Lecompton Meeting Against the Lecompton Fraud, held at Philadelphia on February 8, 1858, he asserted that the Lecompton convention had no authority to ordain a constitution and put it in force without the consent of Congress. The document should be repudiated by every Democrat who cherishes the doctrine of popular sovereignty. He proffered similar views in a Senate report.

Douglas the Democrat, protagonist of popular sovereignty, was now being taken up in a strange political relationship by certain Republicans, protagonists of the doctrine that Congress had a right and duty to prohibit slavery in the territories. Greeley's *Tribune* praised Douglas and urged that he not be opposed for re-election in Illinois. *The New York Times,* which was Seward's organ, the Springfield, Mass. *Republican,* and *The Independent* (a New York religious weekly) joined in the editorial chorus of laudation. Many Republicans now seemed to agree with Douglas's 1854 claim that popular sovereignty, fairly exercised, could result in excluding slavery from Kansas. Henry Wilson favored not opposing Douglas for re-election, and Seward in the Senate chamber announced that he would cooperate with Douglas.

How far was all this intended as a stratagem to divide the Democracy? it may be asked, but the apparent compromise of principle profoundly disturbed Trumbull of

Illinois, who wrote Lincoln that the Illinois Republicans could not support Douglas as long as he supported the Dred Scott decision, denied the right of Congress to exclude slavery from the territories, and upheld repeal of the Missouri Compromise. The Republican flirtation rankled with Lincoln, as we shall see, for it would deny him a chance to contest Douglas for the Senate seat.

Other party stalwarts like Julian recognized the "serious peril to the Republican party"; and Chase wrote Seward, "I regretted the apparent countenance you gave to the idea that the Douglas doctrine of Popular Sovereignty will do for us to stand upon for the present." Chase could perhaps find solace in a discerning letter from a former law partner: "our work is being done to our hands better now by Douglas than we could do it ourselves, & . . . it is no time to attack him, but rather to give him comfort & encouragement. No one need be even troubled with the idea that he will ever be a leader of the Republican forces. But until the Democratic party is broken, we cannot succeed." [7] And, importantly, Illinois Republicans were not willing to defer to outsiders' suggestions.

In addition to Douglas's report the Senate received from the Committee on Territories a majority report favoring Lecompton and a third report offering the Republican view. From the outset it was clear that not enough northern Democrats would join Douglas to defeat the constitution in the Senate. Buchanan made Lecompton an Administration measure. When Bigler asserted that the Democratic Party supported Buchanan, Wade sneered, "I suppose if he takes snuff, every true Democrat ought to sneeze, or else be read out of the party."

Although ill, his voice weak and husky, Douglas made a masterful speech the night of March 22. For one thing, he demonstrated that Lecompton was not the voice of

Kansas. But equally important, he made crystal clear his conviction that the great issue before the country was public policy toward the Negro. He rehearsed the principles on which he said the campaign of 1856 was waged and won, and for which he still stood. To him they were three in number.

First of all, policy toward the colored population was a local matter. Next, the Negro, who was not a United States citizen and hence not entitled to political equality, should have such rights as he was capable of enjoying, consistent with the welfare and safety of the community where he lived. And finally, each state and territory must decide for itself the nature and extent of these rights. With his recognition of racial inequality and of diverse responses to it, he epitomized the problem of the fifties.

Without avail he reminded his auditors of the Democracy's ideals. The next day Lecompton came to a vote. It passed the Senate 33 to 25. Only four northern Democrats voted nay; only two southerners, Crittenden and Bell, voted nay. The real struggle was in the House.

As in 1854 with the Kansas-Nebraska Act, so now in 1858 the more popular branch of the national legislature resisted Administration Kansas policy. Again as in 1854 the parliamentary tactician of the Administration in the House was Stephens, who had seen the President's message before it had been sent to Congress.

Buchanan could count on 100 Administration votes in the House, but he needed 118 to enact Lecompton. There were 92 Republicans, 14 Americans, and 21 anti-Lecompton Democrats. Douglas transferred his activities to the House, seeking to harden opposition, exploiting his advantage in the impending elections in the North. Buchanan, notwithstanding his constitutional theories about a weak executive and the separation of powers, exerted himself to secure passage. His biographer

Klein writes: "The president used every means he could to pick up the few votes needed, dismissing friends of Douglas wholesale, holding up new appointments, and offering patronage, contracts, commissions, and in some cases cold cash."

The House proved obstreperous. When Stephens moved that the Lecompton constitution be referred to his territorial committee, he was defeated 114–113. Speaker Orr then named a special committee of 15, neatly balancing factions by naming a pro-Lecompton majority of 8 and making a Douglas man, Harris, chairman. Stephens wrote the committee report, adopted 8–7, contending that Congress had no power to go behind the work of the Lecompton convention and that its adoption had been regular and lawful. The House opposed reading the report; and Harris charged the committee with not performing its duty.

On April 1 the House took up the Senate bill, turning away from its own bill. Montgomery of Pennsylvania offered an amendment, similar to the one unsuccessfully offered to the Senate by Crittenden. Noting that "it is greatly disputed" whether the constitution was "fairly made, or expressed the will of the people of Kansas," the Montgomery amendment provided for resubmission to the people. If the constitution was approved by a majority of voters, the President by proclamation was to announce the admission of Kansas. If the constitution was rejected, the people were authorized to draft a new constitution. To the dismay of Administration Democrats, this statesmanlike measure passed 120 to 112. Twenty-two Democrats and six Southern Americans had united with the solid Republican bloc to carry the substitute. Stephens, "never so much worn with care and anxiety in my life," blamed the southern independents for loss of the Senate bill.

The Senate unwisely rejected the Montgomery substitute and requested a committee of conference. In a
dramatic roll call on the request, the House deadlocked
108–108. Orr then used his casting ballot in favor of a
conference committee. As a member of the joint committee Stephens took the lead in devising a compromise.
Uncounted persons called on him, and though ill, he
had, he complained, "to give audience to all sorts of views
and suggestions." Before agreeing to report the compromise, he took the plan to Jefferson Davis, who was too
sick to come to the Capitol, and to "all the leading men
from the South." The name of committee member William H. English, an anti-Lecompton Democrat, was assigned to the proposal. Seward and Howard, who had
headed the Kansas investigation in 1856, dissented.

The English bill fastened upon the land grant to Kansas as the mode of compromise. The Lecomptonites had
asked for the gigantic Federal largesse of 23,592,160
acres of land—about the extent of Indiana—despite
their state-rights protestations. The English bill, following the Crittenden bill's proposal, cut this down to less
than 4 million acres—the usual proportion offered a new
state. White, male Kansans were to vote upon the land-
grant proposition, and if a majority voted "Proposition
accepted," the state would be immediately admitted under
the Lecompton constitution. If a majority voted "Proposition rejected," Kansas must wait for statehood until it
had a population equal to the number required for a
member of the House of Representatives, and only then
could a new constitution be submitted to Congress. The
waiting period, it was expected, would be about two
years.

The proposal placed Douglas on the horns of a dilemma. Buchanan had been forced to recede from his
insistence upon admission under the Lecompton consti-

tution. Douglas had prevailed in his insistence upon re-submission. If he were to vote for the compromise he might simultaneously claim a victory for popular sover-eignty and recoup his political fortunes among Admin-istration Democrats. Former Governor Walker and former territorial secretary Stanton declared for it. On the Saturday night before the anticipated Congressional vote, Douglas met with Walker, Stanton, and Forney. While the Little Giant listened to Walker's eloquent per-suasion, he paced the floor, large beads of sweat start-ing from his forehead—"they were almost drops of blood." Finally, Douglas agreed to support the English bill.

On Sunday he met with the irreconcilable anti-Le-compton Democrats to inform them of his change of heart. Passions rose high. Senator David Broderick of California turned livid with anger.

"Sir, I cannot understand, you will be crushed between the Democracy and the Republicans. I shall denounce you, sir. You had better, sir, go into the street and blow your damn brains out," stormed this hot-tempered Irish-man, who would later be mortally wounded in a duel with the chief justice of California.

The storm signals over Illinois loomed at least as ominous as the threats and fulminations of his col-leagues. At the Democratic State convention on April 21 ninety-seven of ninety-eight counties had been repre-sented by anti-Lecompton delegates. Douglas tacked and set his course in opposition to Lecompton.

On April 29, laboring under emotion, Douglas told the Senate that after careful study he could not find the principles of popular sovereignty and Congressional non-intervention in the bill. Instead, he found "intervention with a bounty on the one side and a penalty on the other." The bounty interfered with "the principle of freedom of election." Therefore he could not conclude it "was a fair, impartial and equal application of the principle" of popular sovereignty.

The Buchanan Administration made extraordinary exertions to secure passage. It spent $30,000 to $40,000, as a Congressional investigation later disclosed, to encourage wavering Democrats to support the compromise. On April 30 the Senate approved the English bill by a vote of 31 to 22, the three northern Democrats, Douglas, Broderick, and Stuart of Michigan, siding with the Republicans. On the same day the House approved, 112 to 103; nine northern democrats and one southern American who had voted against Lecompton now supported the English bill.

Under this measure Kansans voted August 2, 1858—the same day that an election was being held in Missouri. The balloting, supervised by a board of commissioners including Governor Denver, was unmarred by fraud. "Mind—I bet on the people of Kansas," Greeley had written his friend Colfax. The expected outcome of this third plebiscite on Lecompton was a resounding freestate victory. Kansans rejected Lecompton 11,300 to 1,788. Kansas preferred territorial status and no slavery to statehood and slavery. If those who had hoped to see another slave state were disappointed, so were those who had hoped to see another Democratic state. As a Kansan told Chase, "The bad faith of Congress in entertaining the petition of the Lecomptonites has placed the Republican element in the ascendancy." [8]

The English bill was the last Congressional compromise before the Civil War. Its great merit lay in resolving the Kansas controversy—no mean achievement. Final disposition of the Lecompton constitution—about which *The New-York Tribune Political Textbook* said, "From first to last, it had been the cause or the subject of more speeches in Congress than any measure ever brought

before that body"—is perhaps enough to ask of any act
of Congress.

But it lacked statesmanship. It placed immediate admission of Kansas on the basis of Lecompton—a constitution
decisively rejected by the people of Kansas. Lecompton
itself was conceived in trickery. Stephens later admitted
Lecompton was a cheat.

The English expedient evaded the issue of self-government. It bartered the historic right of statehood. It said:
approve the land proposition and Lecompton and become
a state at once; or reject the proposition and you must
wait for statehood until you have more than 93,000 citizens. If the boon of statehood could be conferred under
a constitution of shameful chicanery, it could be extended under a constitution of popular consent. The
English amendment, in this view, was much less satisfactory statecraft than the Crittenden-Montgomery
amendment, which would have promptly started up the
machinery for a new convention, should Lecompton be
rejected.

Outraged by the measure, Senator Henry Wilson
branded it "a conglomeration of bribes, penalties, and of
premeditated fraud." He pointed out that the Federal
government had advertised thousands of acres of land for
sale in July. Should Kansas enter the Union, she would
receive by the terms of the bill 5 per cent of the sales
proceeds, running to hundreds of thousands of dollars.
If she remained a territory, she would not receive this
money.

The English bill was a bribe, not because it offered an
extravagant land grant, which it did not, but because it
promised certain benefits—a land grant, a percentage on
land sales, and immediate statehood—on acceptance of
Lecompton, and deferred or ignored these benefits if a
majority of the people rejected the constitution. Finally,

land officers in Kansas offered an oblique bribe to the settlers if they voted for the "Lecompton contrivance." Land sales in two of the three districts were ordered for July. Thousands of squatters were unable to pay up and faced the prospect of losing land they had developed. Land officers were telling settlers "that if they vote for the Lecompton Constitution, and pass it, the land sales will be *put off*. This is a very tempting bribe," wrote the Kansas settler John Everett, "as thousands can not now pay up without ruinous sacrifices, and some not at all." Everett concluded that the forthcoming land sales were being used as a screw to force the poorer pioneers to vote for Lecompton.

It would be two and a half years before Kansas would be admitted as a state. Under a constitution drafted at Wyandotte that confined the right to vote to "every white male person," Kansas entered the Union a free state. Its anti-Negro sentiment soon took form in the segregated schools that inspired a landmark decision of the Supreme Court of the United States, when in 1954, nearly a century after the Dred Scott case, the court struck down school segregation. The race problem of the 1850's had taken a new shape a century later as the nation faced desegregation.

"We have scotch'd the snake, not kill'd it," spoke Macbeth, in words appropriate to the English bill which left the serpent's sharp tooth exposed. The compromise widened divisions among Democrats, now rent into moderates who had endorsed the measure, Douglasites who had opposed it, and southern extremists who had suffered disappointment. From a doctrinal point of view the compromise was fraught with peril for the future, northern Democrats claiming a victory for resubmission while southern extremists denied the principle of resubmission, claiming only the land proposition had been voted on. A party split over popular sovereignty portended, as the Democrats emerged from the five months of intra-party strife.

Beyond the English bill lay the impact of the entire Kansas crisis upon the American nation. Emerson observed in February, 1858, "All the children born in the last three years or eight years should be charged with love of liberty, for their parents have been filled with Kansas and Anti-slavery." The Kansas-Nebraska Act had fostered nearly five years of bitter sectional quarreling. Offered as a great principle of self-government, it had elicited the worst traits from the American people: fraud in voting, guerrilla fighting, sophistical logic, trickery, terrorism, passion, insult, extreme partisanship, murder, and—underpinning all else—a vicious racialism.

The continuing crisis disclosed weaknesses in the American constitutional system: the ambiguity of the Constitution on the territorial question, the document's failure to define citizenship, its failure to say whether state or Federal authority should return fugitive slaves, and its rigid maintenance of an unpopular Administration in power during a crisis.

The politics of Bleeding Kansas could be nothing but an embarrassment to a proud republic. Two Presidents had been elected because of their malleability, because they shared the views of the proslavery minority in the South. It is a remarkable commentary on the period that neither Pierce nor Buchanan had a serious breach with the South before secession. Pliable Presidents had sanctioned bad laws in Congress—the Nebraska Act and the English bill—and in Kansas—the Shawnee laws and the legislative provisions for Lecompton. Pierce had failed to maintain law and order and had repudiated good governors whom he had appointed. Buchanan had betrayed

Walker whom he had entreated to accept appointment. Lesser leaders disgraced the Kansas landscape: Atchison, Sheriff Jones, John Calhoun, Jim Lane, and John Brown. Congressional leaders, for the most part, appear partisan, narrow, casuistical, immoderate: Douglas, Davis, Stephens, Seward, Sumner, Chase, and Wade. A Crittenden seems a Cassandra against this background.

Buchanan, though relieved that the English bill had eased the spring crisis, could write in November: "I feel a proud consciousness that I have done my duty; and had my recommendation been sanctioned by Congress, Kansas would this day have been a State in the Union with just such a Constitution in regard to Slavery as a majority of the people might have thought proper to adopt." [9] He failed to comprehend the power of principle in politics—the principle that Kansans preferred to accept territorial status to statehood under a constitution obnoxious to them.

Popular sovereignty, crippled in its administration, had at last prevailed—that is, almost prevailed—in Kansas. It had permitted the people to reject a frame of government devised by an unrepresentative minority and offered in a unilateral choice. It had withheld from them the right to frame a government devised by the majority of its citizens. It had encouraged formation of a slave state and discouraged formation of a free state. Popular sovereignty, as dispensed under Pierce and Buchanan, in short, had not permitted the people of Kansas to determine their own institutions. It had not reduced slavery to a local problem; it had not removed slavery from the realm of national politics. Popular sovereignty could never find favor among the most ardent advocates or fervent foes of slavery.

The English bill reflected the deterioration of American political skill. The compromise of 1850 had maintained a truce for less than four years. The compromise of 1858 placed northern and southern extremists in aggressive postures, demanding the overturn or effectuation of the Dred Scott principle that slavery was lawful in the Federal territories. In the compromises of 1820 and 1850 each sectional partner could feel it had secured a principle. In 1858 no one—not Buchanan, Douglas, Stephens, Seward—could feel he had secured a principle; he had, instead, accepted an expedient.

The English bill reflected the deterioration of sectional harmony. Four and a half years of abrasive politics had rubbed raw the nation's nerves, created sectional distrust, and turned northerners against the "slave power" and southerners against Yankee "aggression." The Nebraska issue bequeathed a legacy of bad faith, as charges and recriminations rang back and forth: Douglas and the South had violated the sacred Missouri compact, New England had leagued with abolitionist emigrants, the South had leagued with Border Ruffians, Presidents had been putty in the hands of a southern Directory, Black Republicans supported Osawatomie Brown, fanatical Puritan abolitionists were inciting a race war, northerners obstructed the Fugitive Slave Law with their personal liberty laws and Underground Railroad, southerners were bent on spreading slavery through all the territories and into Central America and Cuba, and on reviving the infamous African slave trade.

And so it went. The future appeared ominous. The bonds of Union were breaking, and political parties—the last great bond—were sectionalizing. Almost no one was making efforts at rapprochement.

In the ensuing two years, as the nation moved toward electing a President on a nonextensionist platform, race prejudice was blatant. Democrats and southerners hurled charges of racial equality against their opponents, who countered with denials. A Republican reaction set in, as party leaders strove to prove the party stood for white supremacy.

Seward explained in 1860 that "the motive of those who protested against the extension of slavery" had "always really been concern for the welfare of the white man" and not an "unnatural sympathy for the negro." Speaking in Hartford, Lincoln, referring to a shoemakers' strike in Massachusetts, warned his auditors: "If you give up your convictions and call slavery right as they [the South] do, you let slavery in upon you—instead of *white* laborers who can strike, you'll soon have *black* laborers who can't strike."

This hardening of conviction in the Negro's inferiority hampered Americans in dealing with the slavery problem. It ruled out projects for ameliorating the lot of the slave, or even the free Negro, and for gradually extinguishing slavery. It tarred nonextension of slavery with racial equality and amalgamation. It caused Republican leaders to espouse an impractical and unpopular scheme of colonizing a segment of the population that numbered nearly 4 million. It excited hysterical fears among southerners, and some northerners as well, about the security of American society, now resting upon the legal segregation of Negroes in the form of slavery, should the preservative mold be broken. It was the obdurate substratum of all political argument, beyond which a blundering generation could not penetrate.

EPILOGUE

The great fact of race

The 1850's comprise a complex decade. While railroad, mine, factory, and city were transforming America, rushing it into the modern era, the country was retrogressing into civil strife. Why Americans went to war against one another has absorbed attention for several generations. The grand theme has seized the minds of distinguished historians, James Ford Rhodes, Charles Beard, and Allan Nevins among them.

Scholars have advanced an astounding variety of interpretations of the causes of the American Civil War. In their quest for causation they have discovered the origins of conflict, among many places, in a constitutional crisis, in an aggressive slave power, in slavery, in economic rivalry, in sectionalism, in moral attitudes toward slavery, in blundering statesmen, in political disorganization, in fanaticism, and in slavery conjoined with race adjustment.

This confusion of tongues evidences the diversity of forces at work in the fifties. Accepting the weightiness of many of the

The title of the Epilogue is quoted from the *History of the United States* by James Ford Rhodes (1906).

opinions of previous scholars, I have sought to invite attention to neglected racial attitudes in the Kansas crisis. This small book, then, seeks to demonstrate the burden of racialism borne by the generation of the fifties, without, I trust, overbalancing the measurement of causation.

The Massachusetts abolitionist Thomas Wentworth Higginson, who led a Negro regiment during the Civil War, in 1901 rebuked William Jennings Bryan and severed relations with him for such "ignorance . . . [of] American History" as to think that "no man or party has advocated social equality between the white . . . and the black. . . . The simple fact is," Higginson flamed, "that no man concerned in the great anti-slavery movement . . . advocated anything else."

How far wrong he was! Antislavery men as well as proslavery men, northerners as well as southerners, disfavored social equality between the races. Presidents and politicians, statesmen and lickspittles, poets and preachers, planters and plowmen, artisans and poor whites shared a nearly universal aversion to racial equality. Acceptance of Negro inferiority, as these pages seek to demonstrate, pervaded American social thought. Call the roll of the burdened generation's leaders, and we shall find each name a subscriber to the notion of inequality: Pierce, Buchanan, Douglas, Seward, Sumner, Wade, Trumbull, Wilson, Lincoln, Wilmot, Giddings, Corwin, Toombs, Davis, Stephens, Hammond, English, Blair, Walker, Benton, Bell, Crittenden, O. H. Browning, A. G. Brown, Hunter, Thayer, Owen Lovejoy, Emerson, Theodore Parker, Lowell, and Stowe. Indeed, Higginson may be quoted to rebut his rebuke to Bryan. For his indignation of 1901 ill consorts with his lament of 1863, written from Camp Shaw, South Carolina, "It is the fashion with philanthropists who come down here to be impressed with the degradation and stupidity of these people [the

Negroes]. I often have to tell them that I have not a stupid man in the regiment." Higginson himself appears among a saving remnant who doubted the white consensus.

It was a blundering generation, flawed by its belief in the inferiority of the blacks amongst them. Historians have traditionally overlooked the evidence of the racial gulf in the fifties. Concerned with academic themes like constitutionalism, politics, and economics, they have brushed aside, as if embarrassed, the abundant evidence. A few historians, it is true, have emphasized racial bias in this crucial decade, but no prior writer, I believe, has examined the interrelationship between politics and race throughout the great crisis occasioned by the Kansas issue.

Historians long assumed race prejudice resulted from Reconstruction. They created a myth of benign race attitudes before vengeful Radical Republicans imposed Negro suffrage upon a prostrate South. Southerners, it is said, understood and loved the Negro; and northerners in turn sympathized with the slave, assisted him in his flight to freedom, and resolved to curb the spread of the evil institution of slavery. Racial prejudice, in this view, was an outgrowth of the latter part of the nineteenth century, reinforced by Darwinism. However, an antipodal record of race attitudes is quite clear. Southerners and northerners, in the crucial years before the outbreak of the Civil War, shared a conviction of Negro inferiority. The testimony of the times—in Congressional debates, in state papers, in newspapers, in private correspondence, in statutes, in court decisions, in state constitutions, in sermons, in tombstones, and elsewhere—is overwhelming. It was a rare American who doubted the anthropological assumption of African inequality, an occasional one who favored legal equality, a nearly nonexistent one who favored social equality. Even most abolitionists seemed ambivalent about racial equality. Negro Americans, both slave and free, were denied equal opportunities for education, employment, and with some exceptions for electing government officials.

Historians have repeatedly pored over the pages of the *Congressional Globe* for the fifties, extracting evidence of political, constitutional, and economic factors exerting influence on the events of the times. But they have seen through a glass darkly, for the great debates in Congress were rife with racial preconceptions. When statesmen of the fifties fatefully discussed repeal of the Missouri Compromise and passage of the Kansas-Nebraska bill, admission of Kansas under either the freestate Topeka or slavestate Lecompton constitutions, or the English bill's effort to compromise the Lecompton controversy, they, if not historians, were alert to the racial import of what they were about.

Historians, for example, have cited speeches like Senator Hammond's "Cotton is King" declamation, or Alexander H. Stephens's "cornerstone" address, interpreting the one as about economic sectionalism and the other as about slavery, whereas the underlying theme of both is Negro inferiority. They have written about slavery as though it were mere servitude, comparable to Russian serfdom, and not a racial arrangement. Negro servitude, it is true, began as a labor arrangement in the seventeenth century, but it soon was set off from white labor, free and indentured, by the color bar. Slavery formalized the racial difference. Thereafter it became impossible to extinguish slavery because of racialist preconceptions.

The ante-bellum educator, President Elliot of Planters' College, Mississippi, uttered a home truth when he pointed out that the word "slave" in the United States described not a kind of servant but "the African race." If historians have often failed to distinguish between slavery and race, they also have often neglected or misread the insights of contemporaries. Thomas Jefferson and Alexis de Tocqueville, American democrat and French aristocrat, alike were prophets of conflict over the ineradicable racialism in the American democracy.

Frederick Douglass observed in 1854, "*One seventh part of the population of this country is of Negro descent. . . .*" The question of recognizing the human brotherhood of persons of European and African descent, this Negro abolitionist believed, "is at the bottom of the whole controversy, now going on between the slaveholders on the *one* hand, and the abolitionists on the other." The vice-president of the Confederacy, Alexander H. Stephens, candidly explained the racial basis of the Confederate States of America. The Confederate cornerstone was not, as his long apologia later said, state rights, nor, as some historians stated, slavery, but racial inequality. The question of "the proper status of the negro," he said at Savannah in March, 1861, "was the immediate cause" of secession. "Our new Government is founded," he continued, "upon the great truth that the negro is not equal to the white man. . . ."

Similarly, the Richmond editor, E. A. Pollard, found "the true ground" of the South's defense of slavery to have been the race barrier. "The true question which the war involved," he declared, "and which it merely liberated for greater breadth of controversy was the supremacy of the white race. . . ." The felt necessity to maintain an inferior race in slavery was the fundamental cause of the Confederacy's effort at independence. When the war was well on its way, indeed nearly lost, the fear of forcibly imposed racial equality impelled the South to fight on. In an "Address of the Rebel Congress to the People of the Confederate States," the Confederate Congress anticipated that the horrors of conquest would entail "The destruction of our nationality, the equalization of whites and blacks . . . we would be made slaves of our slaves, hewers of wood and drawers of water for those upon whom God has stamped indelibly the marks of physical and intellectual inferiority."

Southerners and Britons have been more aware of the racial basis of the Union's disruption than northerners. Southern self-awareness is well illustrated by the literary historian, William G. Brown, who at the turn of the century rejected the tariff, internal improvements, banking, and expansionism as sources of the Civil War. "The real cause of all the trouble was not slavery," he also concluded, "but the presence of Africans in the South in large numbers."

The same insight distinguished the professional historian, Ulrich B. Phillips, a native of Georgia, who forthrightly framed his view in his essay "The Central Theme of Southern History." The central theme he found to be not slavery but the South's resolution to keep the land of Dixie a white man's country; the South defended slavery as a guarantee of white supremacy and Caucasian civilization. Slavery was the means of solving the problem of race control. The Phillips thesis has attracted generous attention among historians, but very few have essayed to apply it to the course of southern history. Since Phillips wrote in 1928, historians have continued to search for political, constitutional, economic, emotional, cultural, and social differences between the South and North.

The two northern historians who have most nearly appreciated the racial origins of the conflict have been James Ford Rhodes and Allan Nevins. Rhodes, to be sure, simplistically states, "of the American Civil War it may safely be asserted there was a single cause, slavery." Yet a close reading of his pages proves his awareness of race as a factor in the troubled fifties. He failed, however, to formulate racialism as a cause of conflict independent of slavery and believed antiextensionism to be the product of morality. Belatedly, in dealing with Reconstruction, he seemed to recognize the place of race in the sectional struggle when he criticized Senator Charles Sumner for having no appreciation of "the great fact of race."

It remained to Nevins, whose work, *The Ordeal of the Union,* is superseding Rhodes, to discover "the main root of the conflict" in "the problem of slavery *with its complementary problem of race-adjustment;* the main source of the tragedy," Nevins went on, "was the refusal of either section to face these conjoined problems squarely and pay the heavy costs of a peaceful settlement." Nevins asked, "Was the Negro to be allowed, as a result of the shift of power signallized by Lincoln's election, to take the first step toward an ultimate position of general economic, political, and social equality with the white man?" But in his skillful, broad-gauged treatment, Nevins accented slavery, missed much of the racialism suffocating political choice in the decade, and made Lincoln and the Republicans precursors of racial equality.

Contemporary British travelers underscored the color question instead of slavery. W. H. Chambers described the general white repugnance to persons of color as "an absolute monomania." He thought all efforts at emancipation valueless so long as northern society condemned Negroes to inequality. This fixed opinion about Negro character, he wrote, "lies at the root of American slavery. . . ."

The present-day British historian, Alan A. Conway, in a summary statement of the war's causes sustains the view that slavery was crucial, and he lays stress on Phillips's and Nevins's emphasis on racial slavery. He accepts Nevins's argument that race was a major unifying force in the South, but takes exception to Nevins's argument that Lincoln's election signified a first step by the North to racial equality. The rank and file of northerners, Conway contends, feared "that, if slavery could not be contained, they would be faced with the competition from Negro slave labour in the free states and territories." Northerners in 1860 dreaded economic competition and loss of status from free Negroes, if there should be emancipation, and from slaves, if there should be expansion of slavery. Southerners in 1860 dreaded Negro assimilation into southern society, if there should be emancipation. "They both fought out of illogical fear. . . ." "The Negro as a Negro rather than as a slave," he concludes, "was the critical point. . . ." Yet Conway, while only attempting to synthesize the historiography of the causes of the American conflict, accented economic competition between races, attributed equalitarianism to abolitionists, and in a little more than a page on this interpretation could not particularize the racialist origins of the war.

In his brilliant study *North of Slavery,* published in 1961, Leon Litwack applied a scalpel to northern discrimination against Negroes. His book comprehended the period 1790–1860 and dealt with discrimination in numerous areas, including a single chapter on "The Crisis of the 1850's."

Eugene H. Berwanger in 1967 examined frontier anti-Negro prejudice and the slavery-extension controversy. Four fifths of the voters in Illinois, Indiana, Oregon, and Kansas, he declared, voted to exclude free Negroes "simply because of their prejudice." Before 1854 nonextension had failed to find success because it was tainted with abolitionist support. After 1854 nonextension, as offered by the Republican Party, shorn of the ideas of racial equality and interference with slavery where it already existed, won the support of many westerners. Confronted with the new party, Democrats tried to tar Republicans with abolitionism and Negro equality. Frontier racial prejudice, he concluded, significantly figured in the slavery-extension controversy.

Some previous writers, then, have distinguished between slavery and race, have viewed race as the fundamental cause of conflict, and have traced aspects of the racial origins of the Civil War. So far as Kansas and the racial question are concerned, however, they have done little more than plot the field, leaving it yet to be cultivated.

In retrospect, we can agree that the American Civil War comprehended a constitutional crisis. But it did not come about from the bloodless abstraction of state rights or dry arguments over interpreting the Constitution or its manner of framing. The state-rights dogma was given lip service at the convenience of both parties, professed, for example, both by South Carolina Democrats and Wisconsin Republicans. As Arthur M. Schlesinger, Sr., showed long ago, the dogma was usually the fetish of the "outs" assailing the "ins." In actuality, contemporaries rationalized their views in constitutional language. Alexander H. Stephens, a leading post-bellum interpreter of constitutional conflict, spoke realistically in 1861, when he dedicated the Confederacy to racial inequality. He wrote romantically seven years later, when he asserted the war "was a strife between the principles of Federation, on the one side, and Centralism, or Consolidation, on the other. Slavery, so called, was the question on which these antagonistic principles" collided.

We can agree, too, that the war in a sense was promoted by a slave power. One need not accept Henry Wilson's charge of a proslavery conspiracy to destroy the

Union, or even the existence of a well-organized power. There is no conclusive evidence proving a slave-power conspiracy. What is meaningful is a widespread northern belief in the existence of a slave power. Many contemporaries watched with alarm the reversal of the traditional policy of containment of slavery in the fifties. They beheld the election of the "doughface" Presidents Pierce and Buchanan, the repeal of the Compromise of 1820, the Ostend Manifesto's outrageous demand for Cuba, the Supreme Court's infuriating denial of Congressional authority to restrict slavery in the territories, followed by fresh cries for Cuba and a Federal slave code for the territories. Evidence abounds of contemporary belief in a southern slave-power conspiracy. Besides Henry Wilson, Greeley, Giddings, Benton, Garrison, Seward, Lincoln, and numerous others subscribed in whole or in part to the notion of an aggressive slavocracy. Conversely, many southerners accepted the idea of an aggressive North, intent on denying rights to the South. Calhoun gave the idea classic exposition in 1850, and Davis expounded it in his speeches of the 1850's and his history of the struggle published in 1881. Presumptions of aggressive sectionalism helped to promote sectionalism and to stiffen resistance to compromise.

With respect to slavery as a cause of the Civil War, it may be acknowledged that it stands to the fore. We find it impossible to accept Charles Beard's summary dismissal of slavery as an unimportant cause of conflict. Neither, however, can we accept Rhodes's monistic stress on slavery. Slavery, in actuality, touched nearly all aspects of American life: politics, economics, culture, and all the rest. But what must not be lost sight of, as so many commentators and historians have done, is the distinguishing badge of slavery in the United States—the black skins of the slaves. Slavery alone need not have caused civil war; the American political genius probably could have coped with Caucasian slavery, painful as emancipation might have been to the body politic. It was *African* slavery, an institution fixing the separate status of a race almost universally regarded as inferior and unassimilable, which eluded the political skill of mid-nineteenth-century white America.

The economic tensions between the sections, emphasized by Beard in *The Rise of American Civilization,* were in reality subordinate to slavery. The tariff issue did not loom large in the fifties; the internal-improvements issue no longer sharply divided political parties by 1860; the banking issue had receded to the background; the homestead issue, shorn of the Negro slave question in the territories, was not a conspicuous grievance during the crisis of 1860–61. North and South in 1860 were not divided between a planting interest on the one side and capitalists, laborers, and farmers on the other, who because of opposing economic interests were sucked into the vortex of an irrepressible conflict that became the second American Revolution.

Sectional considerations related to slavery, it is true, often influenced thinking about economic issues, but about as often in East-West terms as North-South. The two sections developed distinctive cultures, but this was in essence an incident of demography. The two cultures developed separately because the two sections contained disparate numbers of Negroes. The true line of division in the United States was not the Mason-Dixon line but the color bar. The republic was not compartmentalized into thirty or more sovereign states so much as into two nations—not southern and northern—but Caucasian and African. The disproportion of Africans in the southern states nourished southern nationalism. Southerners harbored fears of emancipation and insurrection through northern influences. Northerners held an aversion to slavery, "the peculiar institution," as well as to Negroes, and harbored suspicions of southerners' intentions to extend Negro slavery and to dominate public policy. The issue bringing northern sectionalism into focus was the possibility of the expansion of slavery into the territories formerly restricted to white men. Northerners who joined the Republican Party intended to keep America a white man's country, with no black slaves and few free Negroes in the western territories, and with the national government in hands friendly to white northern interests. They did not intend to emancipate the South's Negroes or promote racial equality.

Because the Negro was emancipated and did receive civil rights at Republican hands, historians have perpetrated the error of supposing the party intended these things in the 1850's. They have labored to discover humanitarianism toward blacks in a party largely dedicated to the rights of whites. If we recognize the force of Republican protests against charges of favoring racial equality, it is difficult to embrace Nevins's argument that the election of Lincoln signalized "the first step toward an ultimate position of general economic, political and social equality with the white man." Lincoln himself, abolitionists (who did not support Lincoln), and humanitarians may, to be sure, have wished to place slavery in a position where the public could be assured of its ultimate extinction, but it is one thing to say such persons favored gradual emancipation and quite another to say they favored racial equality. The evidence of bias among antislavery leaders and the masses as well as of day-by-day discrimination against Negroes is so overwhelming as to make one doubt whether more than a few northerners shared the equalitarian goal. Rather, it seems, Republicans desired to arrest the advance of slavery, subdue southern influence in the nation, secure their own rights, and defer indefinitely decisions on the dread questions of emancipation and equalitarianism. Reconstruction precipitated a new crisis, during which some Republicans coquetted with Dame Equality but soon jilted her.

Most Republicans clearly were not emancipationists. Emancipation, to be sure, must eventually have come to the United States, but it did come in the first Republican Administration only as an accident of war. If, to be fanciful for a moment, Stephen A. Douglas in 1854 had proposed a plan of compensated, gradual emancipation without colonization and the Pierce Administration, with its broadly national and strongly southern basis, had enacted it, the names of Douglas and Pierce today would be extolled, a Republican Party might have been organized as an antiemancipationist, anti-Negro party, and the Civil War might either have been averted or taken an unfamiliar form—to secure northern white superiority. In this guise the White Republicans might have been the foes of a Democratic conspiracy to turn the territories over to free black labor. But to make Douglas the Great Emancipator and Pierce the staunch champion of enlightened emancipation is visionary, and may serve chiefly to keep us undeceived about the realities of antebellum American. What is real is the common aspiration of southern Democrats and northern Republicans to maintain white supremacy.

With respect to the moral issue, in defense of slavery southern apologists proclaimed it a positive good and gave it moral sanction. In assailing slavery, abolitionists and publicists condemned it as evil and termed it immoral. Yet, historical evidence is lacking to prove that the moral division ran deep. It is doubtful whether southerners in their hearts believed the peculiar institution to be moral. It is doubtful whether northerners, who refused to support abolitionist parties (the acid test of applying morals in politics), were moved to adopt nonextension of slavery in the territories or popular sovereignty because they believed slavery immoral. If northerners were so moved, they alloyed their morality with racialism. What is certain is the compounding of convictions by southerners and northerners with a shared distaste for Negroes.

Northern sectionalism, then, embraced a dislike for the institution of slavery, for Negroes, and for abolitionists. Historians wrongly have labeled as abolitionists men who merely opposed extension of slavery, wrongly have interpreted nonextension as a first faltering step toward abolition, and wrongly have supposed northern foes of slavery to be friends of Negro rights. When Democrats branded opponents Black Republicans, they might more accurately have arraigned White Republicans.

The distinguished historian James G. Randall termed the men of the midcentury a blundering generation. There would have been no war, he judged, without the "elements of emotional unreason and overbold leadership." If he were to choose one word to account for the war, he said it would be "fanaticism" on both sides. Similarly, Avery Craven traced the coming of the Civil War to "a complete breakdown of the democratic process." Like Randall, he judged that differences between the sections reached a point where "men feel more than they reason." Both historians suggested that rational statesmen would have repressed the conflict. Pursuing the themes of political failure, Roy Nichols painstakingly and brilliantly traced the complex disruption of the Democratic Party in the 1850's. He joined Randall and Craven in finding the American political machinery and its operators defective and in discovering "hyperemotionalism" as the cause of the war.

None of these explanations satisfies. None explains

why a generation blundered, *why* fanaticism dethroned reason, *why* the democratic process completely broke down, *how* the conflict could have been repressed, or *why* the Democratic party ruptured and thereby ushered in a civil war.

We may agree on the existence of each of these historical phenomena. We may agree upon the partial validity of the cardinal explanations of the coming of the Civil War. But in most of them something central has been left out. The 1850's presented a crisis in constitutionalism *and* in color, in economics *and* in ethnology, and in slavery *and* in sociology. The element of race was indispensable to the making of the Kansas crisis. The rationalization of race over a long span of time into constitutional, political, economic, and social issues is at the core of the causation of the Civil War.

It was the inability of that generation to see a viable alternative to slavery as a means of race relations that caused men variously to invoke state rights, give allegiance to party creeds of evasion, localism, or nonextension, succumb to the political economy of slavery, and sanction the maintenance of the peculiar institution. It was their deeply rooted race bias that caused men to become fanatical, to discard compromise, and to march blindly toward secession and a brothers' war. It was the inability of the American political system to cope with the expanding problem of race, as the possibility of extending Negro slavery arose, that caused a generation to blunder, the democratic process to break down, and the Democratic Party to split apart. It was the universal folk belief in Negro inferiority, limiting the alternatives of political action, that made the Civil War an irrepressible conflict.

Historians, seeking rational explanations, trained in political, economic, and institutional history, have often missed this home truth. Puzzled by their failure to discover rational explanations, they have attributed the war to fanaticism or excessive emotionalism, ending up mystified about the fundamental cause of fanaticism—race *mores*. They have sadly concluded, looking at the small dimensions of the territorial and fugitive-slave problems, that the great holocaust was a needless war.

Just as historians have not appreciated the force of racialism in the war's origins, neither have they in general appreciated the factor of racialism in United States history. It underlies our Indian policy, leading to near extinction of the first Americans; our Mexican relations, leading to the war of 1846 and its territorial spoils; our immigration policy, leading to limitations including exclusion, restrictions, and quotas; and our foreign relations, leading among other places to the imperialism of 1898.

In short, at the root of the causes of the Civil War lay diversity of responses to the phenomenon of racial incompatibility. The American spirit was imprisoned by race prejudice. The Kansas crisis was a crisis in color. It intensified existing prejudice. Considering the racialist outlook of white America, the Civil War was an irrepressible conflict.

In summary, the Civil War erupted because of the presence in the United States of the Negro race. The Negroes' presence was largely limited to one geographical section—the South—and their status was largely governed by a peculiar institution—slavery. African slavery, reposing in a single section, contained the seeds of conflict.

The institution of slavery, separating the white race from the black, also differentiated white interests of many kinds. And although the institution of slavery violated United States ideals of liberty and equality, it ironically sustained the ideals of racial purity and the separation of an alien, inferior race, which nearly all Americans favored.

In 1854 the Kansas-Nebraska Act thoughtlessly repealed an earlier compromise and replaced it with the mischief-making dogma of popular sovereignty. Repeal stung many northerners into an instant response, expressed in forming the Republican Party.

The new party was an *ad hoc* coalition, aimed at the seeming clear and present danger of the expansion of slavery into the territories. What did slavery expansion mean? It portended competition of Negro slave labor with white, addition to the political power of the slave-holding South and its northern allies, continuation of southern dominance of national affairs, preservation of an obnoxious institution, disapprobation abroad of America's reputation, and frustration of majority rule.

Many northern whites avoided the Republican Party as an agent of disunion and social disorder. They placed paramount their obligation to preserve the republic and social stability. To achieve these ends they supported the American, Constitutional Union, and Democratic Parties. They preferred the evils they knew to the evils they knew not of.

The antislavery interest of most northerners was not abolitionist. Matters touched by slavery were *white* interests, as Republicans sought to secure national ascendancy for white northerners. Most Republicans were not abolitionists, and most abolitionists opposed the Republicans. Most Republicans, like most white Americans, believed Negroes were racially inferior, and notwithstanding the fact that some spoke for ultimate emancipation, few contemplated extending as much as legal equality to Negro freedmen. It was a rare American who strove for complete equality for blacks.

The pervasiveness of racialism—what I have called the Caucasian consensus—made it impossible to mount a major abolitionist movement in the United States. Efforts even to contain slavery provoked a white backlash. The consensus made it impossible to adopt meliorative measures, which could reduce the inhumanity of slavery. It made it impossible to dig at the roots of the firmly entrenched problem—African slavery. Neither northerners nor southerners desired to uproot the Negro, for where would he be transplanted?

Thus the problem arose over slavery in the territories. It was a white man's problem, a struggle between white groups, less over the future of the Negro than over the future of opposing groups as their interests were affected by the Negro in slavery. It is misleading to regard the Republicans as covert emancipationists, for while the sense of moral indignation against the institution of slavery was strong among many of them, the sense of repugnance to Negroes was equally strong. And, again, while a sense of slavery's injury to Negroes was felt, the sense of slavery's injury to northern white men was resented.

Republicans were concerned less about black skins than their own. If historians have sometimes misunderstood this reality, so too did contemporary southerners. Southerners were concerned less about slavery than racial supremacy. They distrusted the Black Republicans, believing the northern antiextensionists in actuality aimed to subvert race relations by introducing emancipation, equality, and amalgamation. The South's defeat in Kansas, John Brown's invasion of Virginia, and the accession to the Presidency of a northern antislavery man, whose true racial views were ignored, triggered secession and civil war.

APPENDIX

The court would be condemned

How much did Buchanan know about the secret deliberations of the justices? What influence, if any, did he have
on the tribunal? An interesting account of his relations
with the court may be pieced together from his personal
correspondence. A month before his inauguration Buchanan wrote his old friend on the bench, Justice John
Catron of Tennessee, inquiring whether the court was
likely to pronounce its opinion in Dred Scott's case before
March 4. Catron promptly replied that the justices had
not yet conferred, but that he would inform Buchanan, as
his due, when and whether the cause was likely to be
decided.

On February 19 Catron confided that the justices had
discussed the case several times. He furnished Buchanan
with a proposed paragraph for the inaugural, reading
that the court, it may be supposed, "will decide & settle
a controversy which has so long and seriously aggitated
[*sic*] the country." He asked the President-elect to urge
Justice Robert Grier of Pennsylvania to cooperate in settling the constitutional controversy. Buchanan compli-
antly wrote Grier that he thought it desirable at this
time to have a court opinion on the troublesome question.
Grier showed the letter to the chief justice and Justice
James M. Wayne of Georgia. They agreed with Buchan-

The title of the Appendix is a remark made by Supreme Court
Justice James M. Wayne in 1857.

an's view. With their concurrence, Grier in confidence revealed to Buchanan an inner history of the judges' deliberations and informed him of the probable decision.

At first the majority of the judges had determined merely to sustain the lower court, leaving Scott a slave under Missouri law. They would leave untouched the difficult questions of the right of a Negro to sue in the Federal courts and the validity of the Missouri Compromise. A minority, however, including Justice John McLean, intended to write dissenting opinions dealing with these questions. Those justices who differed with McLean and Benjamin R. Curtis of Massachusetts felt compelled to write their opinions on the questions, which Grier acknowledged were in the case. Grier agreed to concur in the chief justice's opinion; and he and Wayne sought to urge Daniel, John A. Campbell of Alabama, and Catron to do the same. This would make at least six justices concurring that the law of 1820 was of no effect, and with Grier's participation would avoid a decision made entirely by southern justices. He assured Buchanan, "We will not let any others of our brethren know any thing about *the cause of our anxiety to produce* this result." [1]

The meaning of this judicial politics becomes more clear when one recalls the hoary northern accusation that the Dred Scott decision was the deed of proslavery justices seeking to advance the southern cause. As if in retort to this, Professor Frank Hodder fastened responsibility for the decision upon two antislavery northern justices. According to Hodder, the court would not have ruled on the political questions had not McLean and Curtis forced the majority to rule. Self-interest actuated each of the two northerners, Hodder charged. McLean, who had been considered for the Republican Presidential nomination in 1856, "still hoped for the nomination in 1860." Curtis hoped to return to law practice in antislavery Massachusetts. He did resign from the bench soon after the decision, and from a lucrative law practice over the years received $650,000 in legal fees. In Hodder's view, which has been accepted by many historians, the ultimate decision—so divisive of the nation—would have been avoided, except for the ambition of two northern justices.

Hodder's hypothesis, however, does not hold water. To begin to reach a clear understanding of this curious episode, be it remembered, the President-elect plainly intervened in the court's deliberations; his intervention began before the conference of February 14 when McLean and Curtis announced their intention to write full opinions. Buchanan made clear to Catron, and later to Grier, his concern for a judicial statement on popular sovereignty.

Moreover, the Catron and Grier letters are suspect as ample historical evidence. The two men did not know one another's minds or activities; on February 19, Catron asked Buchanan to urge Grier to write an opinion on the Missouri Compromise issue, while four days later Grier wrote Buchanan that he would try to get Catron to write an opinion on it. More important, this correspondence omits the significant role of Justice Wayne.

This justice was close to his fellow Georgian, A. H. Stephens. When the reargument began in December, Stephens revealed to his brother: "I have been urging all the influence I could bring to bear upon the Sup. Ct. to get them no longer to postpone the case on the Mo. Restriction before them, but to decide it. They take it up today. If they decide as I have reason to believe they will that the restriction was unconstitutional . . . then the . . . judicial question as I think will be ended. . . ." A fortnight later Stephens said: "From what I hear *sub rosa* it [the decision] will be according to my own opinions upon every point as abstract political questions. The restriction of 1820 will be held to be unconstitutional. . . . The Chief Justice will give an elaborate" opinion.

Various sources—Justice Campbell, Justice Curtis, and Senator David Yulee of Florida—agree in fixing primary responsibility for a full decision upon Wayne. The Georgian, doubtless influenced by Stephens, had commenced to write his own opinion before the conference on February 14. At that conference, before Nelson read his limited opinion, Wayne moved, Campbell relates, "that the Chief Justice should write an opinion on all of the questions as the opinion of the Court. This was assented to. . . ."

We may doubt, too, that McLean, who would be seventy-five years of age in 1860, still cherished Presidential aspirations. As for Curtis's imputed motives, it is certain neither that he intended to resign from the court at this time nor that he was motivated to hand down a judicial opinion in expectation of thereby obtaining a lucrative private practice. Curtis's son and biographer declares that Curtis's and McLean's opinions were written after the two men had heard the chief justice's opinion read in conference. On the problem of motive, it does seem plain that certain southern members of the bench— Catron, Grier, the chief justice, Wayne, and Daniel—all shared with Buchanan concern to achieve a political end through their decision. Consultations took place among them in order to avoid contradictory opinions. They were not "forced" to write a full opinion by McLean and Curtis; they could well have confined themselves to the narrow ground of sustaining the lower court. In that event there would have been a striking disparity between minority and majority opinions, but as the ultimate verdict reveals, there were striking disparities among the majority any-way. Nor in assessing responsibility and ascertaining chronology should one forget that Catron stated on February 6—eight days before conferences began—that Daniel "will surely deliver his own opinion in the case, *at length.*"

We should in fact take a broader view of the Dred Scott decision's motivation than looking for individual justice's responsibility for leading the court to a full opinion. Actually, it was the court's obligation to write a full opinion. Justice Wayne, for all his partisanship, put this matter in proper perspective when he pleaded with his fellow justices, as Campbell relates, that "the case had been twice argued with thoroughness; that public expectation had been awakened and a decision of the important question looked for; that the Court would be condemned as failing in a performance of its duty, and that his own opinion was decided that the Chief Justice should prepare the opinion of the Court, and discuss all of the questions in the cause."

Wayne was quite right. The nation expected the highest tribunal to pass upon the vexatious questions of the validity of the Missouri Compromise and the right of a Negro to sue. These were not obiter dicta; as Grier conceded, both points were *in* the case and might legitimately be considered. And as Vincent Hopkins, the historian of the decision, has suggested about the men on the bench: "If they had not spoken, they would have been attacked as delinquent. If there had been no decision, men would probably ask, in the years to come, why the last peaceful means of settling the issue that precipitated the Civil War had not been tried." All but one of the justices thought the question of Congressional power belonged to the case.

Our look into the inner councils of the Supreme Court

discloses how the Kansas issue had agitated the highest court of justice. The American political system had established an independent judiciary founded upon Anglo-Saxon wisdom. A partisan member of Congress, Stephens, and perhaps others had succeeded in getting the ear of a member of the court. The President-elect, who in theory respected the separation of powers, had been betrayed by his anxiety to enter into an improper correspondence with two members of the court. Keenly aware that the majority of the court was Democratic and prosouthern, he let his two correspondents know he wanted a decision, which of course, would fortify his own political position. As Allan Nevins has written, he wanted a decision "so that the Court would save him from the peril of independent action on the disputed interpretation of popular sovereignty, quiet that disruptive question, restore unity to the party, and strike a crushing blow at the basic doctrine of the Republicans." Buchanan may be acquitted of conspiracy, with which some contemporaries, like Lincoln, charged him. But he may not be acquitted of impropriety, if not complicity. Certainly, he had a large responsibility for the decision, and his may well have been the determining influence, for he encouraged the wavering Grier to act. And if Grier had not joined the five southern justices, who disagreed among themselves on various points of law, that group might not have acted, and the Supreme Court of the United States might not have ruled on the great question riving the nation.

To sum up the matter of responsibility for the Dred Scott decision, we can see that there was no proslavery conspiracy and no evidence that northern justices, actuated by self-interest, forced a decision. In a large view, the decision was a response to a felt public need. The court's decision to rehear the case in 1856 and to give a full opinion in 1857 must be seen in the context of national crisis. The hardy historian who would assess responsibility for the full decision must take into account the maneuverings of Stephens, the motion of Wayne, the intervention of Buchanan, the willingness of Catron, Grier, Wayne, and the chief justice, and perhaps others, to concert together in a prosouthern decision, the early intention of Daniel to write an extended opinion, as well as the resolution of McLean and Curtis to write full minority opinions. Clearly, prosouthern judges cooperated with one another in an effort to arrive at a majority view; there is no evidence that McLean and Curtis cooperated to arrive at a northern or Republican view.

In its composition the Supreme Court was partisan and sectional. Seven of the nine members were Democrats; only McLean, a Republican, and Curtis, a Whig, represented other political affiliations. Five were southerners, to whom the prosouthern Grier may be added. Of the partisanship of Catron, Grier, and Wayne, we have already taken notice. Daniel was a Virginia gentleman of the old school, for whom the Virginia and Kentucky Resolutions and the right of secession were articles of faith he never tired of expounding. He had broken with Van Buren in 1847 over the Wilmot Proviso, and after 1848, his biographer states, "he was a Southern sectionalist of the most extreme sort, his hostility to the North becoming a passion." Campbell was the most moderate southerner on the bench. Nelson of New York, the fourth northerner, was nonpolitical; he was the only justice who did not write an opinion on the territorial issues.

FOR FURTHER READING

This work is based upon a diversity of materials: manuscripts, public documents, newspapers, published letters, diaries, biographies, monographs, and scholarly articles. In a separate table (p. 292) I have listed the manuscript collections, which often afford a rich, private history of the period.

The best general histories of the 1850's are Allan Nevins's two books, *The Ordeal of the Union* (2 vols., New York, 1947) and *The Emergence of Lincoln* (2 vols., New York, 1950), the brilliantly written outcome of vast research. Of value still is the older general history by James Ford Rhodes, *History of the United States from the Compromise of 1850 to . . . 1877* (7 vols., New York, 1893–1906). An acute analysis of historical writing on the problem of Civil War causation is Thomas J. Pressly's *Americans Interpret Their Civil War* (New York, 1962). A British scholar, Alan A. Conway, has written a short, suggestive survey, *The Causes of the Civil War* (London, 1961).

The American economy in the ante-bellum era is skillfully examined by George Rogers Taylor in *The Transportation Revolution, 1815–1860* (New York, 1951) and Paul W. Gates in *The Farmer's Age: Agriculture 1815–1860* (New York, 1960). Two pathbreaking books in political history are W. Dean Burnham *Presidential Ballots 1836–1892* (Baltimore, 1955), which collects and analyzes county returns, and Thomas B. Alexander's *Sectional Stress and Party Strength* (Nashville, 1967), which subjects Congressional voting behavior to computer analysis. *Seventh Census of the United States* and *Eighth Census of the United States* (Washington, 1854, 1865) are mines of data.

A modern history of Kansas is William Frank Zornow's *Kansas; A History of the Jayhawk State* (Norman, 1957). For the interrelationship between land policy and political conflict the great authority is Paul W. Gates, *Fifty Million Acres; Conflicts over Kansas Land Policy, 1854–1890* (New York, 1966). James C. Malin is the author of two meticulous studies, *The Nebraska Question, 1852–1854* (Lawrence, 1953), which explores the forces at work for opening the territory, and *John Brown and the Legend of Fifty Six* (Philadelphia, 1942), which among other matters probes the milieu in which Brown executed his massacre. Samuel A. Johnson, *The Battle Cry of Freedom; the New England Emigrant Aid Company in the Kansas Crusade* (Lawrence, 1954), and Wendell H. Stephenson, *The Political Career of General James H. Lane* (Topeka, 1930), treat unemotionally subjects once swirling in controversy.

For national politics the *Congressional Globe* is indispensable. So too is *A Compilation of the Messages and Papers of the Presidents, 1789–1908*, James D. Richardson, ed. (11 vols., Washington, 1908). The breakup of the Democratic Party is the theme of Roy F. Nichols's *The Disruption of American Democracy* (New York, 1948). An able survey is George H. Mayer's *The Republican Party, 1854–1964* (New York, 1964).

Biographies contain much valuable political history of the period. The two Presidents are depicted at length in Roy F. Nichols's *Franklin Pierce; Young Hickory of the Granite Hills* (2nd ed., Philadelphia, 1958) and Philip S. Klein's *President James Buchanan* (University Park, Pa., 1962). Stephen A. Douglas is best approached through the old life by Allen Johnson, *Stephen A. Douglas* (New York, 1908). The more recent biography by George Fort Milton, *The Eve of Conflict; Stephen A. Douglas and the Needless War* (Boston, 1934), exploits new materials and argues a debatable thesis. Glyndon G. Van Deusen's glowingly written *William Henry Seward* (New York, 1967) so compresses its subject as to make advisable the use of Frederic Bancroft's *The Life of William H. Seward* (2 vols., New York, 1900). James A. Rawley draws on hitherto unexploited Morgan papers to relate the activities of the first Republican national chairman in *Edwin D. Morgan, 1811–1883* (New York, 1955).

The best one-volume life of Lincoln is Benjamin P. Thomas's *Abraham Lincoln* (New York, 1953). For a series of brilliant revisionist essays, see Don E. Fehrenbacher's *Prelude to Greatness; Lincoln in the 1850's* (New York, 1964).

Racial prejudice in ante-bellum America is dissected in Leon Litwack's *North of Slavery; The Negro in the Free States, 1790–1860* (Chicago, 1965) and William Stanton's *The Leopard's Spots; Scientific Attitudes Toward Race in America, 1815–59* (Chicago, 1966). Eugene H. Berwanger's *The Frontier Against Slavery; Western Anti-Negro Prejudice and the Slavery Extension Controversy* (Urbana, Ill., 1967) documents his theme. Fresh approaches to their subjects may be found in Stanley Elkins's *Slavery; A Problem in American Institutional Life* (New York, 1963) and Martin Duberman, ed., *The Antislavery Vanguard; New Essays on the Abolitionists* (Princeton, 1965).

In addition to general works I have listed special studies under the chapter where their subjects are introduced. However, in many instances these studies pertain to large portions of this book.

The following abbreviations have been used in the essay on bibliography.

AH	*Agricultural History*
AHAAR	*American Historical Association Annual Report*
AHR	*American Historical Review*
AI	*Annals of Iowa*
AQ	*American Quarterly*
CWH	*Civil War History*
IMH	*Indiana Magazine of History*
JAH	*Journal of American History*
JISHS	*Journal of the Illinois State Historical Society*
JNH	*Journal of Negro History*
JSH	*Journal of Southern History*
KHQ	*Kansas Historical Quarterly*
MVHR	*Mississippi Valley Historical Review*
NH	*Nebraska History*

Chapter 1

Of particular value are the lives of leading Congressmen: William E. Parrish, *David Rice Atchison of Missouri; Border Politician* (Columbia, 1961); J. W. Schuckers, *The Life and Public Services of Salmon P. Chase* (New York, 1874); H. L. Trefousse, *Benjamin Franklin Wade, Radical Republican from Ohio* (New York, 1963); David Donald, *Charles Sumner and the Coming of the Civil War* (New York, 1961), an acute Pulitzer Prize winner; Henry Cleveland, *Alexander H. Stephens . . .* (Philadelphia, 1866); and Joseph H. Parks, *John Bell of Tennessee* (Baton Rouge, 1950). The story of the nation's most famous editor is told in Glyndon G. Van Deusen's *Horace Greeley; Nineteenth-Century Crusader* (New York, 1964).

Significant articles include two by Robert R. Russel, "What Was the Compromise of 1850?" *JSH*, XXII (1956) and "The Issues in the Congressional Struggle over the Kansas-Nebraska Bill, 1854," *JSH*, XXIX (1963). A masterly analysis of an historian's controversy is Roy F. Nichols, "The Kansas-Nebraska Act; A Century of Historiography," *MVHR*, XLIII (1956). James C. Malin, ed., offers new evidence in "The Motives of Stephen A. Douglas in the Organization of Nebraska Territory; a Letter Dated December 17, 1853," *KHQ*, XIX (1951). Charles Desmond Hart, "The Natural Limits of Slavery Expansion; Kansas-Nebraska, 1854," *KHQ*, XXXIV (1968) examines Congressmen's beliefs about the extension of slavery.

Chapter 2

Edmund Wilson, *Patriotic Gore; Studies in the Literature of the American Civil War* (New York, 1966) has a valuable chapter on the author of *Uncle Tom's Cabin*. The religious atmosphere of the fifties is suggested in Ray A. Billington's *The Protestant Crusade, 1800–1860* (New York, 1938) and Timothy L. Smith, *Revivalism and Social Reform in Mid-Nineteenth Century America* (New York, 1957). John L. Thomas, *The Liberator; William Lloyd Garrison* (Boston, 1963), limns his figure, warts and all. Myths are stripped away in Larry Gara's *The Liberty Line; The Legend of the Underground Railroad* (Lexington, 1961). George Fitzhugh, *Sociology for the South* (Richmond, 1854) is a classic apologia.

Articles of unusual significance include Bernard A. Weisberger, "The Newspaper Reporter and the Kansas Imbroglio," *MVHR*, XXXVI (1950), a study of "yellow journalism"; Robert P. Swierenga, "The Ethnic Voter and the First Lincoln Election," *CWH*, XI (1965); Gerald Wolff, "The Slavocracy and the Homestead Problem of 1854," *AH*, XL (1966); and M. M. Rosenberg, "The Kansas-Nebraska Act; A Case Study," *AI*, XXVI (1964).

Chapter 3

The *Collections* and *Publications* of the Kansas Historical Society (Topeka, 1881 to date) are rich mines to be quarried for settlers' reminiscenses, public documents, etc. The important Howard Report is *House Reports* (No. 200, 34 Cong., 2 sess.). William E. Connelley's massive, *A Standard History of Kansas and Kansans* (5 vols., Chicago, 1918) is very useful.

Individual aspects of Kansas settlement are treated in James C. Malin, "The Topeka Statehood Movement Reconsidered; Origins," *Territorial Kansas* (Lawrence, 1954); W. H. Isely, "The Sharps Rifle Episode in Kansas History," *AHR*, XII (1907); R. V. Harlow, "The Rise and Fall of the Kansas Aid Movement," *AHR*, XLI (1935); Horace Andrews, Jr., "Kansas Crusade; Eli Thayer and the New England Emigrant Aid Company," *NEQ*, XXXV (1962); and John and Sarah Everett, "Letters of John and Sarah Everett, 1854–1864," *KHQ*, VIII (1939), the correspondence of two settlers.

Chapter 4

Biographies that illuminate the scene are Richard H. Sewell, *John P. Hale and the Politics of Abolition* (Cambridge, Mass., 1965), analytical; Barton H. Wise, *The Life of Henry A. Wise of Virginia, 1806–1876* (New York, 1899), filiopietistic; William Y. Thompson, *Robert Toombs of Georgia* (Baton Rouge, 1966), scholarly; and William E. Smith, *The Francis Preston Blair Family in Politics* (2 vols., New York, 1933), a dynastic story. Charles Warren, *The Supreme Court in United States History* (2 vols., 1926) is judicious. Oswald Garrison Villard, *John Brown 1800–1859* (New York, 1943) is the best life.

Among articles of importance are James L. Sellers, "Republicanism and State Rights in Wisconsin," *MVHR*, XVII (1930), a northern instance of state rights; Fred H. Harrington, "The First Northern Victory," *JSH*, V (1939), Banks's election as speaker; R. L. Meriwether, ed., "Preston S. Brooks on the Caning of Charles Sumner," *SCHGM*, LII (1951), publishes two revealing letters by Sumner's assailant.

Charles Robinson, *The Kansas Conflict* (New York, 1892), by a pioneer who became the first state governor; and T. H. Gladstone, *The Englishman in Kansas* (New York, 1858), by the London *Times* correspondent, are by perceptive contemporaries.

Chapter 5

Biographies include Robert Rayback, *Millard Fillmore* (Buffalo, 1959); Marvin Cain, *Lincoln's Attorney-General; Edward Bates of Missouri* (Columbia, 1965); Ivor D. Spencer, *The Victor and the Spoils; A Life of William L. Marcy* (Providence, 1959); Louis M. Sears, *John Slidell* (Durham, 1925); William N. Chambers, *Old Bullion Benton* (Boston, 1956); and L. G. Tyler, *The Letters and Times of the Tylers* (2 vols., Richmond, 1885).

Proceedings of the National Convention held at Philadelphia, on the 17th, 18th, and 19th June, 1856 (n. d.)

details the work of the first Republican nominating convention. Two special studies are Harvey Wish, "The Slave Insurrection Panic of 1856," *JSH*, V (1939) and James A. Rawley, "Financing the Frémont Campaign," *PMHB*, LXXV (1951) the latter based on the Republican chairman's account book.

Chapter 6

Basic reading on the Dred Scott case, of course, is the Supreme Court's opinions, 19 *Howard*, 393–633. A convenient compilation, which contains both contemporary materials and historians' interpretations, is Stanley I. Kutler, ed., *The Dred Scott Decision* (Boston, 1967), with extensive bibliography. Vincent C. Hopkins, *Dred Scott's Case* (New York, 1951) is the standard monograph. "Responsibility of McLean and Curtis for the Dred Scott Decision" is brilliantly probed by Allan Nevins in *The Emergence of Lincoln*, II, 473–77. Carl B. Swisher's *Roger B. Taney* (New York, 1935) is superb.

Two important articles are Harvey Wish, "The Revival of the African Slave Trade in the United States, 1856–1860," *MVHR*, XXVII (1941), and Ronald Takaki, "The Movement to Reopen the African Slave Trade in South Carolina," *SCHGM*, LXVI (1965).

Chapter 7

The Covode committee report on political corruption is House *Reports* (No. 64, 36 Cong., 1 sess.). James P. Shenton, *Robert John Walker; A Politician from Jackson to Lincoln* (New York, 1961) is an able biography. Elizabeth Merritt, *James Henry Hammond, 1807–1864* (Baltimore, 1923), well delineates that southern spokesman.

A well-documented view is presented in George D. Harmon, "President James Buchanan's Betrayal of Governor Robert J. Walker of Kansas," *PMHB*, LIII (1929). Robert W. Johannsen, "The Lecompton Constitutional Convention: An Analysis of Its Membership," *KHQ*, XXIII (1957) is revisionist.

Chapter 8

Don E. Fehrenbacher, "Why the Republican Party Came to Power," *The Crisis of the Union, 1860–1861* (Baton Rouge, 1965), George H. Knoles, ed., commands attention. *Studies in Southern History and Politics; inscribed to William Archibald Dunning* (New York, 1914) contains thoughtful essays. *The Record of Hon. C. L. Vallandigham on Abolition, the Union, and the Civil War,* (12th ed., Columbus, Ohio, 1863) offers the views of the most notorious Copperhead. A prominent politician is portrayed in Mark M. Krug, *Lyman Trumbull; Conservative Radical* (New York, 1965).

Frank H. Hodder's argument, which I accept only in part, is in "Some Aspects of the English Bill for the Admission of Kansas," *AHAAR,* I (1906).

Epilogue

In addition to the writers mentioned in the text, two studies of special interest are William H. and Jane H. Pease, "Antislavery Ambivalence; Immediatism, Expediency, Race," *AQ,* XVII (1965) and George O. Virtue, "Marxian Interpretation of the Civil War," *NH,* XXX (1949). C. E. Cauthen and L. P. Jones, "The Coming of the Civil War," *Writing Southern History* (Baton Rouge, 1965), A. S. Link and R. W. Patrick, eds., has merit.

Manuscript Sources

My original typescript submitted to the publisher bore fully fifty pages of footnotes. Reluctantly, I have radically (and painfully) cut the documentation to only direct quotations from manuscript sources, which, generally speaking, are both unique and difficult to locate. The notes that follow, then, do not adequately reflect the profound influence on my thinking of extensive searching in manuscripts.

On the other hand, to my surprise, while reviewing the typescript before taking this decision, I discovered I had already incorporated in the text clues which often would enable the alert reader to find my sources. For example, I have drawn heavily upon the *Congressional Globe,* and my references in the text to names and dates will permit the inquiring student to discover precise pages in it.

In addition, the foregoing critical essay describes many but not all the numerous general and special works I have used. Beyond all this, I have retained a copy of my original typescript for those who want exact citations. These, then, are the tactics of documentation and the reason therefor.

Manuscript Collections. I have consulted the following collections. Abbreviations used in the notes are given after the name of the repository.

Bowdoin College (BC): W. P. Fessenden (transcript furnished by M. W. Whalon).

Columbia University Library (CUL): S. H. Gay.

Kansas State Historical Society (KSHS): John Brown, Emigrant Aid Society, Charles Robinson.

Library of Congress (LC): N. P. Banks, F. P. Blair, John C. Breckinridge, James Buchanan, S. P. Chase, Jefferson Davis, Stephen A. Douglas, R. M. T. Lincoln (microfilm), John McLean, Franklin Pierce, Alexander H. Stephens, Benjamin F. Wade, Elihu Washburne (transcript furnished by M. W. Whalon), and Gideon Welles.

Nebraska State Historial Society (NSHS): J. Sterling Morton.

New York Historical Society (NYHS): James Buchanan, Lysander Spooner.

New York Public Library (NYPL): Greeley-Colfax.

New York State Library (NYSL): Edwin D. Morgan.

Pennsylvania Historical Society (PHS): James Buchanan.

Princeton University Library (PUL): Blair-Lee, Andre de Coppet Collection, Richard Rush.

University of Chicago Library (UCL): Stephen A. Douglas.

University of Virginia Library (UVL): R. M. T. Hunter.

University of Rochester Library (URL): Thurlow Weed.

Notes identifying manuscript sources

Chapter 1

1. Ira Mayhew to J. Sterling Morton, June 11, 1856, Morton Papers, NSHS.

Chapter 2

1. Pierce to Davis, Jan. 12, 1853, Pierce Papers, LC.
2. Cobb to Stephens, Feb. 23, 1853, Stephens Papers, LC.

3. Fessenden to his wife, Mar. 14, 1854, Fessenden Papers, BC.
4. I am greatly indebted to Professor Jack Rabun of Emory University for permission to draw upon a paper he presented at the Organization of American Historians convention in Cincinnati, Ohio, April, 1966. He was commenting upon a paper by Robert W. Johannsen, subsequently published in a revised edition as "Stephen A. Douglas and the South," *JSH*, XXXIII (1967).
5. William C. Dawson to Linton Stephens, Dec. 21, 1853, Stephens Papers, LC.
6. Cox to Douglas, Mar. 24, 1854, Douglas Papers, UCL.
7. James M. Morgan to J. C. Breckinridge, Mar. 16, 1854, Breckinridge Papers, LC.
8. Seymour to Douglas, April 14, 1854, Douglas Papers, UCL.
9. Fessenden to his wife, June 14, 1854, Fessenden Papers, BC.

Chapter 3

1. Norman L. Rosenberg, *Personal Liberty Laws*, MS. M.A. thesis, University of Nebraska, 1967, iv, 41–62.
2. L. B. Dickerson to Breckinridge, Mar. 12, 1854, Breckinridge Papers, LC.
3. Greeley to Schuyler Colfax, Mar. 12, 1854, Greeley-Colfax Papers, NYPL.
4. Breckinridge to Douglas, Sept. 20, 1854, Douglas Papers, UCL.
5. Amos Tuck to Elihu Washburne, Mar. 18, 1854, Israel Washburne Papers, LC.
6. Preston King to F. P. Blair, Oct. 14, 1854, Blair-Lee Papers, PUL; quotations from Blair-Lee Papers by permission of Mr. P. Blair Lee.
7. Browning to McLean, Dec. 5, 1854, McLean Papers, LC.

Chapter 4

1. Charles Robinson to E. E. Hale, April 9, 1855, Emigrant Aid Correspondence, KSHS.
2. Dallas to Rush, Jan. 1, 1855, Richard Rush Papers, PUL.
3. George Plitt to James Buchanan, Jan. 29, 1855, Buchanan Papers, LC.
4. F. P. Blair, Jr., to M. Blair, Mar. 16, 1855, Blair Papers, LC.
5. John Brown to wife and children, Dec. 16, 1855, John Brown Papers, KSHS.

Chapter 5

1. Sheahan to Douglas, Feb. 8, 1855, Douglas Papers, UCL.
2. Chase to E. L. Hamlin, Feb. 9, 1855, Chase Papers, LC.
3. R. K. Meade to Hunter, Feb. 10, 1855, Douglas Papers, UCL.

4. Pierce to Douglas, May 28, 1855, Douglas Papers, UCL.
5. Preston King to F. P. Blair, Nov. 21, 1855, Blair-Lee Papers, PUL.
6. C. S. Tarpley to Douglas, Nov. 15, 1855, Douglas Papers, UCL.
7. W. H. Seward to F. P. Blair, Dec. 29, 1855, Blair-Lee Papers, PUL.
8. Buchanan to David Lynch, Sept. 21, 1855, Buchanan Papers, LC.
9. King to F. P. Blair, Jan. 5, 1856, Blair-Lee Papers, PUL.
10. Weed to Banks, Feb. 3, 1856; Charles Congdon to Banks, Feb. 5, 1856; Samuel Morse to Banks, Feb. 18, 1856, Banks Papers, LC.
11. Frémont to Robinson, Mar. 17, 1856; Reeder to Robinson, Feb. 16, 1856, Robinson Papers, KSHS.
12. H. B. Stanton to Banks, Feb. 18, 1856, Banks Papers, LC.
13. H. F. Benjamin to Banks, June 2, 1856, Banks Papers, LC.
14. Morgan to John Bigelow, June 2, 1856, Morgan Papers, NYSL.
15. Giddings to Brown, Mar. 17, 1856, Brown Papers, KSHS.

Chapter 6

1. Buchanan to Slidell, May 28, 1856, copy in Breckinridge Papers, LC.
2. Rives to Breckinridge, June 2, 1856, Breckinridge Papers, LC.
3. Wise to Buchanan, June 26, 1856; Buchanan to Wise, June 28, 1856, Buchanan Papers, PHS. Wise's distress gainsays Rhodes's assertion (vol. II, 202) that Buchanan's letter of acceptance, June 16, showed any doubting ones in the South he was sound on Kansas policy.
4. Abolitionist circular in Lysander Spooner Papers, NYHS.
5. Morgan to J. Bunce, April 17, 1856, Morgan Papers, NYSL.
6. Banks to Robinson, Mar. 19, 1856, Robinson Papers, KSHS.
7. Isaac Sherman to Banks, April 3, 1856, Banks Papers, LC; Greeley to Schuyler Colfax, May 16, 1856, Greeley-Colfax Papers, NYPL; William Bigler to Buchanan, June 23, 1856, Buchanan Papers, PHS.
8. J. Glancy Jones to James Buchanan, June 27, 1856, Buchanan Papers, PHS.
9. Faulkner to Buchanan, July 4, 1856; Bigler to Buchanan, July 15, 1856, Buchanan Papers, PHS.
10. Pierce to John Breckinridge, July 22, 1856, Breckinridge Papers, LC.
11. Boutwell to Banks, July 1, 1856, Banks Papers, LC.

12. Buchanan to J. C. Breckinridge, Sept. 25, 1856, Breckinridge Papers, LC.
13. Everett to Buchanan, Jan. 19, 1857, Buchanan Papers, PHS.

Chapter 7

1. Geary to Pierce, Dec. 22, 1856, Pierce Papers, LC.

Chapter 8

1. Geary to Buchanan, Jan. 16; P. F. Smith to Buchanan, Feb. 3; Bancroft to Buchanan, Feb. 21; Bennett to Buchanan, Feb. 7, 1857; Buchanan Papers, PHS.
2. Walker to Buchanan, June 23, 1857, Buchanan Papers, PHS.
3. Douglas to Walker, July 21, 1857, Walker Papers, NYHS.
4. Robinson to wife, Oct. 3, 1857, Robinson Papers, KSHS.
5. Cass to Buchanan, July 31; Buchanan Papers, PHS.

Chapter 9

1. James B. Eads to Douglas, Nov. 14; Richard McAllister to Douglas, Nov. 15; Sheridan P. Read to Douglas, Nov. 23; E. M. Huntington to Douglas, Nov. 29; Bancroft to Douglas, Dec. 2; Sheahan to Douglas, Dec. 4, 1857, Douglas Papers, UCL.
2. Tallmadge to Douglas, Dec. 14, 1857, Douglas Papers, UCL.
3. Wade to his wife, Dec. 12, 25, Wade Papers, LC; John Allison to McLean, Dec. 12, 1857, McLean Papers, LC; Welles to Douglas, Dec. 12, 1857; Forney to Douglas, Dec. 13, 1857, Douglas Papers, UCL.
4. Sumner to Chase, Jan. 18, 1858, Chase Papers, LC.
5. M. C. Fulton to Stephens, Mar. 30, 1858, Stephens Papers, LC.
6. E. D. Morgan Papers, March–June, 1858, NYSL; Edward Dodd and others to T. Weed, May 17, 1858, Weed Papers, URL.
7. Chase to Seward, March 11; George Hadley to Chase, April 3, 1858, Chase Papers, LC.
8. Greeley to Colfax, April 24, 1858, Greeley-Colfax Papers, NYPL; J. M. Walden to Chase, April 7, 1858, Chase Papers, LC.
9. Buchanan to Dr. Kaufman, Nov. 13, 1858, Buchanan Papers, LC.

Appendix

1. Catron to Buchanan, Feb. 6, 19; Grier to Buchanan, Feb. 23, 1857, Buchanan Papers, PHS.

INDEX